ALLIES INVADE ITA
Sheriff Beaten and Stabbed in Halting Break
REDS WIN 2 KEY TOWNS; CRACK NAZIS' 1941 LINE
Daily Tribune
FINAL
SAKES HIS THRONE!
EDWARD AGREES TO QUIT; PRE FLIGHT TO JOIN MRS. WALLIS
Britain's Monarch Bids Farewell to Family.
Chicago Daily Tribune
ALLIES INVADE FRANC
Hit North Co
FIERCE BATTLE R NORMANDY, BER
Daily Tribune
MB WARSAW!
RMY ORDER
Tribune
ELT IS DEA
Truman Sworn In, Pled
NEW EXECUTIVE SAYS HE PLANS NO CHANGES
Daily Tribune
UITS; PETAIN
Chicago Daily Tribune
ATOMIC BOMB STORY
Tribune
PS AT WA
ES, GUAM, SINGAPORE
Chicago Daily Tribune
V-E DAY-TODAY
Tribune
FINAL
AP FLEET!
GREATEST AIR AND SEA BATTLE 'CEASES TEMPORARILY,' MacARTHUR DECLARES
Allies Vow to Continue Attack After Blasting 17 Enemy Ships; U. S. Losses Undisclosed.
Tell How Japs Dived Off Two Fiery Carriers
SCORE OF SEA BATTLE
Chicago Daily Tribune
GREAT WAR ENDS
Will Surrender to Gen. M'Arthu
Chicago Daily Tribune
COL. R. R. McCORMICK DIES
Tribune Editor-Publisher Ill Two Years
U. S. INDICTS PRECINCT AID AS VOTE BUYER
Girl Victim of Kidnaper Found Slain
UNION BACKS AVERY IN HIS

McCormick of Chicago

McCORMICK OF CHICAGO

★ ★ ★ ★ ★

An unconventional portrait
of a controversial figure

By
FRANK C. WALDROP

PRENTICE-HALL, INC.,
Englewood Cliffs, New Jersey

Library of Congress Catalog Card Number: 66-10711 / Printed in the United States of America / T 56675

Prentice-Hall International, Inc., London / Prentice-Hall of Australia, Pty., Ltd., Sydney / Prentice-Hall of Canada, Ltd., Toronto / Prentice-Hall of India (Private) Ltd., New Delhi / Prentice-Hall of Japan, Inc., Tokyo /

to the Manito that made Chicago what it is today

CONTENTS ★★★

FOREWORD ★★★ There was a funny movie of the thirties in which one of the characters described his way of reaching decisions: "First I ask myself, 'What would General Motors do?' and then I do the opposite." For many of us, over more than a generation, the views of Colonel Robert R. McCormick, in the Chicago *Tribune,* provided an equally satisfactory reverse shibboleth.

It would be no surprise to discover Colonel McCormick had been kind to animals. There is a shock of recognition in discovering the humanity of a person previously seen only as a symbol or a caricature. But the shock is predictable, both in its immediate impact and in its more lasting consequences. It was perhaps best described in the *New Yorker* Magazine's surmises on the reflections of J. P. Morgan and the Midget Lady after their celebrated encounter at the Pecora hearings. Morgan, the *New Yorker* suggested, must have gone home and told Mrs. Morgan the Midget Lady really wasn't a bad sort at all, while the Midget Lady went home and said approximately the same thing to her husband.

It was predictable that, on close inspection, Colonel McCormick would turn out to be a man and not just a moustache. What manner of man he was and how he grew to manhood are questions that must await the results of the inspection.

The results are full of surprises, and many of the surprises are to be found in attendant characters, such as Big Bill Thompson, the Midwestern populist whose antecedents were so distinctively Bostonian, or Joe Patterson, founding father of the New York *Daily News,* who began his career as a Socialist, was one of the very few major journalists to support Franklin D. Roosevelt from 1933 to 1941, who then ended crying that his only aim was to outlive the man he had come to hate. But the greatest surprises are to be found in the relevance of Colonel McCormick's quarrels to the issues that still divide us. The specifics must await their telling. But it is not unfair to stir up speculation at the outset on the underlying question: Why did Robert R. McCormick so conduct himself that he became perhaps the best-known American symbol of reaction? How did he manage to swim, or float, so far out of the main stream?

I am inclined to look for the answer in the arena of his theories of politics. Of course anyone's theories are woven of many strands of personal experience, both visible and submerged. For whatever reasons, Colonel McCormick seems early to have become a devotee of the conspiracy theory of history. At first he adopted the theory in its less virulent form, simply as a belief that inner politics—the preferences of individual men at the center of power—were what counted, rather than the movements of peoples and nations. Later, he came to believe that what went on in the corridors of power was determinative by itself, and that what went on there was never accidental or uncoordinated. It was all a plot, and from there, as it is so easy to do in these visions, it disclosed itself to be a plot against the central figure in the landscape, the narrator, McCormick himself.

Colonel McCormick seems never to have learned how little one man can affect the course of government—perhaps because his own accomplishments in private life, both in Chicago and in the wilderness of Northern Canada, were so considerable. He discovered very early what a practical man of affairs could achieve in business, if he set his mind to it, and he assumed that the change in scale from business to government carried with it no essential qualitative changes.

Then, too, Colonel McCormick's career began when we were still very much in the age of royal cousin diplomacy, so that rulers all sat on their thrones as if they were sitting to a well-schooled horse, even if in fact the horse was about to bolt—and sometimes to throw his rider as he bolted.

Colonel McCormick's eventual prescription was to do away with government, or at least with the new forms of government that had emerged to deal with new problems. His proposed substitute for the United Nations—the opportunity, going all the way back to 1789, for other nations to seek statehood in the United States—is characteristic. Let them join Us!

The Tribune Company is a tribute to the Colonel's powers as an organizer. He was not inexpert at the arts of public persuasion, as the columns of his newspaper testify. But he was no politician, because he did not understand the limitations within which politicians—and even statesmen—work. In business, he knew when to quit and cut his losses because he knew that business is governed by the inexorable realities of the profit and loss statement. But in politics he refused to recognize that even the highest affairs of state are governed by what men far below the summit of power will and will not accept. It was this calculus of consensus, whether expressed in Harry Truman's observation that "I sit here all day trying to persuade people to do the things they ought to have sense enough to do without my persuading them . . ." or in Lyndon Johnson's exhortations to reason together, that escaped Colonel McCormick; and ignorance of it drove him from one frustration to another.

As a public man, therefore, the Colonel stands in dismaying contrast to that other Illinois Republican, who was called the Great Emancipator, but who put the preservation of the Union even ahead of the emancipation of the slaves. In sum, the Colonel was a radical. If his economics anticipated Milton Friedman, his sociology anticipated C. Wright Mills. And although Mills might have labeled him as In, he would unhesitatingly have classified himself as Out. No matter that the Establishment he attacked was not existent. It's easier to attack an Establishment that isn't there, because you can blame it for the things it hasn't done.

Colonel McCormick's strictures on the fate of the Republic no longer require an answer as to specifics. But they are relevant. Their relevance lies in the perspective they provide on today's radicals, whose fulminations were so accurately foreshadowed by the Colonel's own sad progress down the road to unreason. They remind us that unreason staggers under a terrible burden of confusion and danger, to itself as to others. The only answer to the Colonel's heirs is not to succumb to a petulant defense of our partial solutions to the great problems all of us face alike, but rather to go on drawing attention, with as much patience and good humor as possible, to the unregenerate reality of the problems themselves.

ADAM YARMOLINSKY

OF NAMES AND PERSONS ★★★ Unlike the writers of fiction, biographers are bound by the evidence and may not invent in aid of clarity.

In the pages that follow, therefore, it will be found that people sometimes alter the spellings and even the content of names with which they began. Favorites are mixed, as to generations and as to persons, in rich profusion.

Nothing can be done about it except to offer here a brief sorting out among certain of the principals, joined with a regret that fact is so inconsiderate of sense.

In 1847, three brothers from Rockbridge County, Virginia, began the development in Chicago of a farm machinery business, almost exactly on the day that the Chicago *Tribune* opened up as a newspaper. The brothers were:

Cyrus Hall McCormick, great-uncle of the subject of this book.

William Sanderson McCormick, paternal grandfather of the subject.

Leander James McCormick, great-uncle.

In 1855, a Canadian-born journalist, reared in Ohio, came to Chicago as an editor on the *Tribune*. He was Joseph Medill, maternal grandfather of the subject.

Robert Sanderson McCormick, son of William, married the eldest Medill daughter, Katherine, and of this marriage there were three children:

Joseph Medill McCormick.

Katrina McCormick (died as infant).

Robert Rutherford McCormick, subject of this book, also known as Robert Sanderson McCormick, Jr.

In 1833, a Presbyterian minister, born in Tennessee and reared in downstate Illinois, came to Chicago as pastor of the city's principal church of his denomination. He was Robert Wilson Patterson.

Robert Wilson Patterson, Jr., his eldest son, married the second Medill daughter, Elinor, and succeeded Medill as editor of the *Tribune*. Of the marriage, two children:

Joseph Medill Patterson.

Elinor Josephine Patterson, who had her name changed in court to read Eleanor Medill Patterson.

All that follows can be summed up best by saying it is an attempt to discover a man. In his day, McCormick was closely noticed and frequently characterized as he moved among the manipulators of public power in most parts of the world. He expected attention and he got it. Contusions and abrasions, if not physical yet not one whit less painful, usually marked victims of his disapproval, and these were not few. I can best suggest the effect he had on other people by mentioning that some citizens, of whom he was one, came to feel he would make an admirable President of the United States. Others, including a President who had known him since boyhood, found themselves wishing him in the dock, charged with the gravest of crimes against the United States imperiled by war.

Yet nobody seems to have done a total study to show just what helped make him the sort of man he was. Indeed, it was only in his very last years that he disclosed any consistent effort of his own at introspection. Quite in keeping with his nature, when he did get around to it he conducted the exercise in the columns of the *Tribune* and on its radio and television stations, to impress the largest audience he could assemble. Even so, many details passed unmarked by those who might have used them effectively, for him or against. As usual, his mere presence, rather than the content of it, kept the beholder in thrall.

Here, then, is what I offer as the very first total effort to organize Robert Rutherford McCormick as a human being and to define him according to the facts of his existence. But I cannot claim to be an unbiased witness. My judgment has been affected by personal experience, and it is part of McCormick's achievement that nobody who had much to do with him was left indifferent.

I met McCormick on March 26, 1929, in Nashville, Tennessee, while he was there on a brief visit and soon learned to marvel at his capacity to make other people anxious. For a while, I kept up with him in the news, but nothing he did was of any special importance to me until July 31, 1933, on which date I entered the employ of W. R. Hearst, with the then Washington *Herald*. The executive editor was Eleanor Medill Patterson, McCormick's cousin.

In the years following, I evolved as Mrs. Patterson's envoy, negotiator and pacificator with "my lordly cousin," as she called him on the good days, in matters gravely affecting not only her intensely personal approach to publishing, but his more generalized and conventional system. It should give some idea of what this assignment entailed to say that McCormick could be found conventional by comparison with anybody.

In 1949, as an executor, trustee and beneficiary under Mrs. McCormick's will, and as an officer and director of the Washington *Times-Herald,* which had become her own newspaper, I found myself opposite McCormick at the bargaining table, with large money at stake. Each of us wore the several hats of principal and fiduciary, accountable to persons and institutions with extraordinary power to hold us liable. There was much stress and many difficulties as the work was done. There was even more complaint about the result—but that is another story. In this record it is appropriate to deal only with the parts in which McCormick was the central figure. These were not minor.

In 1949, I ventured for the first time directly into McCormick's employ, as an officer and director of his attempt to publish the Washington *Times-Herald*. It was an effort begun with the highest hope and confidence, at least on my part. But on June 1, 1953, just short of twenty years from my beginning in Washington journalism, I was allowed to resign, in an amiable fiction for being fired, as business defeat and personal humiliation threw a mournful shadow across McCormick's final years.

All of these matters are explored in detail at proper points in the general narrative. Here I add only that in bargaining with McCormick I asked no quarter and gave none. At the forming of his Washington effort he neither invited me to pass judgment on his intentions nor did he offer any apologies on discovering the consequences of his own. There was never the slightest tinge of personal rancor in our acquaintance and I have come to feel it was very bad manners, not to mention my loss in the humane sense, that I made no effort to maintain communication with McCormick after 1953. Sheer curiosity and interest, if nothing more elevated, were excuse enough. But the truth is that I was so generally shattered by the total circumstances I spent several years trying to put all memory of them out of my life. Failing that, I have since done what I could to understand.

And so, this book. In a chosen place I try to give all credits due. I have used only materials of record, to which I had rightful access and against which I have set out my speculations, so plainly marked that one cannot fairly be mistaken for the other. So far as I know there are no misplacements of fact, but of course I am bound to be wrong about more things than one. In a single vanity do I feel secure. However short it may fall of justice, this account would surely stir a certain response in one reader if it could only be made available to him. In every sense, I regret that he is beyond reach for comment.

FRANK C. WALDROP

Washington, D.C.
April 1, 1965

McCormick
of Chicago

CHAPTER ONE ★★★ The first of many contradictions which beset the man here examined has to do with his birth. It is certain that he was born in the city of Chicago on July 30, 1880, but on other points there is conflict among the authorities.

He was known to the world as Robert Rutherford McCormick, and so shall he be called here. But his widow says he told her his childhood name was different. Other family members agree. His birth certificate gives no name at all.

He believed himself born at one address but his birth certificate gives another and independent evidence is only confusing. He was generally thought to be one of two children, yet the official document shows there were three.

The great world through which he moved all his life casually supposed his hard certainty of behavior was based on a huge family fortune, his to command at will. Not so. It is incorrect to say he was domineering, but certainly true that he was dominating by nature. And he had great skill at employing his nature to gain his purposes.

He was best known for his distinction as a journalist. But he was also a lawyer, public official, historian, soldier, cut-and-try engineer, woodsman, inventor, manufacturer, proprietor of very large properties, linguist, world traveler, radio and television performer, social critic, and even, in one especially romantic circumstance, the secret agent of two foreign powers at once. He did nothing in that role contrary to the interests of the United States and was soon in uniform at war against the very nations which could have held him to account if his exploit had been discovered.

On the evidence, therefore, it may be said that as a man of action, over long years, McCormick performed with great effect in a broad variety of important fields, to the never-ending surprise of his many critics. These seemed to feel that underestimating him offered more comfort than acknowledging his demonstrated capabilities.

He analyzed the constitutions of states ancient and modern; wondered whether the vibrations of leaves on trees affected the rise of sap from their roots; advised kings, emperors and presidents of their duties; had an automobile monogrammed for his favorite bulldog; managed thousands of employes with art and generosity; was twice married and had no child, except for the newspaper operation he rescued in young manhood and vastly multiplied both in dollars and in power. Then, he left his share of it to the benefit of employes and the public welfare.

At his death the argument for Social Darwinism as the perfected essence of the good passed from the American scene. McCormick was the last important man in the country who then still believed in that idea, propagandized for it and, in every way his ingenious mind could conjure up, dared the hazards of attempting to live by it in a society which no longer cared enough to recognize its name.

For more than forty years he held primary responsibility for the operations of the Chicago *Tribune* and was the executive head of its many enterprises. In that role he managed to convince—and to concern—many people, that he embodied an unknown territory of wayward surprise, "the Middle West."

The *Tribune* has been published in Chicago since 1847, and it has a record in the shaping of public attitudes difficult for any journal of our time to match. Certainly, McCormick operated the *Tribune* with great gifts of inheritance, knowledge, ability and determination. And certainly, the Middle West long rested under his hand, almost literally, as he built the *Tribune* into the most widely circulated newspaper of standard size in his day. More than that, out of the *Tribune* in his period flowed capital to extend its interests throughout the United States and almost everywhere else on earth people had learned to read print, look at pictures or follow drawings in caricature.

If McCormick had ideas of what society should be, and he certainly had them, he also had superb means to distribute his ideas for the consideration of others. He was at his peak in the years before radio and television on the one side, and magazines on the other, had shaken the rasping self-confidence of daily journalism and driven it from the pleasure of being feared to the hope of being appreciated.

Sir Shane Leslie, a friend of McCormick's from their childhood meeting at school in England, remarked after long years of moving among newspaper proprietors that no other citizens make quite so much noise in passage as these gentry, but that when dead, none lie more quietly. It is true, and yet it is not altogether true. Something depends on how the grand noise-maker occupied himself in other ways.

McCormick, to be sure, was as loud as he could manage at living political dialog. And if anybody expected a blessed silence to fall after he was gone it must be noted that the Republican Party, ten years after his death, was in convulsion for reasons directly traceable from his final attention to it. But even if his effect as noise-maker is set aside, there is further, and better, reason to argue that McCormick is worthy of some study.

Both in his native city and in the wild country of Canada, McCormick did truly significant and enduring work entirely outside journalism as such that had profound effect on social and economic developments.

It is possible, now as in his lifetime, that any two critics of political journalism will disagree flatly about McCormick's views and about his performance as an editor. It is not so easy for anybody to find fault with him as a public official or as a creative, risk-taking capitalist.

Before he ever got into journalism, McCormick, at the age of twenty-five, chanced into administrative charge of Chicago's most important public work, the Sanitary and Ship Canal that links the Great Lakes with the Mississippi river system and the Caribbean sea. It was a moment of municipal crisis and if he had not proved to be able, incorruptible—and ruthless in a fight—Chicago might now be a very different, and less fortunate, city.

As capitalist, he invaded the North Shore of the St. Lawrence river in country so rough nobody had dared tackle it for such purposes, and built in the heart of its spruce forests a newsprint manufacturing system that is now one of the principal industries of Canada. His tact and skill at multilingual and multinational politics were a total confusion to critics on each side of the border who liked to think of McCormick only as a monster of blind, stubborn prejudices.

Stubborn he most assuredly was, and afflicted with prejudices to the point of mania, but seldom really blind to the cost, for he knew very well the risks inherent in the things he chose to do. And, as will here be shown, again and again, it paid nobody to assume that in any situation he could be counted on to behave reliably according to type-casting by superficial observers.

And so, what was he like? How did he look? What were his parts and his purposes?

For all the confusions mentioned at the outset, there is none whatsoever as to certain elements we need to know. McCormick was born into an environment of record making and record keeping. The families of his immediate constellation began posing for photographs as early as any were to be had. Uncounted numbers of period likenesses yet gather dust in hatboxes, trunks, attics, newspaper libraries, safes and bankboxes, waiting someone to codify their graphic evidence of how citizens of a particular kind looked and lived when they felt very much in command of themselves and free to do about as they pleased.

The first so far turned up of McCormick is at age three, in a ruffled dress with a large bow at the left hip, hair fluffed out and cut squarely across the small, stern forehead. The baby face that looks full and directly out at the world is impassive, unsmiling and unyielding, unaware of the costume so feminine in design and yet in effect not effeminate. There is a reason he is dressed so, and it has nothing to do with that high crime against small boys known as Little Lord Fauntleroy, which had not yet been perpetrated.

The family account is that McCormick's mother, at the time of his birth, still mourned the loss of an infant daughter. She dressed the new baby in girl's clothes for as long as she could and refused to accept him for what he was.

That earliest pictorial expression finds support at every following period. There is preserved a hard, unyielding look, intended to disclose nothing. Indeed, it is not until his old age and away from his ordinary circumstances that McCormick is ever caught allowing himself a small, engaging smile, as if he were now indifferently willing to let others think what they like and be damned to the whole lot.

McCormick, at maturity, stood six feet, four inches. He had large head, hands and feet, was rather awkward in the small movements and condemned always to be careful where he sat. He tried hard to keep his weight down to 215 pounds with boxing, polo, shooting, riding to hounds and other blood-sport notions of masculinity, but was never satisfied with the result.

In his early years he was clean-shaven, but came out of World War I with the bristly moustache which thereafter summed up an austere old-fashioned look, his trademark, and gave those who sought to caricature him an endless inspiration. He kept a full head of hair, had brown eyes which, for all their occasional bulging with rage, were mild enough in general. And it is proper to his personality that when he died at seventy-four his teeth were still essentially his own. In keeping, too, he used a plain, straight razor right to his very last illness, no matter how much his elderly hands trembled, chasing off wife and valet who watched from a distance as he wavered through the fearful possibilities each defiant morning.

His hats, suits and leather goods came from London, and, if he could manage it, from the same establishments his father had used before him. His shirts were made in Paris and young ladies of his acquaintance learned to send him neckties of vigorous color. His usual style of dress was naturally as solemn as his expression, yet on occasion he liked to burst out in strong, though never unattractive, combinations. Color was one of many instruments of attention fascinating to him, and he made the *Tribune* its pioneer at run-of-paper use of four colors in daily journals. So were uniforms. He maintained a wide variety of regalia, bearskin caps and similar amusements, including sets of knickers and belted coats of a sort not seen since 1912 except on certain English politicians out with their cronies at ritual grouse murder.

At the table, McCormick was no glutton, but he was not finicky, either. He fancied himself something of an expert on wines, in light of his cosmopolitan upbringing, but in fact paid them little enough attention. He was rather a frequent user of the best Scotch whiskies and suffered no known remorse on such occasions as he allowed one to get the upper hand. Whisky went well with his favorite dishes of corned beef hash, roast beef, cold steak and vegetables of matching simplicity, produced to his exact orders on the farm he had roamed from boyhood. There he liked to pick the garden fruits, rumbling to himself a jingle in language hardly imaginable from the editor of the *Tribune:*

> "Pa ain't got no peas and corn,
> Pa ain't got potaters,
> Pa ain't got no lima beans,
> But Jeeesus—what tomaters!"

Whereupon, he would salt one, hand it to whoever had been summoned to ramble with him, salt another for himself, and give off, like as not, one of his unsignaled generalizations. These, his executives came to cherish and cautiously to exchange as clues to what might happen, next. Of politics: "California, next to Wisconsin, is the nuttiest state in the Union." Of the English: "They don't like to admit anybody else can have ideas." Of the French: "Never been happy except in a monarchy." Of two wrist watches keeping separate time: "Men love gadgets." Of inherited money: "The easiest way to get it." Of Illinois voices: "It's the combination of northern and southern influence that makes them so beautiful."

His own voice was a muffled baritone, not made easier to understand by his mode of speech, which he held to have been influenced by his brief period as a schoolboy in England. He once invited his radio audience to judge for itself whether he had an English accent. It required little shrewdness for anybody to gather how McCormick himself felt about it. From childhood, relatives had the habit of calling him "Bertie," but as he matured he let it be known that intimacy, if any, should be signified by calling him "Bert." One of the duties assigned to his second wife was explanation that "Bertie is a Cockney word," but his first wife called him "Bertie" and so did his cousins, often to his face, and not only in moments of conscious spite.

It could be argued quite sensibly, examining the facts all from one direction, that McCormick was really an example of a common enough American type, the romantic and sentimental Anglophile. In demeanor, dress, gestures and speech, he came off a work of art as first gentleman of his county, its hereditary law-giver toward whom bloods, yeomen and vagrant tinkers alike could turn for equal justice according to their deserts.

But against any straightforward interpretation of appearances there must be set formidable objections, the first being that great comic feat for which he was known all over the world, his word war with the British Empire. Simplistic critics tried to dismiss this with the vague charge that McCormick was "anti-British," or else that he was just another journalistic hypocrite, baiting the credulities of the ignorant for low, political purposes. McCormick's own estimate of why he did it was full enough of holes, but at least it was more complex. He held himself not anti-British but "pro-American," and claimed proper Britons agreed. He saw modern England in the grip of parasites in the church, the law and most especially in the Foreign Office, who could not make a living at honest work and so were out to suck the blood of an obsolete colonial empire, into which they would like to embrace the United States. Only "pseudo-Americans," he said, were taken in by their spurious grandeur. And to educate his readership he would at regular intervals review the plan of Cecil Rhodes to build a secret society for world conquest. He nominated Benedict Arnold as the first member of "Union Now."

But, of course, there was much more than that to McCormick's fascination with English political, social and military history, on which he produced a polemical literature inviting a separate book in itself. It is now commonplace to examine any man's affairs according to a sort of theory of opposites. If there is no letup of talk about love after the honeymoon, look to see what the difficulty is in suppressing something else. And what, after all, is hate, except a shocked response to the thought of not being loved?

This reduction of human feeling into a sort of reciprocating steam engine can, of course, be over-simplified, and it has long since become one of the banalities of literature. But even so, it can be a power in the study of real life. Truth has a way of rising to it.

In McCormick's case, the evidence is copious that his feeling toward the British welled from some secret knowledge, not all of which could he discuss even with himself, and that it was cross-connected throughout all his affairs. There was nothing simple and straightforward about any of it. The influences governing him on

Britain began to form before he was born. They did not arise out of any one aspect of his experience but permeated the whole, with an effect powerful as money itself, or the lack of it. It would be meaningless, therefore, to exhume them abruptly. They must be allowed to emerge as they will, to appear and reappear in the disguises and forms they assumed in the first instance, if they are to be appreciated in their potency.

As a matter of fact, McCormick's attitude on money, though definite, was calm enough. He never pretended to hold any prejudices against luxury. He had been taught by his parents to think in terms of first quality and so he unashamedly lived. He was by no means indifferent to the pursuit of dollars, for he had painful family knowledge of the punishments that can fall upon a financial dependent. But his contempt for money hogs was conspicuous, and more than one so defined in his mind came to discover how merciless he could be. Money, rather, was something he needed in the exercise of power, so he kept it well available. Yet he was by no means unwilling to risk it all. He could challenge the times, his readers, his advertisers and all the powers of what he considered the political darkness, and put in hazard not only his own purse but that of all tied to his impulse. The effect could be shocking to behold, not to mention endure.

His formal education began at the Ludgrove School in Middlesex, while his father was a diplomatic attaché in London. It continued in the United States at Groton and Yale, as good as the country had to offer. His academic record and personal deportment were of high order, but he considered that his real impression of life's purpose came from experiences lived with his grandfather Joseph Medill and the *Tribune,* a forceful combination for any mind to grasp. But one exception must be taken immediately. McCormick was a pupil of William Graham Sumner, who was then at the summit of his influence as Yale's philosopher of Social Darwinism. At his own life's closing, McCormick remembered to mention emotional and intellectual debt to Sumner. It was just that he should. No two men ever were more alike in considering the times, and not themselves, out of joint.

In sum, McCormick was encouraged by all he learned to approach life soberly, sure that he had been born into the most responsible and best-equipped element of the most envied people in the world. He was expected to turn in a good report card and he meant to do it.

This general purpose, his tendency to commune with himself, and his somber public manner, led the uninformed to suppose McCormick pretty much of a bore. Nothing could have been more unsound. If he felt like it, he could hold his own in any sort of company. Certain ladies beautiful enough, clever enough and mature enough—but not too mature—learned that he had a vast knowledge of scandal and could be induced to swap. He was adept, too, at the role of man-among-men, when allowed to play it on his own terms. That is to say, he moved easily among all varieties of *Tribune* workmen and gauged nicely the moments when it was possible to let fly a shattering men's room joke. It is not easy to find out how he learned these, for nobody was ever heard to come up with a competitor. Other editors and publishers, if he had known them very long, came to appreciate his rather biting sense of wit and dry, abrupt declaratives, but very few could claim to be on really easy terms with him. If any.

As to religion, both his training and record were uneven. His ancestry on all sides were Calvinists and the McCormicks in particular had a history of splendid doctrinal rows on Presbyterian practice. But his earliest schooling was all among members of the Church of England and New England Episcopal converts. These latter he delighted to ridicule for abandoning their heritage for the soothing effects of a more elegant ceremonial. He once tried to get a rise out of J. P. Marquand, whose novels on Boston manners were then at their peak of popularity, only to discover that Marquand had much the same view as his own. He had little patience with ordained churchmen of any denomination, as a matter of fact, and if one dared heckle him he was quick to confute with deadly contradictions from the King James Version, of which he knew a dazzling set.

Even so, as his end approached, he took his usual care to have all in order for any contest that might develop. First, he went privately to chapel and affirmed himself true to the faith of his fathers. As he left he muttered to his wife that he felt like a fool. But then, at a dinner in celebration of his seventieth birthday, the spectacle of his life in review moved him to call on the minister present as witness that he was "a good Christian."

In his daily work, McCormick made the seconds count. Whenever he might choose to sleep, there when he awoke would be his personal bundle of fresh *Tribunes.* He would begin dissection at once. If he were anywhere in the vicinity of Chicago an appropriate chauffeur would move him by plane or helicopter or strapped in the back seat of his limousine [McCormick had seat belts in his cars long before other people thought of them], as he scrawled on margins, tore out bits marked for department heads and read with minute attention to detail. By the time he had got to his tower fastness he knew that morning's product from the line across the first page to the last want ad. Misery was inevitable for any who supposed otherwise.

There was grave risk, too, for any who might be tempted to treat any McCormick marginalia as confidential information, to be exploited for individual advantage in the office politics inevitable in any large enterprise, but fifty times more intense among many able men all reporting to a single absolute monarch.

McCormick's handwriting was such a threat that experienced executives formed a sort of insurors' pool or defense committee of deciphering experts. Even so, not only the script, but even the idea, could escape everybody. The *Tribune*'s chief correspondent in Washington, Walter Trohan, once got a passage from one of McCormick's speeches, and the query: "What do I mean by this?"

McCormick was perfectly well aware of the defense committee and the trouble he gave, but all he ever did about it was to keep an eye out for script contesting with his own for obscurity. If he found it interestingly bad he would ask where his rival had studied penmanship.

At his desk in the room about which so many stories were spread in his lifetime as to trick doors, concealed machine guns, guard dogs and other such fright-wiggery, he proceeded, with the aid of three lady secretaries who henpecked him unmercifully, to lay about him in the fashion by which the great world knew him. Gifted technicians of his editorial will came and went. By telephone and by crisp, if sometimes also cryptic, correspondence, he directed those beyond his immediate presence. No man ever gave a better appearance of knowing exactly what he wanted, how to get it or what to do with it.

None of which should be taken to suggest that he suffered any fetish for consistency, in small things or in large. He read dictionaries and encyclopedias as others do novels. Books of historical reference were usually stacked at his elbow, for instant resumption of his hunt for facts. But no orthodoxy governed except his own. If some version of events sat well with him yesterday that meant nothing now, even less tomorrow. He would, without the least apology, contradict anybody, including himself.

Those who knew him took care not to smoke in his presence, for he suffered—or gave out—the notion of throat ailment from exposure to gas in the First World War. And woe to him, also, who dared light a cigarette in the *Tribune*'s handsome elevators, each bearing on its walls a warning that such was against the law.

What was the real reason for this necessity? As against that business of gas inhalation, McCormick was on record elsewhere as having claimed that in college he discovered smoking a waste of time. Still a third explanation was given in the autobiography of John T. McCutcheon, most famous and most widely loved of all *Tribune* cartoonists of the twentieth century. McCutcheon said that McCormick told him how he found himself, in a very early critical encounter with another Chicago publisher, stubbing out one cigarette after another, and decided to discipline himself by quitting altogether. He fancied himself a demonstration of the man who manages himself shrewdly in all things to gain his ends, and remarked to McCutcheon that he noticed men who catch the eight o'clock train to town manage to do it with regularity, but the man who means to take the nine-fifteen is apt to miss the one going at a quarter past noon.

Just what smoking story fits the facts, if any, is beyond saying. The point is plain. Any man who could not resist such a small vice as smoking quite likely would be overcome by a worse one. In this, as in so many other instances, it was McCormick's gift to use the instrument at hand for his own good end, so that abstinence was one more small warning to those around him that they must look alert, take care and not offend.

Those who saw him the most would be the first to deny that he was at all a cruel man in personal relations, nor should the small insight just given be taken as any such suggestion. But he most certainly could be ferocious in his role as editor and social critic. He had a memory to intimidate a whole herd of elephants, vast resources for revenge or favor and a child's passion for omnipotence, his own way exactly on terms of his own imagining. It is remarkable, all things considered, that in so many circumstances he was able to be kind and generous, that in private manners he could be the soul of courteous gentility and that when he died he was genuinely mourned, not least by those who saw the most of him around the *Tribune*.

In short, like John D. Rockefeller to whom he was related by marriage, and Henry Ford with whom he collided in one of history's most absurd lawsuits, McCormick turned out to be another true American original. He was and now is not, gone with the carrier pigeon and the novels of William Gilbert Patten, whose muscular invention, Frank Merriwell, was often mentioned by McCormick as the hero he would most have wished to be.

CHAPTER TWO ★★★ Long before McCormick was born the *Tribune* had an international reputation for intrusion upon major problems of public policy. It had been central to the elections of three Presidents of the United States and had been credited by one of these with primary influence in bringing on an unprecedented convulsion in the national life.

The President was Abraham Lincoln and the convulsion was the American Civil War.

So, too, the McCormick family had distinguished itself with the invention of a grain harvesting machine, "the Virginia reaper," which is noted in civilian economic history as having worked a world-wide revolution in agricultural practices. Military economists commonly agree also that the Virginia reaper had as much to do with the victory of the Union in the Civil War as any combination of men at arms.

The entanglements of Lincoln with the McCormicks and the *Tribune,* and the entanglements of the McCormicks with each other, have inspired enough books to fill a fair-sized library. So, too, the mythology that has grown out of the truth. One such myth is that McCormick's paternal grandfather was Cyrus, founder of the present-day International Harvester Company, who brought the McCormicks to Chicago. If brains, vigor and sheer lunatic contrariness were enough, it would be so. In fact, McCormick's paternal grandfather was William, a younger brother of Cyrus.

Another such myth has left the impression that Joseph Medill, McCormick's maternal grandfather, organized the Chicago *Tribune,* founded the Republican Party and elevated Abraham Lincoln from country lawyer to folk hero. Not one of these suppositions is true, though McCormick certainly encouraged belief in them. And as in the myth about Cyrus, there was just enough fact entangled in belief to make it all too easy to accept.

The third myth, growing out of the first two, is that McCormick himself "owned" the *Tribune* and a great deal else besides, so that it was confidently asserted, even by people who should have known better, that he was "one of the richest men in America." In fact, when McCormick died in 1955, the administrators of his estate put a fair market value on it of $20,711,037.68, the most of this sum representing 381.83 out of the 2,000 shares of common stock issued by the Tribune Company of Illinois. To be sure, McCormick died richer than most men, and his administrators were interested in the lowest possible valuation of anything subject to the tax collector's scrutiny. But $20,000,000 does not qualify him as a magnate in the class with Rockefellers, Fords, Mellons and Duponts, if money is the measure. McCormick was a magnate, all right, and he had all the money he needed to live up to his role. He could have had a lot more if it had interested him enough, for he proved he could both get it and keep it. But he had something much more satisfying to his taste than the largest possible pile of dollars. He had a role and a status that allowed him to arouse concern in any quarter that drew his notice. The facts about how he came to achieve this capacity need no element of myth whatsoever to enliven them.

Since McCormick's Grandfather Medill was the ancestor about whom he talked most the facts about Medill are first in order of exploration. Medill was born on a farm near the village of St. John in the Canadian province of New Brunswick, April 6, 1823. His parents had emigrated from Belfast, aiming for the United States, but it was not until Medill was nine years old that they made it down to Stark County, Ohio.

They were the simplest and plainest of members in that great stream of the Scotch-Irish which poured in through Pennsylvania and along the edge of the Great Lakes. This group populated the Middle West from one direction, as another such stream ran south through the troughs between the Allegheny ranges to occupy the back country of Virginia. In Belfast, Medill's father had been a shipwright. In Ohio, he tried farming, but made little success of it. Medill, except for brief schooling in the county seat, Massillon, educated himself.

From earliest times in small-town America, young men of little means and large ambition have found the triangular relation between law, journalism and politics holding within it that which they really wanted most, the power to make other people jump. Medill's approach was by way of the law, but he found that he could pick up cash around newspaper shops, setting type. And because he had a disputatious mind and ready tongue, it was not long until his arguments with his employers about the issues of the day resulted in his setting editorials and political commentaries directly into type without bothering first to write them out. At New Philadelphia, the principal town of Tuscarawas County, he came into collision with James Patrick, judge of common pleas, Presbyterian elder, Indian agent, manager of Whig politics for that whole sector of the Northwest Territory and owner of the New Philadelphia *Chronicle*. It was from Patrick that Medill learned the uses of power.

In 1849, Medill bought his own paper, the Coshocton, Ohio, *Whig*. He renamed it *The Republican* and put his brothers, William, James and Samuel, to running it. He had another idea for himself. On September 2, 1852, Joseph Medill and Katherine Patrick were married at New Philadelphia, very much against the judge's wishes. Miss Patrick was an expert typesetter and thoroughly familiar with the journalistic life, so that when Medill carried her off to Cleveland, where he had organized another paper, the *Leader*, she was a great help to him in business until their first child was born there on July 11, 1853. They called her Katherine Van Etta Medill. She grew up to be the mother of Robert R. McCormick.

Medill traveled the classic route from Whig to Free Soiler to Republican activist, in search of a leadership that would both save the American Union and rid it of the doctrine that human beings could, of right, be owned as chattel goods. And he lived to see it all come to pass, with him having much to do with the outcome.

But by no means did he have any part in starting the *Tribune*, which dates its official career from June 10, 1847. Medill was then still learning how to compose hand-set copy back in Ohio. The

Tribune began in a single room of a building on the southwest corner of Lake and LaSalle streets with a hand press on which one of the editors cranked out its first edition of four hundred copies. The originators were J. K. C. Forrest, James J. Kelly and John E. Wheeler. Only Forrest made any serious effort to stick out the exactions of running a newspaper. Within a month, Kelly sold his interest to Thomas A. Stewart, who promptly set the tone by which the *Tribune* has been known from that day to this. In 1847, Chicago was already taking on its now settled role as the point of transfer for men and goods crossing the North American continent. There was great trouble in the primitive harbor and the *Tribune* suggested editorially that the captain of a U.S. Naval patrol vessel should make himself useful at helping merchant ships find their way. This insult to his rank and station fired up the naval officer to challenge the editor to a duel. The *Tribune* merely published this demand of honor as news and in the municipal uproar that followed, the captain sued for peace, escorted the merchantmen to safe anchor, and the *Tribune* found an identity.

Not until the spring of 1855 did Medill come to Chicago, and not until 1874 did he get a controlling interest in the *Tribune*. But there cannot be any doubt he was a true mover and shaker in his day. He did become a major figure in Abolitionist politics after 1850 and had as good a claim as anybody to having popularized the name "Republican" for the rising new political faction. He was certainly one of Lincoln's most effective promoters, and from 1860 until his death in 1899 moved freely in the innermost circles of influence among those who triumphed out of the Lincoln legend. He was intelligent and courageous, a wholly effective journalist, if puritanical in taste and harsh as Cato in his pursuit of the most radical Republican doctrines on Reconstruction as due punishment for defeated rebels. It is undeniable that Medill was the unifying figure in *Tribune* affairs. He did not found the paper, but he certainly did preserve it.

In 1871, Chicago's very heart was destroyed by fire. The *Tribune,* which had been warning against just such a disaster, was last of the city's papers to be burned out and in two days was back on the streets. Medill drove the paper straight through the catastrophe and then, if *Tribune* official histories are to be accepted, he wrote its famous editorial, "Cheer Up," which called on the public will to survive. He next announced himself candidate for mayor on a "Fireproof" ticket and was overwhelmingly elected.

Medill was not much of a churchgoer and was far too much the critical journalist to be a literal believer in Bible-pounding, but he did have a severe fix against whisky among the working classes or licentious behavior by anybody. He conceived it his duty in the purification of Chicago to close down its bawdyhouses and gambling hells, which not even the catastrophe of 1871 had checked. He might as well have set out to bail Lake Michigan with an eyedropper. He finally resigned in August, 1873, and took off for Europe. Under his leadership the city had more than recovered its physical plant. It had grown and thrived. But its wild, animal spirit would have none of his meddling with its folkways. Even the police joined in open rebellion against his attempts to close down Sunday service in saloons. And though he remained abroad more than a year, animus had not cooled when finally he returned to buy control of the *Tribune*. Never again was he seriously considered for public office in the city which owed him so much for leadership in its darkest hour.

The Medills' marriage produced no sons, but three high-spirited daughters, Katherine, Elinor and Josephine, were all reared in a Chicago version of blue-stocking drill in journalism, literature and government. Josephine died before marriage. What the other two were like is reflected in a scrapbook kept by Elinor. She thought her elder sister exactly right to play the feminine lead in *The Taming of the Shrew*.

But if Miss Medill was a true Kate, the husband she caught was hardly qualified as Petruchio, though in his case, too, "such wind as scatters young men through the world" had something to do with his presence at the altar. Robert Sanderson McCormick was born July 26, 1849, on a farm in Rockbridge County, Virginia, the eldest child of William Sanderson and Mary Ann Grigsby McCormick. The McCormicks, too, were part of the Scotch-Irish stream from Pennsylvania. It was on that farm somebody invented the grain harvesting machine so powerful in altering the course of development in nineteenth-century Europe and America. Cyrus McCormick, William's older brother and road salesman for the machine, early got control of the patents and the money. In 1847, just exactly at the time the *Tribune* was establishing its real identity in Chicago, Cyrus McCormick settled on the city by the lake as the ideal site for taking world agriculture by the throat. By 1855, when Joseph Medill came to Chicago, Cyrus was already reckoned a millionaire. His younger brothers, William and Leander, were at first unsure whether they wished to risk the city life, especially since their stake in the business was limited to straight salaries, William as business manager and Leander as head of the manufacturing force. Cyrus remained on the road, fighting lawsuits, seeking business. The younger brothers, in 1857, threatened a sort of managerial strike if not given a better cut. The best they could get was a word-of-mouth approval to draw five thousand dollars a year each in cash and a beneficial interest to be gained out of investing 50 percent of the net profits to their account in equal shares. All property and principal were held by Cyrus.

William Sanderson McCormick proved to be a masterly, natural administrator. Furthermore, he was an extremely shrewd investor. He needed, to become one of the great magnates of the age, only enough gall to cope with Cyrus, a measure which would, indeed, have set him apart from the run of mankind. But a destroying sadness overtook him.

When the Civil War came on, all McCormicks in Chicago were torn by divided loyalty. Cyrus was even foolish enough to collide with the *Tribune,* not only by trying to compete with it in journalism, at which he was an immediate and total failure, but also in running for Congress as a Copperhead Democrat, critical of both Lincoln and the war. The *Tribune* went after him in a fashion any modern reader of its editorials will recognize as up to standard. It defined his claim to the reaper patents as fraudulent and held his only true invention to be the lie that he had any right to them. What the *Tribune* had to say about Cyrus McCormick as general citizen and candidate for office can only be given in its own language:

"Mr. McCormick has not an instinct that is not in sympathy with the rebellion. Like all poor white trash of Virginia, he left the State a better friend of slavery than the slaveholders themselves, and the prejudices of his youth have built upon a defective education, a perfect monomania in behalf of man-stealing."

None of which penetrated Cyrus' hide in the least. As late as March, 1865, he announced himself ready to go to Richmond and negotiate a settlement, if Lincoln at last realized it impossible to down Jefferson Davis.

William S. McCormick was less insensitive, if no less disturbed. The war was piling up cash in the company's till, but William had no confidence whatsoever in the Union Government's money, any more than he had belief in its war. He became so agitated as to urge the company be liquidated and its assets transferred to England.

By 1864, William's health was gone. He turned the management back to Cyrus, the division of profits and beneficial interests between the brothers an unsettled question. Within a year he was taken downstate to the Illinois hospital for the insane and there died, in September, 1865, imploring his brothers to "forbear one another in love" and not fight over money. That monumental difference, begun well before they left the farm in Virginia, was still unsettled at the time of Robert R. McCormick's death. In 1955 a descendant of Leander published a book holding that the reaper was really invented by Cyrus' father, Robert Hall McCormick, with an important assist from Leander.

McCormick himself took the view that his great-uncle Cyrus was guilty of overreaching and more than once said so in semipublic circumstances. He also got some sort of satisfaction out of saying, "all McCormicks are crazy, except me," and once startled Walter Trohan, chief of the *Tribune*'s Washington bureau, by adding: "You wouldn't agree with that, would you, Walter?" Trohan, who had sometimes frightened himself with the thought of what it would be like to head the *Tribune*'s political service with his employer in the White House, records that he confessed there were times when he had doubts. In that, as both knew, he was hardly alone.

But it may as well be stated in brief that all the quarreling was to no avail against Cyrus. By 1868, he was the largest payer of income tax in Chicago. By the time he died in 1884, he was world-renowned for his philanthropies, for his attempts to dictate Presbyterian doctrine, for his lawsuits and for his power at making money. So overawed were his contemporaries that he was accepted outside the family, if not within it, as the true patriarch of the herd by then assembled in such number along Rush Street that the neighborhood was known as "McCormickville." From there he dispensed his brand of justice. To the widow and five children of the defeated William, this resulted in a $400,000 cash settlement on the undistributed profits of the Civil War period. And that was all they got out of the ever-blooming Harvester Works harvest.

The record is mute on the entrancing question of how Robert

Sanderson McCormick, the relatively impecunious eldest son of William, ever dared approach Joseph Medill to ask the hand of Kate, truly a formidable father's imperious daughter if ever there was one. It took nerve, for the McCormicks were still Copperheads and Democrats and Medill was implacable as ever on vice inherent in all those ever indulgent of "man-stealing." But Robert S. McCormick certainly was a University of Virginia model of a gentleman, esteemed in polite society for his quiet good manners, courteous attention to elders and interest in matters literary. He was educated to be a lawyer, but had gone into the grain brokerage business in Chicago and St. Louis in hope of building his modest competence into something more muscular. On the side he acquired merit as a student of the vast literature on Napoleon then so much in vogue. He also was much interested in seeing Chicago have a good public library.

On June 8, 1876, Katherine Medill and Robert S. McCormick were married at the Second Presbyterian Church of Chicago by the Reverend J. Monro Gibson. She was twenty-two, he was twenty-seven. At that time, Chicago was the Rome of North America for Presbyterians and the Second Church was as near to a St. Peter's as propriety may permit suggestion. The pulpit of the Second Church had known only one other pastor, the Reverend Robert Wilson Patterson, who resigned in 1874 after thirty-two years and led a movement toward a sort of churchly colonization in the suburbs, called Lake Forest. Dr. Patterson and his family, too, are part of this account and will be brought into it more fully in due course.

On May 16, 1877, the McCormicks' first child was born, christened Joseph Medill McCormick by his intelligent young parents. Instantly it was accepted on all sides that one day this baby would succeed to the *Tribune* editor's chair, and so he did. But he could not hold it.

On January 17, 1879, a second child was born. Having produced a son, the mother prayed for, and had, a daughter. The baby was first called Katherine, but in consideration of Dutch influences in the mother's ancestry, this was changed shortly to Katrina. On July 6, the baby died. Its mother was shattered but certain the Almighty would not deny her another little girl. Katrina's clothes and trinkets were saved and there was even some talk of naming the next baby Katrina as if, somehow, that would erase the pain.

On July 30, 1880, that next baby was delivered, and with it the McCormick-Medill-Tribune mythologies already made and yet to come took on a burnish that has kept them ever since a subject of entertainment and absorption in Chicago.

McCormick's formal obituary in the *Tribune* of April 2, 1955, gives his birthplace as 150 East Ontario Street on Chicago's Near North Side, a neighborhood once all fashionable, but now the worse for wear. According to the *Tribune,* McCormick set out one evening in his later years, wearing smoked glasses and following one of his German shepherd dogs, harnessed after the fashion of the Seeing Eye. It was a thing he had done before.

As McCormick told it later, he went around to 150 East Ontario, then occupied by a night club, and was so overwhelmed with courtesy shown a supposedly blind customer that he soon left in shame. But it is unlikely any Chicago headwaiter was really so innocent as not to recognize Haroun-al-Raschid out on the town in defense against boredom. McCormick's striking appearance and his habit of roving the streets in that particular disguise were both of long standing as spectacles for the city's special entertainment. In any case, McCormick next arranged a dinner at the night club and called for a toast to all the famous men born there. Then he revealed to the guests all these famous men were himself, and the disclosure became dogma.

His birth certificate is the usual ruinous eyewitness contradicting a good story. But if so, it at least comes up with another just as interesting. The certificate was returned by H. Webster Jones, M.D., on August 31, 1880, but quite obviously was made out by an entirely different hand, not now known. It is a portent of McCormick's whole life, a rich mixture of error, omission and misdirected fact.

The certificate recites that on July 30, 1880, at 101 Pine Avenue in the 18th Ward of Chicago, there was born a male child, the third of their marriage, to Katherine Medill McCormick and Robert Sanderson McCormick. The father's occupation was given as grain shipping and commission business, which was correct, but put his birthplace as Cleveland, Ohio, and the mother born in Rockbridge County, Virginia, just exactly opposite to the facts, and a fair indication of the general stress that surrounded the whole event.

It is part of the family recall that Mrs. McCormick's third pregnancy was so fear-haunted and unsettled a time that her own mother had, in a literal sense, been obliged to keep a watch over her. This may account for the birth certificate's reading 101 Pine Avenue, for a manual of addresses gives that as Joseph Medill's residence in 1880. Robert S. McCormick's business address is given for that year as 174 LaSalle Street, but no home address at all, until 1882, and that as "Flat 6, The Ontario," a now long-vanished apartment building of undisclosed location. Searches of title do not reveal any such building on the site which would now be 150 East Ontario Street, in any case, nor do they show Robert S. McCormick ever owning property there or near it.

But the most important of all the birth certificate's oddities is that it has a blank where the baby's name should go. There is a stipulation on the form that if this is not filled out at the time of birth it must be, within the year, as a necessary step in establishing secure legal identity. Clerks in the Vital Records office of Chicago have been unable to find that it was ever done for the third McCormick baby.

These matters might seem of picayune significance, except for their relation to others not of documentary character. But when all the points are coupled together, it requires no more than ordinary sympathetic insight to understand the origin of powerful governors in McCormick's behavior, whether that in itself is thought worthy or not.

When Kate at last was made to realize her third child could not sensibly be named Katrina II, so the family story goes, she simply refused to conform to the sensible. She had the baby dressed in the ordained feminine pink and called it "Roberta" until the child's tantrums, when it was almost seven years old, finally impressed her to quit the punishment.

From the start, according to family account, the little boy was to everybody else Robert Sanderson McCormick, Jr. In the end, if Kate lost her battle to save Katrina, she did her worst to destroy the identity of her husband in the son. For when the boy was ten years old she declared Sanderson too common a name to be endured. So, she called him Rutherford, on the theory that she had discovered kinship, through such a family relation, with Sir Walter Scott. And Rutherford was his name of record throughout his youth and college years. Not until he was a man did he manage to revive connection with his father and sign his letters "Robert R. McCormick."

CHAPTER THREE ★★★ Early in January of 1952, McCormick announced over the *Tribune*'s radio station, WGN, that on the first Saturday night of each month he would broadcast a chapter from his memoirs. He would not cover modern times, he specified, becausc his listeners were familiar with these, "but perhaps the first half-century of my recollections will bring out many things not generally known, especially the years of my boyhood in Europe."

For the rest of his life he regaled a fascinated radio and television audience with some rare material, which was regularly printed, also, on the editorial page of the Sunday *Tribune* following; deservedly one of the most popular, if one of the least accurately evaluated, features ever to appear in the paper.

McCormick not only had a real gift for narrative but also a near to total recall for minute details of his experience and so this series, which he did not live to edit into a proper book, is invaluable to the biographical investigator—so long as he can keep firmly in mind the colloquy between Holmes and Watson in the *Silver Blaze* case on the "curious incident of the dog in the night-time."

Watson: "The dog did nothing in the night-time."

Holmes: "That was the curious incident."

As with dogs, so with men. McCormick's memoirs are always informative, though not always in the fashion he means them, as much for what he does not tell as for what he does.

This is all well illustrated in his very first broadcast, which begins:

> I was born on July 30, 1880. My first vivid recollection is the day that the anarchists were hanged in Chicago, November 11, 1887. Children were not allowed out of doors because riots were feared. The police were armed with rifles.
>
> The widow of one of the men, Miss Van Zandt, who married the anarchist [August] Spies by proxy after his conviction, lived in our neighborhood. We were deadly afraid of the poor woman and I am afraid I shouted at her on the street.
>
> My older cousin, Robert Hall McCormick, had a high bicycle. I used to ride on the step behind him. One day her pug dog ran out and we rode over it, but fortunately did not kill it.

And that is all he has to say about an event of the profoundest influence on the life of Chicago, in the affairs of his own family and finally, though it is doubtful he ever had any conscious realization of it, of powerful effect upon his own outlook. The very next paragraph of his memoir deals with a divorce sensation of the day involving the wife of a prominent Chicago attorney. From there, McCormick went on to tell of his boyhood abroad and to other subjects of great fascination, but not another word about that matter of the anarchists, which to this day remains a galling memory to Chicago. But anybody who wishes to know about McCormick must refresh his understanding of that long-ago municipal fright.

History, seen as a record of the crimes and follies of mankind, cannot hold very much against the year 1880 anywhere, if we let the surface record stand alone. In England, Queen Victoria was said to fidget at news the electorate had sent her dear Earl Beaconsfield home to stay, for now she would have to hear Mr. Gladstone again, addressing her as if she were a public meeting. In France, the struggle between church and state led to a presidential decree ordering the Society of Jesus to dissolve and disperse. Nothing much came of it. In the rest of Europe the public was so calm that even in Russia only two attempts were made to blow up the Tsar's minister of the interior. Undoubtedly, in Asia and in Africa the usual famines, pestilence and tribal wars claimed their thousands, but as far as the Western world knew all that vastness was the domain of militarists and explorers, whose writing industry furnished the romantic literature of Empire.

In the United States, President Rutherford B. Hayes and his abstemious wife, "Lemonade Lucy," retired from politics with pleasure. Mr. Hayes had never much wanted prominence and had made it plain he would serve but one term in any case. Promptly, he insured this by attempting reconciliation between war-torn factions, North and South. For this he got small thanks from anybody.

But, of course, the surface record is, as usual, a deceit. At Harvard, a young enthusiast named Theodore Roosevelt, on being handed his diploma, thought he would make a career at writing history. Instead, his career turned out to be the making of history, much of it with special effect on the child soon to be born to the young McCormicks in Chicago.

In Washington, another Harvard man whose estimates of men and events also throw much light on the influences that were to shape the baby's life, chose 1880 in which to hand around among friends an appraisal of the American scene as he found it at that moment. His name was Henry Adams, and he titled his estimate *Democracy,* but what he had to say was not meant to praise it, as practiced just then in the United States.

When Adams was born, in 1838, government in the new Republic still enjoyed some reputation for heroic creativity. Men still lived who had seen King George's Redcoats in their village streets. Some tottering few claimed to have fought in the sacred Revolution itself. Men who took to government quite usually assumed themselves responsible, in the best sense, and it was not at all extraordinary to find some philosophic and abstract in their approach to duty. No household in the country more conformed to this pattern than did Adams'. It was natural, therefore, for him to think of government as the prime instrument of society, to expect leadership's unselfish wisdom from men in office, and from the country at large grateful concurrence.

Adams fought the Civil War from London as confidential clerk to his father, the United States Minister. It was exacting, important work, all very much to his credit, but remote from the terror of the guns. In 1868 he came home still under the influence of his dry family expectation that Order can be imposed on Creation at once.

For seven years he studied the scene from a professor's chair at Harvard, then came down to Washington for a close, continuous examination of government in the hands of the New Men. He was revolted. His indictment was put about as a novel and he was careful not to sign it, but "everybody," the rarefied society of scholars and statesmen, knew it as his denunciation of Hayes and the Republican oligarchs in the Senate. Generations of writers since have been affected by it to misconstrue the realities of political existence in the American period from the first inaugural of Ulysses S. Grant in 1869 to 1901, when an assassin felled William McKinley and, in the immortal words of Marcus A. Hanna if he really said them, put "that damned cowboy" in the White House.

Adams himself came to realize there was more to the case than he had thought. In 1905, after much personal sorrow and many deepening experiences with the tribulations of his countrymen, he offered in his *Education of Henry Adams* that famous metaphor of the United States after the Civil War, "the profile of a long, straggling caravan, stretching loosely toward the prairies, its few score leaders far in advance and its millions of immigrants, Negroes and Indians far in the rear, somewhere in archaic time." He found the old world replaced by one of "energies quite new," in the hands of men with time for nothing more than the day's work, quick to resent being told what to do by those who "took their ideas and their methods from the abstract theories of history, philosophy or theology."

The United States to which Adams returned in 1868 was of necessity a caravan of stragglers. And it had good reason to be sick of all who set up to be leaders of men. Government had been the agent of a near-lethal rupture in domestic society. Men in office had hounded one another—and hounded also millions of other men, women and even little children—into the frenzy of Civil War. It was a degraded act of which nobody had cause to be proud. The bitter essence of it is all in Francis Parkman's reflection on what he thought the failure of universal suffrage. It was the nation's shame, he held, that the American people had not virtue, temperance and wisdom enough to abolish slavery peacefully and harmlessly.

In light of all the ordinary human being had been through, therefore, it was only natural that the caravan's first lurch toward peace turned out to be a cruel struggle of every man for himself and no inclination to look in awe on the pretensions of an office-holder, whether at the courthouse or the White House.

Adams' *Democracy* is, after all, no more than a mannered version of the charade acted out by sophisticates in Washington. If a valid literary summary of the general reality can be found anywhere it is in *The Gilded Age: A Tale of Today,* brought out in 1873 by Mark Twain and Charles Dudley Warner, editor of the Hartford *Courant.* As literature it is almost impossible to bear, but as social history it is illuminating in every way that *Democracy* is not. The theme of the work is pursuit of money by men and women hardened alike in times of disorder. The very vulgarity and rawness of the personifications give insight and convey feeling of real people in action in their time.

When McCormick was born in 1880, the harshness of the earliest struggles in the Gilded Age had just begun to temper, but it would not do to say that in the public mind government had begun to recover its antique dignity. It is one of the essential purposes of this work to search out just why, in McCormick's estimate, that recovery never did take place in his lifetime.

He had a unique invitation to lead such a recovery himself, to be one of Adams' few score leaders in advance of the caravan of pathetic searchers after a new life. Naturally, he considered himself thoroughly well equipped with the proper abstractions to insure a leadership of wisdom and generosity. He had an instrument, in the *Tribune,* beautifully fitted for the work. And certainly the fluidity of life in Chicago made it seem inevitable that he could lead the stragglers in the right direction.

No doubt it would be McCormick's estimate that he did, and despite the malicious interferences of less noble men. But if it can be said that he sought a role as one of the leaders in Adams' metaphoric caravan, he also acted out the role of the new men, too, so quick to resent being told what to think and how to behave. It was often said of him in his lifetime that he wished to set the clock back; that he feared and resented change; that he could not bear submission to superior authority. In one sense, these are just the usual misleading generalities of political hard language; but there is also a deeper truth in every one of them. For certainly, all his life long, McCormick was under the influence of distractions and alarms out of his past. Some were most intensely personal, of which his birth and infant experiences already mentioned are expressive. Other events were outside his immediate family, but certainly tangent to and weighing upon it.

The Haymarket Riot of 1886 and its aftermath offer an example which sums up many. Adams' caravan of stragglers nowhere cast off new citizens more steadily than in Chicago. Out of Europe poured the thousands who had lost their struggles for power, but not their urge. Chicago was a babel of tongues, quoting every coffee-house thinker from Proudhon to Marx to Sorel; and yet, among the common run of men there was only the slightest marginal interest in the general idea that government ought to intervene in the shaping of social action. Mainly, the common run were interested in getting rich, for Chicago was growing at a fantastic rate. But opportunity was dearly bought in freight yards, slaughter houses, iron mills, and nowhere at more brutal human cost than in Cyrus McCormick's Harvester Works. The men who commanded the industrial power had nearly all, and McCormick was one of them, known the hardest sort of physical labor themselves. They saw no reason for anybody else to be absolved from sweating it out, as they had done.

But not everybody above was unsympathetic toward those below and striving to rise.

In 1873, a 25-year-old lawyer-politician from New York named Henry Demarest Lloyd abandoned Eastern frustrations for a fling at journalism on the Chicago *Tribune*. Within a year he married Jennie Bross, daughter of one of the minority stockholders, and shortly thereafter became financial editor. In that role he developed into a close and critical student of business until 1885, then quit to do independent research which led him finally to bring out *Wealth Against Commonwealth,* an attack on trusts which had great influence on politics well into the twentieth century. It also had special bearing on the outlook of McCormick's brother and on McCormick's cousin, Joseph M. Patterson, his principal colleague and closest friend in life. But in McCormick's memoirs there is nothing to indicate the *Tribune* had ever harbored such a person, though descendants of Henry Lloyd remain important stockholders in the Tribune Company and a namesake sat on its board of directors at the very time of McCormick's memoir broadcasts.

Shortly after Lloyd left the *Tribune,* contention between Cyrus McCormick and the labor community passed beyond peaceful settlement. It had started with demand for an eight-hour day and led from there to a fight on the closed shop. McCormick finally turned the key in a lockout, which set off a great riot at the gates of the plant.

The next day, May 4, 1886, is one Chicago has wished many a time to forget. A crowd gathered in the old Haymarket Square and police arrived in platoons. Someone threw a bomb. One policeman was killed outright. By the time it was over six more policemen were injured fatally and a total official count of the wounded ran to one hundred, but Chicago still supports a firm tradition that many a man unlisted was knocked on the head by the Pinkertons, the reds, the police, the anarchists. Polemical histories for and against the city's industrial power have made it impossible to get a sense of precise truth out of the whole thing, except that it was bad.

Eight men, finally, were charged with the blame. Not one was shown to have made or thrown the bomb, but they were all undoubted anarchists and had declared themselves at open war with the community. No reasonable analyst can deny that their language, in the circumstances of the time, was less than the most flagrant provocation. Seven were sentenced to death, one to fifteen years in prison. The governor, Richard J. Oglesby, was put under terrific pressure both to relieve and to maintain the verdict. One man committed suicide in his cell. Four were hanged and two were let off from death sentences to life terms. Seven years later another governor, John P. Altgeld, himself an eccentric of the most provoking kind, pardoned all three survivors on ground they had not been given fair trials. The actual thrower of the bomb has never been positively identified, though there have been many nominees.

All of which was certainly the dominant event of Chicago in its time, as it is a galling memory even yet. And in every history of the Chicago labor wars, the *Tribune*'s Haymarket Riot editorials, uniformly critical of the dissidents, are featured elements. The editorials are also eloquent evidence that throughout McCormick's infancy and childhood threats from the anarchists, real or imagined, were subjects of constant household concern. So, too, was the great scandal attached to the behavior of Henry Demarest Lloyd, who not only became a socialist tractarian but also was one of the leading men in the argument that the anarchists had not been shown justice.

McCormick had, through his memoirs, every invitation to explore those dramatic times and to discuss their impact on his brother and on his Patterson cousin, to show how the Haymarket Riot laid the foundation for the environment in which both those young men and himself as well entered into Chicago's political life shortly after 1900.

Instead, he abandoned Chicago in a hurry and turned at once to his boyhood in Europe with the valiant proclamation:

> My parents were splendid diplomats because they had no inferiority complex. My father, one of the last of the pre-Civil War school, looked upon himself as of the Virginia aristocracy, the equal of any aristocracy in Europe. My mother reached her viewpoint by another route. Her father had been the intimate, in fact the leading individual in the nomination of President Lincoln, and also a supporter and intimate friend of General Grant.

All accounts of McCormick, Sr., agree that he was, indeed, pleasantly earnest and of meticulous good manners. But he had no luck in the Chicago grain market, which was supposed to build his limited inheritance to such a great fortune as to command respect from his Uncle Cyrus and from his wife's even more imposing father. Before his children were out of the nursery, Robert Sanderson McCormick was plucked like a chicken. And he lost more than his money, for, like all the rest of her family, Katherine Medill had no taste for failures.

There could be no place for McCormick on the *Tribune*. First, he hadn't the slightest bent for journalism. Second, Medill already had one son-in-law in the shop. His second daughter, Elinor, married a thoroughly competent *Tribune* reporter, Robert Wilson Patterson, Jr., son of the mighty pastor of Second Presbyterian. The young Pattersons, too, named their first-born Joseph Medill Patterson. They also had a daughter, Elinor Josephine, who as a woman of middle age, after two marriages and many adventures, had her name changed in court to read Eleanor Medill Patterson. Complications were already brewing which for half a century would add to a lively sense of excitement around the *Tribune,* not to mention fashionable parts of Washington, Vienna, St. Petersburg and Paris.

The Presidential election of 1884 clearly signaled that the day of the oligarchs could not remain forever sunshine. Farmers of the

Middle West, after years of every man happily on his own, were going broke. Their enemies, they decided, were the Gold Standard, the railroads, the "Eastern Capitalists," industrial monopolists, "middlemen" and foreign producers of wheat. Joseph Medill's intimate friend, James G. Blaine, valued next only to Lincoln as a paragon of greatness, was the victim of both intramural Republican quarrels and of general national distemper. One result was that the Democrats found a way to cohere Bourbons, farmers and city workmen into the first of their remarkable associations of opposites, to elect Grover Cleveland as President.

Cleveland's first administration was a flying in the face of settled oligarchic practice. He even went so far as to veto a gift to the Grand Army of the Republic called the "Dependent Pension Bill," and added insult to injury by proposing return of captured Confederate battle flags to whoever below the Mason-Dixon Line thought honor attached to their possession. His final, least explicable taunt to fortune was to propose himself for re-election on the abstraction of reduced tariffs, offered as a weapon against the trusts and high prices.

In 1888, therefore, the Republican Party made its historic commitment to high protective tariff, describing it as the savior of both business and jobs. Government was beginning, again, to be an actual instrument of serious public policy, if still on a severely limited scale. And the Republicans were sensible enough at practical mass politics in those days to offer also a great new pension project for the veterans. Even so, the election turned on a triviality that McCormick, in his day, had the *Tribune* retell in every Presidential year, vainly hoping it would work its magic again. The British minister to the United States was Lionel Sackville-West, second baron Sackville of Knole and long a target of Fenian curses, therefore a potent prospect for disruptions in the shaky tribal organization of the Democrats. A California Republican wrote for advice on how to vote, claiming to be an English-born naturalized U.S. citizen. The baron found for Cleveland. And when the votes were counted, the Democrats found that, even though they had disclaimed all British alliance and handed Sackville-West his passport immediately after the letter was made public, still they lost crucial blocs of non-Anglicans East and West. In consequence the majority of the Electoral College was bound Republican. Medill's problem of what to do with Robert S.

McCormick was automatically solved. The new United States Minister to Great Britain in 1889 was Robert Todd Lincoln, son of the Emancipator and head of the *Tribune*'s law firm. As Lincoln sailed for London aboard the S.S. *Adriatic* his second secretary was McCormick, out to recover through diplomacy the puissance lost in Chicago's savage wheat market.

In England, Mrs. McCormick discovered the importance of genealogy. Joseph Medill was himself a plain and forthright example of the Scotch-Irish in America, unpretentious, uninterested in supposing glories of aristocratic ancestry. The Pattersons were equally plain-style. And if, in fact, the McCormicks were of identical homely stock, by no possible stretch of imagination connected with the grandees of the Virginia Tidewater, there were elevated connections through various female lines. By such constructions did it turn out that Mrs. McCormick's second son, at last, was given the name she could accept and "Rutherford" he was thereafter not only at home but in records at school and in the *Tribune,* for as long as she could dominate. Her own name she revised to read Katharine Van Etten Medill McCormick, and laid much emphasis on the "Van Etten" as Patroon Dutch. Another Dutch ancestral name was Westfall, which she recast as "West Vael."

One popular theory among those who took McCormick to be anti-British in every sense was that he suffered heavily as a schoolboy in England. He did say he was first sent to a boarding school at which the proprietor was indifferent to the boys' comfort and one of the masters so brutal "I have remembered it for sixty years. . . . Not long ago [as of 1952] I met one of my schoolmates who had attended the school and found that his recollection coincided with mine." That, of course, is more or less standard. Hardly any public man, in writing of the nineteenth and early twentieth centuries, has neglected some such revenge.

All the more interesting, therefore, to find McCormick's account of Ludgrove is very much another story. The masters, he said, quite naturally expounded on the glories of England, but always explained that his own duties were to the United States. English and Scotch and Irish boys picked on each other a good deal, "but the American was exempt. The Stars and Stripes on his bed was inviolate." The headmaster was "a splendid and kindly man" who unfortunately died early of heart trouble. His wife McCormick thought also "a lovely, kindly woman," and he corresponded with her as long as she lived.

At Ludgrove he learned to play cricket, "and am, I believe, one of the few Americans who does not make fun of it." McCormick also kept up a lifelong contact with schoolmates, most of whom went into the army or navy or some other public service. This practice, he said, furnished the leadership which created the Empire, but "by making industry and commerce middle class, eventually made England a second-class nation."

With his own testimony, therefore, McCormick destroyed the theory that arrogant blows and knocks by embryo dukes developed his idea of what the proper citizen of the United States should think of Britain. In fact, he even went so far as to say he thought British boys, in his time, were better brought up than American ones. And his version of Ludgrove is supported by an exceptionally independent witness, Sir Shane Leslie, whose mother was a daughter of Leonard Jerome and whose cousin, Sir Winston Churchill, more than once was McCormick's house guest in Chicago in the 1920's and 30's. Sir Shane's account is that:

> When I reached Ludgrove, Robert was a big swell among the small boys. When he heard I was half-American he shook my hand and we became friends for life, with a forty-year gap, but we recognized each other on sight at President's Lodge in Dublin and I came over and stayed with him at Wheaton, recently.
>
> The school was gentlemanly and happy—it collected Norfolk squires, Queen Mother's four brothers, the Bowes-Lyons—an Indian Viceroy, Linlithgow. . . .
>
> It had the finest reputation of any Prep School in England. The First World War decimated the contemporaries of Robert. None survives today unless myself.
>
> It was a small, very happy School and provided we worked and played well and hard there was nothing the masters would not do for us. We were all lucky to get sent there. Our masters were our best friends. One of them, Henry Hansell, was detached to teach and superintend the Duke of Windsor who would have been a different man had he been sent to Ludgrove.

So it is not possible to hold English school days to blame for anything. Nor does it seem reasonable even to accuse Royalty, of which McCormick's account is as follows:

I knew enough Revolutionary history to hate the red-coated soldiers. I saw Queen Victoria in her old age, driving with postillions. There were three gates leading into Hyde Park. She used the center one reserved for royalty. I think it was shortly after her return from her long absence in Scotland. The crowd acted like merry villagers in a comic opera, throwing their hats in the air.

Subsequently, I was spoken to by the Prince of Wales, then with the young kaiser on a good will tour in Germany.

I was dressed in the prevailing style for little boys—in a sailor suit. The hatband bore the name of some British ship—H.M.S. something. The royalties were being popular. I was perhaps the tallest child there.

The Prince of Wales lifted my hat, looked at the name, and said: "Ah, a nice little English boy."

Outraged, I said: "I am not. I am an American."

And the kaiser laughed: "Haw, haw, haw."

That awoke his parents to his feelings, McCormick said, and he was switched to a midshipman's uniform with an American hatband. So was his brother. But even so, the encounter seems to have done no permanent harm to international relations, for McCormick added:

One reads a good deal about the hauteur of the nobility. From what observations I have been able to make, that is a matter of the past. I have never met anything but extreme good manners and extreme courtesy from the nobility anywhere, even in Royalist Austria and Poland, where families insisted that husbands and wives must both have sixteen quarterings of nobility, that is, indentifiable noble ancestors back to the great-grandparents.

The only snobbishness he ever ran up on, he added, was among unspecified English fortune hunters in the United States, among boys at Groton School, to which he went after Ludgrove, and from a Prince Murat in France, of whom "Royalist nobles said he had to make an effort to pretend he was a real noble."

Mrs. McCormick's first venture into the high life had its satisfactions in genealogy and in making friendships among ladies of international fashion, which certainly she held all her life long. The boys visited the Paris Exposition, saw the brand-new Eiffel Tower, learned to sail on the Mediterranean, and spent part of one year at Versailles, learning French from the widow of an officer killed in the 1870 war with Prussia.

But Robert S. McCormick was struggling along on two thousand dollars a year as Second Secretary of a tiny mission, allowed only to handle internal office accounts and collect routine minor information on American trade efforts. It was the dullest of work. His State Department file shows that in July, 1891, his name came off the Diplomatic list for reasons not given. He was simply noted as "retired." The State Department Diplomatic List does not show his name again until 1901. He did return to London, however, to stay until 1893 as a promoter of the World Columbian Exposition, Chicago's triumphant finale to the nineteenth century. The boys continued at Ludgrove with side ventures on the Continent.

After the Exposition, McCormick, senior, was left adrift as a major turn in the *Tribune*'s course was being rounded. Daily operations were now under control of Robert Wilson Patterson, who was determined to hold the attention of Adams' still streaming caravan of new men with methods entirely contrary to Medill's experience. The whole is epitomized in a many times told occasion on which Medill ordered that whenever the Socialist politician, Eugene V. Debs, had to be mentioned, he must be designated only as "Dictator Debs." Patterson countermanded the order and made the change stick. He concerned himself with building a staff of reporters who understood what he meant by "news." Debs got hard treatment on the editorial page, but so did George M. Pullman, whose refusal to show any sense of conciliation brought on a catastrophic strike among railroad workers.

The *Tribune* was now printing seven days a week. It installed new presses, the first of their kind ever built, and delighted the public with a circulation promotion offering at one cent per copy. Patterson's brother, Raymond, was head of the Washington bureau and won a notable news beat on the Supreme Court's verdict declaring a tax on incomes unconstitutional.

Patterson was a thoroughly conventional Republican of his day, but he was also very much the son of the Reverend Dr. Patterson of Second Presbyterian and had no patience with oligarchs who thought the public power their private property. He was especially merciless toward anybody who thought to approach him about the *Tribune* and came home one night to announce his resignation from the Chicago Club, because "everybody I meet there either wants to get something in the paper or keep something out." His attacks on the Chicago board of aldermen for letting out indefensible contracts to operators of streetcar lines, gas and electric utilities even produced a Municipal Voters' League which, if Chicago had really cared, could have done something of permanent use. But no more then than in Joseph Medill's time was Chicago really ready for reform. Anyhow, much more exciting developments were at hand.

In April, 1898, the United States went to war with Spain. It was a great war for the newspapers and the politicians. The *Tribune* beat the world with news of Commodore Dewey's victory in the Battle of Manila Bay and the managing editor had the exquisite pleasure of rousing President McKinley out of bed to tell him all about it. Colonel T. R. Roosevelt charged with the Rough Riders straight to the center of Oligarchs' Heaven and an intimate, not always happy, association with the Robert S. McCormicks. But that was yet to come. At the moment the really controlling question was how Joseph Medill would handle his daughters' expectations in his will.

The Medill girls, as they liked to be known, were now handsome, in a healthy, buxom fashion, and spent little time in provincial Chicago. They were red-haired and convinced that they were supposed to be highstrung and quick-tempered. Thomas Beer could have used the Medill girls in *The Mauve Decade* as his very models for the suddenly aggressive American women "bullying husbands and fathers for money to be spent on frocks, French tenors, flowers for actresses and actors," and all the rest of his terrifying female horde, running after Oriental philosophers, expensive painters, titled Europeans, "gouging men's eyes out with hatpins," hiding his view of the stage, loading up his house with expensive junk, "making him damned miserable in all ways." Sons, Beer noted, were a generation fated to be "reared in the shadow of the Titaness, aware of her power, protected by nothing from her shrill admonitions." And all of it was so in no families more positively than those gathered around the now rapidly failing Medill. The boys had all been hustled off in their teens to the Reverend Endicott Peabody's Groton

School, about which McCormick in his memoirs was rather waspish:

> After the way I had been treated in England, I was puzzled to find the Boston and New York boys, who composed most of the student body, looked down upon us as Middle Westerners. I told this to my father when he came to see how I was getting along, and he said, "Tell them they are descendants of Boston tradesmen and you are descended from Virginia gentlemen." I did not understand it, but the remark was so successful that the headmaster called me to him and said he did not like sectional arguments. He never objected to the Easterners assuming superiority.

The headmaster, McCormick thought, must have been disappointed in many of his pupils, "especially Franklin Roosevelt and his sons," but he conceded Mr. Peabody's high sense of honor was of incalculable benefit to most of his students. Roosevelt was in the class following McCormick, but neither ever claimed they were intimates.

As a matter of fact, for all his grumbling, McCormick did well at Groton. The *Alumni Recorder* reports that he arrived in 1894 and left in 1898 without waiting for graduation. School records do not show the reason, nor is there any persuasive story. He studied Latin, Greek, mathematics [Harvard Division], English, history, government [Yale Division], German and Sacred Studies. His marks do not survive, so far as the school can find, but a classmate of McCormick's told the *Recorder* he was "very quick-witted." Letters home from his cousin, Joseph M. Patterson, even report him popular and well-received, which is better than his own estimate, then or later.

Of his classmates, the best known to the world in general was Henry F. du Pont, creator of Winterthur Museum. Once, when they were elderly men, McCormick and Du Pont chanced to meet in an elevator of the Ritz hotel in Paris. Mrs. McCormick, who was present, said they spoke as casually as if they had just stepped into a Groton hallway. Du Pont later wrote that "we were always very congenial and I very much regret that we saw so little of one another."

In his memoirs, McCormick complained at the narrow insularity of the teaching at Groton. Except for Washington and Lincoln "all the rest of their heroes were New Englanders. Their sectional patriotism was also evidenced by the reading of mediocre New England poets."

His 1897 copybook indicates there was much official interest in the doings of Palamon and Arcite, Hector, John Milton, Alexander Pope, and the late M. T. Cicero who "took the side of Pompey in the civil war and sank with his party to oblivion." More to the point for a grandson of Joseph Medill, were themes on "Alaskan Boundary Question," "Confederate Prisons," "Our Need of a Navy in Our War with England," "Why We Should Have a Half [sic] Holy Day Today," all presented in straightforward, workmanlike style.

McCormick's examination of the copybook in his declining years reminded him that "there was a sadist at Groton, too." His mother, "a superior musician," was very anxious to have him learn to sing. The sadist's rejection was justified as a musical matter, but "he was unnecessarily nasty about it." Furthermore, the same master squashed McCormick's literary ambitions so hard that "altho [sic] I went thru college and took literary courses, I never tried to write until I had to as a war correspondent in 1915." His retrospective analysis of these early works came out: "They were not precocious, neither were they inferior." And, for all the red ink admonitions in the margins, "awkward," "can hardly be said in a theme," and "weak" [particularly threatening], it is a reasonable estimate.

In his first year at Groton, McCormick had pneumonia, which caused his parents to have him spend the worst of winter thereafter with Joseph Medill, whose arthritis and gout sent him hunting for warm weather, also. One season was passed at Thomasville, Georgia.

> Mark Hanna had a house there with William McKinley, whom he was grooming for the Presidential nomination, as a guest. Also staying with him was Herman Kohlsaat, a successful Chicago baker who had turned journalist and was taking more interest in politics than was good for him. McKinley's candidacy was clouded by the fact that he was bankrupt. Hanna, Kohlsaat and others passed the hat and paid his debts. I suppose that a number of politicians came to Thomasville, but I was unaware of that, being more interested in Mrs. McKinley, who would have epileptic fits at the table.

McCormick was little interested in girls, though he had opportunity. The Hannas had him at the children's table with Kohlsaat's daughter, Pauline, and his Patterson cousin, Eleanor, had her own playmates around to join in the goggling at Mrs. McKinley. That winter his elder brother became engaged to the Hannas' daughter, Ruth. But to McCormick the big event was that he learned to use a bow and arrow so effectively he shot out a neighbor's window.

During those years, too, he learned to love Red Oaks, the farm at Wheaton, just west of Chicago. It had once been owned by his great-uncle, William Medill, and then was his grandfather's. On it he played at cowboy, had scarlet fever and formed an attachment which led him, in time, to establish Red Oaks as his principal residence. There, too, he died. It is now a museum of his life interests and his burial place.

The search for warm weather in the winter of 1898–99 sent the old man and the boy to San Antonio, Texas. Some parts of town were as "safe as Lake Shore Drive," an interesting thought about each place, but others were the Wild West every night. McCormick even claimed that he watched "one rather large killing," but couldn't recall any prosecution. He did remember that a Bostonian opera troupe came to town. When the orchestra played the "Star-Spangled Banner" nobody stood up except himself and a few army officers home from the war with Spain, "altho the Civil War had been ended thirty years."

His grandfather, who resisted Mrs. McCormick's policy on names, called him Bobby. One day, Medill found the boy reading Conan Doyle's *The White Company* and took it away, substituting Grant's *Memoirs*. That, McCormick said, started him on his life-long study of the Civil War and toward his two-volume work on its campaigns, a technical military study which even his most acid political critics found competent. McCormick also noted that after taking away the English thriller Medill read it through himself.

> One evening, my grandfather sent me to the telegraf [sic] office with a message to President McKinley, urging him to take the Philippines. When I went in to see my grandfather the next morning he asked me: "What is the news this morning?" and died immediately after.
>
> Probably because of my sojourn in an English school I had formed

an ambition to become a naval officer. This ambition was not lessened by the presence at Groton of Lyle Evans Mahan, son of the famous author and nicknamed Timothy, and Casper Goodrich, the son of an admiral. It was a great disappointment to me when the naval oculist refused me admission.

The next fall I went to college. My boyhood was at an end.

CHAPTER FOUR ★★★ Just how McCormick managed to get into Yale the record does not show. His attendance at Groton was intermittent and it is the school's evidencc that he did not stay for graduation. In any case, he entered the college on schedule in 1899 and graduated on schedule as a member of the class of 1903, neither at the bottom nor at the top.

His own testimony, supported by recollections of others, is that he had a happy time of it. His brother and cousin had come on from Groton ahead of him. It was a period of unabashed enthusiasm, epitomized in the refrain, "For God, For Country and For Yale." Nobody laughed when it was sung. Laughing was entirely appropriate, of course, at the variety hall skits with Jews, Irish and Negroes in caricature. In the experience of the Class of 1903, the raw and vulgar figurines of *The Gilded Age* certainly had no relation to any known parents or grandparents. Mark Twain was a funny old gaffer who waved his napkin from the head table at monstrous public dinners. He told jokes for a living and was a success, obviously, because it cost a great deal of money to get him into action. As for the Negroes and the Jews, not to mention the Irish and the Dutch, these stragglers in Adams' caravan were not bad fellows, but sometimes they *were* funny, so why not face it? No offense really meant, so no reasonable offense could be taken. The comedians on stage often were Jewish and Irish themselves.

For a man who had come from persecuted stock himself and

never tired of mentioning grievances dealt earlier Americans by political and social oppressors, McCormick all his life long showed a peculiar lack of grasp on the real as against the manipulative value of sensitivity in matters of race. It was not that he misread the polyglot nature of Chicago's population or was unsympathetic with its strivings. The executive staff of the Tribune Company, as it rose around him, fairly reflected native, local talent which had fought its way to the top and demonstrated his willingness to use Chicago's religious and ethnic aspects as they came. In private, McCormick's manners were impeccable. In public, he sometimes behaved as if he had deliberate intent to make strangers think him a boor, a madman or both. Here, for instance, is what he had to say in a broadcast on May 3, 1952, about racial caricature in his youth and Jewish reaction to it:

> Weber and Fields and David Warfield created the stage Jew. Weber and Fields developed their show into the prototype of the Follies; Warfield became a great tragedian, and as far as I know the stage Jew disappeared with them, but he has produced several generations of income for the hired employes of the Anti-Defamation League.

This ungenerous language has been taken by some as settled evidence that McCormick was at heart fearful of Jews, repelled by their company and sneering in spirit as to their aspirations. Certainly it cannot be denied that on occasion in the presence of Americans of Jewish extraction he lacked his usual manners. In one instance he went so far as to mock the accent and forms of speech of an earlier speaker at the same luncheon table. But the Washington office of the Anti-Defamation League finds its files on McCormick difficult for the interpreter who approaches the record sure beforehand of the verdict. He cannot, from that authoritative source of fact and judgment, be all so easily typecast.

For a clearer understanding, the Yearbook of the Class of 1903 is basic. There were 318 men in the class, of whom 280 gave information on how they had lived the full four years. The average spent was $4,316.09. The lowest amount reported was $550.00, but one man's personal expenses added up to $25,000.00. The average weekly cost of board was $5.18, room, $3.13. A surprising nineteen paid all bills through jobs, ninety earned their way "in part." One man reported that his total school expense was $3,750, and that he had not only earned that much on the side but had a stake of $900.00 left over. For all the indulgences granted by parents who had money, '03 had its share of men with the will to get ahead, no matter from where they might start.

Politically, they assayed 152 Republicans, 42 Democrats, 6 Prohibitionists, 5 Populists. Their favorite newspapers turned out to be all from New York, in this order: *The Sun,* now many years gone; the *Herald; The Tribune* [later combined into the *Herald-Tribune*], and the *Times*. As for drinks, beer won 57 votes, water got 40, champagne, 7, ink, 3. Colleges best liked, next to Yale, were Harvard, 85; Princeton, 45; Williams, 30; Smith, 25, and Vassar, 10.

In matters of religion, '03 reported 92 Episcopalians; 73 Congregationalists; 45 Presbyterians; 23 Baptists; 18 Catholics; 9 Methodists; 7 Unitarians; 7 Disciples of Christ; 5 Jews; 4 United Brethren; 4 Lutherans; 3 Dutch Reformed; 2 Friends; 1 Universalist; 1 Christian Scientist, and 1 Adventist. On the basic issue of church attendance, 144 thought it should be compulsory; 57 opposed and 15 felt they had no opinion; but nobody seems to have been bold enough to profess either agnosticism or atheism as grounds for resistance.

The favorite character in history was Napoleon, with 106 votes. Lincoln got 38 votes, Washington 9, Cromwell and Charlemagne, each 3. Among popular personages, Maude Adams was first actress, with Ethel Barrymore as runner-up. Joseph Jefferson stood first among actors, and Richard Mansfield, second. Among the faculty, G. M. Wheeler was voted best lecturer; W. L. Phelps, favorite professor; W. G. Sumner, best teacher; E. P. Morris, pleasantest; H. C. Emery, most popular, and E. B. Reed, brightest.

Into this envelope of experience McCormick appears to have slipped with ease. His first year was taken up with Latin, Greek, modern languages [apparently German], English and mathematics. He found the classics "stupid." McCormick, in his public role, tended to lay on heavily for the utilitarian in formal study and to conceal any weakness for the aesthetic and the abstract. Yet, for all his bravura, he had some small gift for pleasure in all of these, as indicated by his tendency to ruminate and generalize. He even quoted more of poetry and fiction in his memoirs than he might have realized. In his memoirs, too, a single sentence makes clear why he harped so much on values to be found outside books: "I had so few friends before I went to college that I took up companionship at the expense of my studies, but fortunately not to the extent of those useful to me in after life."

McCormick wished it understood that he was a plain, blunt man of affairs. Mathematics he could apply to canal building, dam construction, timber cruising and artillery instruction. Physics was all right because it helped with electricity, paper making and ink. Once, pursuing this vision of himself, he struck his confidant, Walter Trohan, mute, with: "Walter, you and I are just members of the middle class." It was his notion that, having rejected F. D. Roosevelt's grandiosities in world view, he must naturally be the hero of that simple savings-bank depositor so much admired by his college mentor on social values, William Graham Sumner.

As for McCormick's pursuit of companionship at Yale, again the best evidence that he had success is in the class yearbook, with those proofs of notice, nicknames: "Mac," "Bert"—and "Rubberfoot." Whether this last was a comment on his congenital clumsiness or a corruption of the "Rutherford" his mother required is undisclosed. In any case, it appears that in his sophomore year he went out for cheerleader; he campaigned on the campus against Bryan in 1900 with a "sound money" platform; he became president of the University Club, and gave his ambition "to write for the *Tribune*." He criticized "over-conservatism" as the sin of the class of 1903. He even went so far as to condemn a prevailing "mediaevalism," but there is no evidence to show what details he had in mind.

McCormick's own testimony is that he was something of a classroom jawbone and, at Yale as at Groton, sought to argue with professors who marked him with low grades. One, after listening to his protests, said he should be a lawyer, then flunked him just the same. McCormick more than once said he thought his idea of going into the law was germinated by that professorial rejection.

College adventure was a pleasure for him to recall all his life. His sophomore year he went exploring on Hudson Bay and on his twenty-first birthday shot two polar bears. He still had the hide of one on his bedroom floor when he died. His senior year he visited his parents abroad, saw Vienna, Constantinople and the Sultan of Turkey taking the air, with ladies of the harem unveiled and leaning to the windows of their carriage.

On the lighter side of campus life, he went in for carousing at Mory's, was once hid out in a boathouse while friends hushed up a charge that he had assaulted a townie with intent to kill, and made Scroll and Key as his student club. He was little interested in girls and thought his classmates were not much so, either. Except at prom time, he said, the only girls likely to be seen in the vicinity of the Quadrangle were those "looking to increase their acquaintance."

But for all his remarks about the superior worth of things learned outside classrooms, McCormick at Yale came under one powerful teacher's domination and all his life thereafter saw the world as nearly as the master could ask, given their elementary differences in capacity. William Graham Sumner was the son of an English-born artisan employed at the railroad repair shops at Hartford, Connecticut. In 1859, Sumner entered Yale by way of the Hartford public school system, thinking to become a priest of the Episcopal Church. From the start he was sober, incredibly industrious and superior in his class work. He wasn't interested in anything else. And he was ferociously independent. He neither feared the rich nor envied them, and he showed not the slightest interest in being one of them. From Yale he went to study theology at Geneva, Göttingen and at Oxford. Then he tried the pulpit, which could no more hold his passion to see mankind whole than a mousetrap can hold a lion. The smallest parish sufficient to his purposes was his Alma Mater, which created for him in 1872 a chair as Professor of Political and Social Science.

Yale hasn't been the same since.

Sumner's first assault was upon the classics. Then this curiosity among ordained clergy demanded, against the will of the university's hierarchs, the right to use Herbert Spencer's *The Study of Sociology* in classrooms. It may seem no worse than quaint today, but then it was beyond imagining for a professor to take the cause of academic freedom to the country through newspapers. Sumner did, and he won.

There was no stopping him thereafter. His writing ranged from monetary policy to forms of government to anthropology. No Yaleman was thought to be much who had not heard him cry, "Get capital, young man. Get capital." McCormick also studied economics in detail with Albert Galloway Keller, Sumner's assistant and literary executor. For the rest of his life, McCormick kept in touch with Keller and mentioned him affectionately in speeches.

Sumner was a gold standard man, first to last, and hated large, loose promises of all sorts, most especially in politics. His cast of mind is best indicated, perhaps, by the titles of some famous provocations:

"The Absurd Effort To Make the World Over"; "That It Is Not Wicked To Be Rich; Nay, Even, That It Is Not Wicked To Be Richer Than One's Neighbor"; "War and Other Essays"; "Earth Hunger and Other Essays"; "The Challenge of Facts," and two monumental works, "Folkways" and "The Science of Society."

Of all Sumner's mighty output the one essay best known today is "The Forgotten Man." To Sumner, the forgotten man was that savings-bank depositor plodding a quiet round in life, trying to hold a job, trying to stay on the right hand of God—and paying with blood, sweat and gold for the follies of power administered by the state. In short, his own father. The essay is a work of surpassing eloquence and stunning quotability, yet so subtle and many-sided as to be utterly beyond safe use by the careless borrower. Franklin D. Roosevelt got a particularly sharp lesson on this point. In the spring of 1932 his speech writer of the moment, Professor Raymond Moley of Columbia University, was trying to fix in the public mind an image of Mr. Roosevelt as friend of the underdog. Moley scraped up, he later wrote, an old phrase, "the forgotten man," which had haunted him for years. Mr. Roosevelt used it as a most powerful appeal for votes. Yet his approach to the problems of society could never be squared with the fundamental argument of the essay:

> If it is desired to bring about social improvements, bring us a scheme for relieving the Forgotten Man of some of his burdens. He is our productive force which we are wasting. Let us stop wasting his force. Then we shall have a clean and simple gain for the whole society. The Forgotten Man is weighted down with the cost and burden of the schemes for making everybody happy, with the cost of public beneficence, with the support of all the loafers, with the loss of all the economic quackery, with the cost of all the jobs. Let us take some of the burdens off him. Let us turn our pity on him instead of the good-for-nothing. It will be only justice for him, and society will greatly gain by it.

Sumner's essential view was that nobody yet had enough wisdom to be rational or just in executing a detailed plan of social enterprise. Therefore, justice could best be expected from a condition of what came to be defined as Social Darwinism, and the less meddling with the mysterious processes of natural, ungoverned human intercourse, the better life would be. For survivors, only, of course. Modern politicians flee any such locution in well-reasoned terror, but McCormick never recovered from Sumner's impact on his undergraduate understanding. Whether he ever attempted to explore the far ranges of Sumner's inquiry into cultural anthropology it is difficult to say. Nothing in his writing or in his speeches appears to indicate it. But the unyielding spirit, the determination to assert facts as found, he assimilated to the uttermost. And the gross, obvious truth in the economic lesson, "get capital, young man, get capital," really was one thing he carried home from Yale. That meant more than his diploma as a Bachelor of the Arts.

Ordinarily, graduation is for any young man the climactic moment of his year, but for McCormick it was only a preliminary to much more excitement. On June 10, 1903, his elder brother married Ruth Hanna, daughter of the Republican Party's most potent operator. The wedding, McCormick said, was organized on the basis of politics. Senator Hanna meant to run for President himself in 1904. Therefore, it was necessary to scuttle the accidental incumbent, T. R. Roosevelt, who was quite pointedly not asked to the party. But if we are to believe McCormick's account, T. R. simply crashed with his daughter, Alice, "who, of course, became a bridesmaid." And, with teeth and pince-nez gleaming, T. R. brazenly stole the show.

McCormick's friends generally took graduation year off for going around the world. McCormick thought he would do better to learn polo, which he said "was of great value to me." His principal recorded achievement was to ride a horse up the steps of a Chicago house, to the alarm and delight of Miss Alice Roosevelt and another young lady. This boyish showing off, McCormick held, was the basis of "a number of untrue stories of similar conduct in my mature years." By such indirection did he enter denial of a many times repeated tale that he really did once arrive at a picnic of *Tribune* advertising salesmen in a closed horse truck, from which he descended in full regalia astride his pony, to deliver an address from the saddle. Nobody now alive who might know the truth will discuss it.

But the most important thing he did in 1903, polo not withstanding, was to go abroad after all. Just about the same time President Roosevelt was crashing the wedding party at Cleveland, Secretary of State John Hay sent off to the United States Minister in Bogotá a telegram so full of menace, historians ever since have taken it as the precipitant of events which later allowed Roosevelt to boast that he took Panama while Congress was idle and started the canal, leaving the legislators nothing to do "but to debate me."

Naturally, the boil of events in the Caribbean was at least runnerup to the wedding as a center of attention in McCormick's family, as in the *Tribune*. As soon as he could arrange it, McCormick took a boat out of New Orleans for Costa Rica. On board was Minor C. Keith, whose father had been granted the concession to build a railroad in Costa Rica and lost a fortune doing it, but gained another, far greater. Keith, senior, introduced bananas to the breakfast tables of North America. McCormick's report to his parents about all this has more than one sort of historical interest:

> Mr. Keith—the uncrowned king of Costa Rica I spoke about in my last letter—saw fit to take a trip to Panama and impressed one of the fruit ships for that purpose, and the honored guests, of course, went along.
>
> Arriving in Colon we found the *Mayflower* and the *Dixie* and another warship in the harbor. [It was the cruiser *Nashville*.] The Marines were all on board as affairs on shore were quiet. Affairs were very quiet, the quiet that comes after the storm. The people had not gotten over the scare the Columbians [sic] gave them last month. According to all the American and English residents we talked to, the Marines arrived just in time to prevent a massacre. The Columbian troops, they said, were a lot of bushwhackers, brutalized by years of guerilla warfare and thirsting for the spoil of cities as foreign to them, in fact, as they are to us. That this was a fact and not merely the idle talk of partisans was more deeply impressed upon us every day I was on the isthmus.
>
> We took train for Panama at two-thirty in the afternoon, arriving just before dark. The road was in the general line of the canal and in sight of most of the excavating material. [This would be the French project at which Ferdinand de Lesseps had failed.]

There was miles and miles of it. I might almost say mountains of it, most of it *never in use*. [Emphasis McCormick's.]

Literally, I was unable to grasp the enormity of the swindle. At one time we passed a mile of hoisting machines, at another, several miles of dump cars *with the forest growing through them*. [Emphasis his.] But this is but an item of the whole. Were I to write you all I heard on that subject I would have to charter a ship to carry the letter.

Panama is the most picturesque city I have ever seen, excepting possibly Constantinople. It was built as you know in the sixteenth century. I talked to Gudger, the American Consul, the British Minister, the various members of the Junta and Panamanians of all classes. Everyone was in favor of the revolution and annexation to the United States.

The money to buy the garrison was furnished by Ehrmann, the banker of Panama, upon a draft of the Junta endorsed by the canal company. No one would admit that Roosevelt promised protection to the revolting states but I gathered enough to feel sure that he did.

My last day on the isthmus I spent going over as much of the canal as I could in the company of the French superintendent and a Mr. Peyroutet who worked thirteen years on the canal but is now with the fruit company. He came to Panama just to show the canal to me. He would have crawled, if necessary. Now that we are to finish the work, it is touching and also amusing to see how anxious the Frenchmen are to get credit for what they have done. The Culebra cut is a great undertaking. It is only one-third completed and yet we walked three miles over the refuse taken out of the cut.

I am now on the S.S. *Mount Vernon,* of Bergen. She is a nice little ship of about 600 tons' burden and loaded with bananas and cockroaches in about equal quantities. The captain is a cheerful little Viking with a loving family that he talks about all the time when he is not taking observations.

On the isthmus there were rumors of war between Japan and Russia but no definite news, so I will not know anything about it until I arrive in Mobile tomorrow morning.

Your loving son,
Rutherford

This letter, unfortunately, is not dated, but external evidence indicates it was written near the end of 1903. His parents were by then, all unknowing, caught up in a great complex of intrigues, both public and personal—and all disastrous—and over their heads in trouble. McCormick himself was coming home to take up law at Northwestern University. Events were impending in his life, in the lives of his parents and in the affairs of the United States which would affect him, too, in his life-long preoccupation with the springs which move governments from within.

CHAPTER FIVE ★★★

Joseph Medill died March 16, 1899, and the Day of the Titaness was then upon Tribune Company of Illinois and all-encompassed in its affairs. McCormick summed it up for his radio audience, which was quite naturally entranced by such a burst of confidence from one so notable for family pride not ever denied:

> Toward the end of his life my grandfather worried about the future of his daughters and grandchildren and contemplated selling the *Tribune*. The price mentioned was six million dollars. Mr. R. W. Patterson was very much opposed to the sale, which would deprive him of the editorship and *my mother* [emphasis supplied] wanted to use the paper to obtain a diplomatic post in Europe, so they combined and persuaded him against the sale. Instead, his stock was left in trust with R. W. Patterson, my father, R. S. McCormick, and William G. Beale, as trustees for his daughters and their heirs.
>
> The plan was carried out. Mr. Patterson became president of the company and my father was appointed minister to Austria, to which he soon became ambassador and then ambassador to Russia and to France.
>
> My brother and Joseph M. Patterson graduated from Yale and went into the *Tribune*. There then arose the great hostility between my mother and her sister and also between my brother and Joseph M. Patterson. Mr. Patterson, secure in his position as president of the *Tribune,* now asked for and obtained the recall of my father.

So far as it goes, that is an entirely fair outline of what did happen. But it does not begin to indicate the far-ranging total effect of the family wrestling match, begun almost at Medill's graveside. When it was reorganized in 1861, the Tribune Company got authority to issue 2,000 shares of common stock, which are all it has out yet. Available records are uncertain, but the best apparent evidence is that Medill's control rested in never more than 1,070 shares, of which he sold ten to his son-in-law, R. W. Patterson. Another ten shares he gave to his Patterson granddaughter. Therefore, when he came on to make his will, control of the *Tribune* depended on 1,050 shares, a bare 52.5 percent of the whole.

Medill met his problem of protecting this control through a will first drafted as of August 22, 1894, to which he added four increasingly elaborate codicils. In the first codicil, he set aside a number of special bequests of a thousand dollars each to old hands of affectionate memory on the *Tribune,* also to various relatives of secondary rank and to namesake children among friends. He gave 100,000 dollars outright to his Patterson son-in-law, whom he also made an executor of the will. To his son-in-law, Robert S. McCormick, he gave ten thousand dollars and "a full and final release and acquittance of all obligations, debts and sums of money he may owe to me at the date of my decease; and I direct that all written evidences of such obligations and debts be cancelled and given up to the said Robert S. McCormick, notwithstanding some of them may be signed, indorsed or guaranteed by another person or persons."

Medill had planned to leave his *Tribune* shares divided equally between his daughters, after saving out a dower right for his wife. But on October 1, 1894, just after he had completed his first codicil, Mrs. Medill died. On December 8, 1894, he made a second codicil, providing that each of the daughters could sell her shares in the *Tribune* "upon such terms as she may see fit, upon the express condition, however, that she shall first obtain of the other legatees of said stock, for the time being surviving, an express written consent to the proposed sale or sales and all the terms and conditions thereof."

Medill's lawyer was William Gerrish Beale, a partner of Robert Todd Lincoln, in whose company Robert S. McCormick had ventured first into diplomacy. Beale came up with something better, finally, and it is the third and fourth codicils, of April 14 and May 5, 1898, which finally allowed Joseph Medill to rest, assured he had done the best anybody could to hold the daughters in line. The all-crucial 1,050 shares, on which the family's responsibilities, power and future depended, were left in a trust which would own and vote the stock and receive its dividends. After expenses, this income would be divided equally between the daughters, who would themselves have no equitable title. The trustees, who must always be three in number, would have full power to sell the stock [as a whole and not in parcels] "at such price and upon such terms as they may deem best."

Patterson and Beale, already executors, were also made trustees. The third trustee was Robert S. McCormick. If either husband should drop out, his wife would succeed him, but thereafter all would have to be settled on appeal to a judge of the U.S. District Court.

It was a perfectly sound will from the legal point of view, and the Pattersons were happy with it. The McCormicks were anything but, and said so. Contention reached the point that the administrators of the estate, in their final account of April 26, 1902, entered on the record a defensive explanation of why it might appear they had given Elinor Patterson $275.49 more than they had paid over to Katharine McCormick. In fact, they had distributed each daughter $371,186.38 in direct personal capital, but the $275.49 had been advanced to Katharine McCormick to help her meet the State of Illinois inheritance tax. Elinor had paid her own out of other funds. As for the 1,050 shares of *Tribune* common, that was set up in the trust and it has been in trust ever since, one way or another. The sisters were, therefore, now well squared away for the combat kept up until they died.

The Honorable Shelby Moore Cullom, Senator from Illinois, was the first of many public officials to find himself entangled. Mr. Cullom was Speaker of the Illinois House of Representatives when the Legislature enacted the *Tribune*'s charter of 1861, and his signature appears on the document. In 1872, he put Ulysses S. Grant in nomination for a second term as President. In 1882, he won for himself the Senate seat some had thought Joseph Medill ought to have, both family members seeking esteem and Illinois politicians hoping the *Tribune*'s meddlings could thereby be diverted. Cullom held the job until his health failed him in 1913, and throughout his many years he was always anxious to keep the *Tribune*'s owners obligated, as near as he could manage. And so on October 23, 1900, he addressed a letter to President McKinley, saying that he had been informed "a few of the friends of Hon. Robert S. McCormick have suggested to you, his name as a fit and proper man for United States Minister to Austria or Belgium. I take pleasure in writing to you a line in his behalf, giving my unqualified endorsement of him for one or the other of these missions."

In consequence, on March 7, 1901, McCormick was sworn as Envoy Extraordinary and Minister Plenipotentiary of the United States to the Court of Francis Joseph, Emperor of Austria and King of Hungary.

In his memoirs, McCormick claimed that when his father went to present letters of credence to the Emperor, Francis Joseph was so struck by the bearing of the new envoy he ordered the court to treat Robert S. McCormick as ambassador, and so caused an actual promotion to come to pass. The official records of the State Department show nothing like that. The United States, after the war with Spain, was making something of a noise among the powers, and Francis Joseph was only following the English and the French, a little behindhand. His ministers explained that on account of old ties and Spanish sensibilities, he had necessarily waited for the dust to settle.

The assignment to Vienna was Robert S. McCormick's happiest hour. He was elevated to ambassador on May 27, 1902, but after a bare four months to savor it, he was transferred, for what reason the record does not say, to the Russian court at St. Petersburg. It was all taken to be a sign of triumphant progress and Mrs. McCormick was delighted that her Patterson niece, already visiting in Vienna, was allowed to go on with her to Russia. She was very fond of the young lady, but that was by no means all. The girl's letters home were proof positive that just getting out the *Tribune* every day was not the only wonderful gift that could come to a person of importance. In fact, the move turned out a disaster for both families. For, in St. Petersburg, Miss Patterson was overcome by a middle-aged Polish horse fancier, the Count Josef Gizycki, out to improve his finances by a method popular among courtiers everywhere. He would endow her with his honor of family and she would meet the bills. In 1904, he married her at her mother's house in Washington and carried her back to Polish Galicia, but he lacked the resources to hold her. The fight that followed between Gizycki and the Pattersons made a great Sunday supplement story in the newspapers of two continents for years. But the papers never got word of the even worse recriminations between the Pattersons and the McCormicks. Nor did the papers then, or ever, discover how Robert S. McCormick suffered humiliation at St. Petersburg at the hands of the President of the United States, egged into action by a British agent. Yet it is so.

On September 6, 1901, while shaking hands with the public at the Pan-American Exposition in Buffalo, Mr. McKinley was shot in the stomach by Leon Czolgosz, a professed anarchist, who explained later that it was nothing personal. He only wished to express disapproval of the social system. Just the same, McKinley died of it.

Colonel T. R. Roosevelt's Rough Rider account of his war with Spain, which Mr. Dooley retitled "Alone in Cubia," had forced Mark Hanna's hand to the point of putting the colonel on as Vice President in McKinley's second term, settled oligarchic practice for sidetracking upstarts. Hanna meant, above all, to follow McKinley into the Presidency himself. But he neglected a place for Czolgosz in his planning, so now there was work to do in order that Mr. Roosevelt could be retired to writing again. As it turned out, Mr. Hanna's planning was a little short on that point, too.

It was a sad chance that moved the McCormicks to St. Petersburg. Vienna was less a center of powerful intrigues and more a baroque museum, in which a final, arthritic remnant of the ancient Holy Roman Empire lay dying. Kings and emperors despaired of it. Not even T. R. Roosevelt could have had the brashness to send his ambassador meddling in the arrangement of its requiem. But Russia under the last of the Romanoffs offered temptations and disasters so all-embracing, and delivered them to so many, that the ruin there of Robert S. McCormick has only the barest mention in dispatches. Yet, for him, it was as total as any.

In 1902, the Tsar still saw himself endowed with a divine right to dispense justice as an absolute and final monarch. An established church taught as much, in the Holy Name. Idiot peasants by the millions and most of the rising industrial classes in the cities took it as true. so that the national custom was to hate the Tsar's government and yet excuse the man himself from his agents' failures. The essence of the court is given in the historical fact that the Tsaritsa, after bearing four daughters, hired a French horse doctor to tell her whether she might again be pregnant and if so, that the child be a boy. The horse doctor held for the negative and when irrefutable Nature proved him fallible, he was fired. His eventual successor as familiar to the Imperial household was the monk Gregory Rasputin, who taught that sin is necessary if one is to know the holy joy of forgiveness. This unique adaptation of doctrine led to some extraordinary encounters among the devout, for it was self-evident that the more lurid the sinfulness, the more joyful the forgiveness. Release came in July of 1918 as "Citizen and Citizeness Romanoff," their four daughters and their haemophilic wraith of a son, saw, at last, the face of reality between the trigger-pull and the bullets.

It was all a long way from Chicago. Miss Patterson decided that she was fascinated by the dashing Count Gizycki, for which romantic lapse from her natural wit she would pay as long as she lived. Her McCormick relatives were barely conscious of the riddle of a court that held all newspapers the devil's handiwork and Chicago mannerisms, however dainty, little better than peasant comedy.

One of the court adventurers, a sometime Colonel Besobrasov, held a sort of concession for timber-cutting along the Yalu River in Korea. It was his view that a dispatch of troops would do much to encourage industry among the woodchoppers. The land and sea forces were all with him. So was the Tsar's busybody cousin in Berlin, William II of Hohenzollern, who gave assurances that he would keep the West all quiet so that Russia could have the honor of saving Europe from the yellow peril. In the mind of the British Foreign Office, it would never do for Germany and Russia to have too easy a success in any such undertaking. That would undermine the balance of power, the stalemate considered essential to Europe's peace with itself. So the English and the French set about to "stiffen the Japanese spine," as if any such thing were necessary, and Russian loathing for all foreigners rose to feverish levels.

The queen of Imperial outposts in Russian Manchuria was Port Arthur on the Yellow Sea, and at midnight, February 8, 1904, it glowed with light. So did the ships of the Far Eastern Fleet, swinging at anchor. It was Name Day for the port admiral's wife and daughter. In the great houses there was dancing and along the streets the hands roared from one cabaret to the next as Admiral Heihachiro Togo, every light doused, led a small squadron around the headland and into the bay. It took Admiral Togo just forty minutes to start the Russian Empire down the chute. The hapless McCormicks, as incomprehending as the Tsar himself, were shocked to find themselves ridiculed and snubbed at every turn. Captain T. Bentley Mott, their military attaché, recorded that the McCormicks suffered not only from a generalized hostility against all foreigners which intensified with every Russian defeat and humiliation, but, further, from a special error of their own. They had leased a house from the Prince Kotchoubey. That in itself was second rate. "People" never leased, but bought. And hardly had the McCormicks moved in before Kotchoubey, sure enough, sold over their heads to the Grand Duke Vladimir, a cousin of the Tsar. McCormick committed the ghastly boner of notifying the Grand Duke that he would be quite willing to vacate his lease if the Grand Duke would find him a house of equal fashion. At that moment, he might as well have packed up, for as Mott observed, the Tsar's relatives were accustomed to having their slightest whims obeyed as much by the diplomats as by the natives. Mott noted in his journal that Mrs. McCormick said to him one day that the vast power of social position is something Americans rarely estimate at its true value. Something else rarely estimated at its true value is the knack of the British Foreign Office at always having one good man buried somewhere for the exact need of a desperate moment. In St. Petersburg, just at that time when Mrs. McCormick was deploring American ignorance to Captain Mott, precisely such a man was writing his friend, T. R. Roosevelt in Washington, and he was writing about Mrs. McCormick and her husband. That Robert S. McCormick's modest heart should break as a consequence was not much of a charge on the bill at the time. But all those who spent so much effort in later years searching for the root of the feeling McCormick's son exercised against the Foreign Office—and with some extraordinary effects, too—could have done their work better if they had bothered to read up the two-volume *Letters and Friendships of Sir Cecil Spring-Rice*.

Spring-Rice was an Old Etonian. His college at Oxford was Balliol. His career was plain ahead of him when he was born in

1859, and by 1882 he was in the Foreign Office. In 1886, he "went out to Canada" for a visit with his brother Gerald, who was following fashion in attempting to develop a holding in the wilds. As he passed back through New York, someone told him that he should make certain to meet a Mr. T. R. Roosevelt, who would be aboard the ship on which he would be going home. Roosevelt just then was thought by most people to be a lonely, dispirited young man. He had been defeated for mayor of New York. His wife and mother had died within two days of each other, and he had been royally knocked around by the Republican oligarchs for objecting out loud to Joseph Medill's friend, James G. Blaine, as head of the party.

Roosevelt and Spring-Rice, by the time the ship docked, were committed to each other for life. And once in London, Roosevelt produced one of those surprises he loved so well. He announced that he was over there to marry Miss Edith Carow of New York City, and it had all been arranged to avoid the chatter. Would Springy be his best man? Springy certainly would. What is more, he also applied to the Foreign Office for posting to Washington. The seniors were surprised, for the British mission in the United States was very modest then, and young men of Spring-Rice's promise were expected to avoid it in favor of the grander assignments. But Spring-Rice knew what he was doing. For the rest of his life, he concentrated on the zoology of American social and political power, and not alone to the great benefit of his own country. Some have argued that in an hour of crisis, Spring-Rice turned the direction of the First World War to rescue civilization itself. However that may be, his countrymen, in keeping with their great tradition, concentrated more on abusing him for being so slow about it than in praising him for the achievement itself.

In 1887, the center of the Washington world—White House notwithstanding—was Number 1603 H Street, where Henry Adams dwelled. Spring-Rice made it in one, and soon knew "everybody." He became fast friends with Senator Henry Cabot Lodge, who loathed British policy but dearly loved Springy. He was on equal footing with Henry Adams' bosom friend, John Hay, invariably described by McCormick as "the first American Secretary of State to become an Anglophile and take orders from the Foreign Office."

Among the ladies, as among the men, Spring-Rice was a great

success. One who liked him especially was Miss Mary Victoria Leiter of Chicago, whose rugged father grew rich out of Chicago's boom in real estate. The Leiter family set up in Washington to enjoy the proceeds.

One of Spring-Rice's closest friends was George Nathaniel Curzon, eldest son of the fourth Baron Scarsdale of Kedleston. Miss Leiter became Lady Curzon and until she died, untimely, in 1906, got her name in the papers even more than her friend Miss Patterson, as an example of the Chicago girl abroad. But in a different sort of way.

It should not be thought Spring-Rice frittered away his time in mere social binding and loosing. When he came to Washington the British Minister was that same Baron Sackville of Knole whose disastrous advice to vote for Cleveland had turned the election of 1888 for Benjamin Harrison, and as one minor consequence had given Robert S. McCormick his first diplomatic post to London as secretary to Robert Todd Lincoln. It is part of the record that when the Baron made that boner, Spring-Rice was back at the Foreign Office on a brief refresher. Sackville-West's successor in Washington was Sir Julian Pauncefote and Spring-Rice moved smoothly back into place with him, the established expert on Americans.

And so it went until 1895, when he was posted to Berlin just about the exact time the Kaiser discovered the yellow peril and had his court painter make a dragon painting of it, with multiple copies for distribution among cousins on thrones all about. In 1901, Spring-Rice did a small tour in Cairo as minder of money collected in the rich vein of gold that was Egypt. In 1903, he was sent to St. Petersburg as secretary and counselor of embassy.

Spring-Rice's letters to the President of the United States from St. Petersburg and to the President's wife make up as a true masterwork of the diplomatist's art. He was a born writer of letters anyhow, and certainly the most sensitive kind of man-watcher. And he needed no specific instructions on his duty, as it became clear to all the world that the Russian Empire was in the deepest sort of trouble. Far from merely bloodying up the Tsar's forces a little, the Japanese were threatening the very self-confidence of the regime itself. Russia was in a turmoil of xenophobia, pogroms, riots and distractions. It had no idea how to save itself, but would not allow either England or France to so much as hint at a rescue.

Step by delicate step, Spring-Rice built an understanding through letters, first to the President and then to the President's wife, to show that the McCormicks, who saw themselves securely in favor because they were effusively pro-Russian, were thought at court some sort of joke in poor taste on Roosevelt's part. The climax was precisely timed. On December 7, 1904, Spring-Rice sent to President Roosevelt a detailed review of the total prospect.

In St. Petersburg, he said, it was freely acknowledged that Berlin was now the capital of Russia. The Kaiser had the Tsar entirely under his influence and would very likely be the true arbiter of Russia's fate for years to come. It appeared that he would have a free hand to turn his attention to the United States and to Great Britain in such a way that whatever agreement might be reached in the Far East through him would have to be a world agreement. In translation, he was warning Roosevelt that unless stopped, Wilhelm would manipulate a peace between Russia and Japan that would profit Germany at the expense of everybody else. And then, the whiplash ending:

"How I wish you had a really good ambassador here. . . ."

Britain's own man, Sir Charles Hardinge, he described as very strong and independent. It was not necessary to add that if Roosevelt could send a proper substitute for McCormick, the pair could work as one to put the Kaiser down and the President up. And that is how it was done. By that time, T. R. had Mark Hanna's scalp at his belt, the Isthmus of Panama in his hip pocket and the Old Guard terrified as nobody knew what blow would fall where, next. He got the message—all of it—with the result that at the American Embassy in St. Petersburg, on January 14, 1905, the head of mission sat down and in his graceful, orderly handwriting, accepted fate as a gentleman of Virginia:

> Dear Mr. President:
>
> I beg to acknowledge receipt of your kind letter of December 26 and to say that I am delighted to meet your wishes in the matter of the transfer suggested by you.
>
> While I naturally have many regrets at the possibility of leaving this post around which so much of interest and importance attaches at this time, and to leave relations here which have become most agreeable, and which might add to my usefulness, I nevertheless view the

prospect of service in the field which you indicate with great satisfaction.

In any policy which you feel it desirable to follow, believe me most anxious to continue to serve you loyally and with genuine friendship.

Yours sincerely,
Robert S. McCormick

It was, quite simply and utterly, for Robert S. McCormick, the living end. He was posted to France for two dull years, with the faithful Captain Mott keeping notes for his own little memoir. The McCormicks kept up appearances as best they could, assuring friends they were happy as larks to be in Paris again, in between trips to Chicago for quarrels with the Pattersons about whose son would have preferences on the *Tribune,* whose Washington house was best and whose fault it was that the Patterson daughter was now the subject of struggle between so many advocates that even the Tsar and the President of the United States had to take notice. Then, they were out of Paris with nowhere next in sight.

In 1908, T. R. designated his successor to the Presidency, a dignified judge from Cincinnati and good Yaleman, who had done such a good job as Secretary of War and head of commissions to bring Cuba, Panama and the Philippine Islands into proper orbit. Mr. Taft had the nation's confidence and his opponent, William Jennings Bryan, was so shopworn that the campaign was looked on by all as no more than a formal walk-through to conform with the rules. So it was, too. Therefore, early in the year, the McCormicks began to lobby for a new assignment. Their eldest son, Medill, had been a wild enthusiast for T. R., and found it difficult to understand his parents' tendency to chill at mention of the hero's name. He was understudy to R. W. Patterson for editor of the *Tribune,* and to help get himself in training had used up all his own capital and borrowed from his mother to buy the Cleveland *Leader,* which his Grandfather Medill had owned before ever coming to Chicago. With his clever wife, Ruth, at his elbow, and his Hanna in-laws everywhere abounding, he regarded himself as established and secure in a life work of importance. But Patterson, senior, only thought him unstable and a threat to the *Tribune*'s survival. Patterson's own son was, by that time, off on a venture in socialism the whole family found it difficult to discuss. Relations between the elder Pattersons themselves were strained to the edge of breaking as they sought to deal with the importunate McCormicks, Gizycki and his endless claims of money due. In consequence of all the uproar, Mr. Patterson's defense was, every now and then, to take a steamer to London and hole up with Brown, Shipley & Co., at 123 Pall Mall.

From there, on August 15, 1908, he sent a letter to William Howard Taft:

> Mrs. Robert McCormick has formally proposed to my wife to help my daughter with the Russian government in some of her domestic troubles, if I will agree in writing to assist McCormick to get another ambassadorship. The suggestion is also that if I do not support her for an ambassadorship, she will oppose my daughter at the Court of Russia.
>
> I shall do nothing of the kind. On the contrary, I protest against the appointment of McCormick to office, if his appointment is supposed to be by way of recognition of the Chicago *Tribune*. I am the editor-in-chief of the *Tribune* and President of the Tribune Company, and I know that three-quarters of the shareholders in the paper do not wish it to be represented in office:-
>
> 1.) Because it is degrading to the paper and injurious to its standing with the public to have it supposed that it is a constant applicant for official favors;
>
> 2.) Because office holding on the part of one of its stockholders destroys its influence with the public, as it is then supposed when it supports the Administration to be earning a bribe that has been given to it.
>
> Mr. McCormick failed disastrously in business twenty-five years ago, and has since been dependent on his wife. He has no independent status and no merit, except that "he is the husband of one wife"; certainly he has no qualification for an important diplomatic office.
>
> He has never written a line for the *Tribune,* never made a campaign speech, nor ever given a dollar to the campaign fund; nor has his wife, unless she has done so this year "in the lively expectation of favors to come."
>
> McCormick and his wife were disloyal to President Roosevelt and to their own country when they were in St. Petersburg during the war with Japan. They wrote home in violent terms concerning their own countrymen and especially of President Roosevelt and Secretary Hay. They said of Mr. Roosevelt, whose personal representatives they were

supposed to be, that he was a "madman in the White House," and of Mr. Hay that he was "giving an exhibition of shirt-tail diplomacy."

For the better part of five more pages, Patterson detailed his feelings on the whole problem of running the *Tribune* for a pack of women, children and, to his mind, malcontent parasites:

> President Roosevelt told me that he was compelled to remove McCormick from St. Petersburg during the peace negotiations because he was incompetent and "a stronger man" was needed there.
>
> I enter this protest at an early day to the appointment of McCormick on account of the Chicago *Tribune* because he was appointed the last time through a misunderstanding and by a "fraud on the court."
>
> The McCormicks represented in Washington that they were the chief owners of the *Tribune* and that the other shareholders would be gratified by their appointment. Neither of these statements was true. Mrs. McCormick inherits under her father's will a small fraction more than one-quarter of the stock of the paper, and that stock is in the hands of trustees, of whom I am one. She does not control it nor vote upon it.
>
> As for the wishes of the other stockholders, I think I may say that they are unanimous in *not* [emphasis Patterson's] wishing to have the influence and character of the paper pawned in order that the McCormicks may enjoy a social distinction which they have done nothing to deserve.
>
> I shall send copies of this letter to Secretary Root, Senators Cullom, Hopkins and Lodge, to Governor Deneen and to Speaker Cannon, and you are at liberty to show it to either or both of the McCormicks at your discretion.

Whether Mr. Taft ever invited the McCormicks to discuss the matter may be doubted, but he was tactician enough to send the letter to the official files of the State Department, where it has been ever since, a silent, secret but powerful witness that the war between the Titanesses and their men, not to say against each other, was by no means a one-sided contest. Patterson, as the letter shows, had a gift of invective to match them all. He so managed to lacerate "the witch of Wheaton," as he called Mrs. McCormick, that she kept lawyers at work, hoping to remove him from the *Tribune* in disgrace. She never did. Neither did her eldest son, Medill, manage a free hand with the *Tribune*'s editorial power. In 1910, the very week Patterson died, suddenly, in Philadelphia, he warned his wife that both he and Beale considered Medill McCormick so degenerated mentally that unless the young man were taken away Beale would refuse any longer to be a director of the company. And his prophecy of disaster was all too promptly verified.

As for Robert S. McCormick, by 1910 he was far gone into melancholia and from time to time had to be dug out of retreat to a country hotel at Natural Bridge, in the Virginia county where he had been born. Finally, his family put him in a nursing home at Hinsdale, on the way to the Medill farm west of Chicago. There, on April 16, 1919, he died of pneumonia. For his widow, it was only a relief and she made no bones in saying so. But the ruin of his father's life was without any doubt the most influential single experience of which Robert R. McCormick was ever conscious. Hardly a dozen persons who knew him in his own old age had ever heard the tenth of it. Of that handful none dared to risk his fury by mention of the facts.

There can be no doubt McCormick's life-long hunger for the sort of father he wanted and his flooding love for the father he had affected his editorial judgment. So, too, did his reaction upon discovering that, grown though he might be and already a man of importance in the public life of Chicago, he could not move without his mother's interventions.

Mrs. McCormick's niece, the bruised but still acute Countess Gizycka, finally spoke in defense of her Cousin Bertie:

"You ruined your husband. You ruined your oldest son. Do you wish to ruin this one, too?"

Cruel words, cruel insight. But incomplete. Robert R. McCormick was tougher than his father and tougher than his brother. He was tougher than his mother. He may even have been tougher than his Cousin Eleanor, but neither ever had a final chance to settle the point because of her sudden death in July, 1948, as she prepared to "sue Bertie right out of his britches."

Just how tough McCormick really was, he discovered for himself in the wards of Chicago. A harder school would be far to seek, indeed.

CHAPTER SIX ★★★ On the subject of "government burocrats," it was McCormick's habit to roar so that he was heard through six continents. Yet he had immense pride in his own performance as one.

All the evidence argues that when he got out of Yale he drifted back to Chicago and the study of law at Northwestern University only because he had nothing better to do. He had no home. His parents had not really tried living in Chicago since the days of Benjamin Harrison and had not yet given up hope of triumph abroad. If McCormick felt lonely and neglected in his callow years, faltering in the wake of his brother and cousins, he had reason. His one firm support was Joseph Medill, who tried consoling him with the prospect that he would yet prove himself as a "late apple." When the old man died, McCormick, emotionally, was on his own.

But in 1904 he found that his grandfather's promise could hold truth, after all. An old, familiar order in American politics lay in ruins, and any apprentice at government could feel himself enticed to take power. There would not be a time like it again until 1932. McCormick himself would discover, then, how it feels to be trapped in the crisis of action as "those behind cried 'forward' and those before cried 'back.' "

In 1904, the man of the hour was Theodore Roosevelt, made President of the United States through the chance lunacy of another of those anarchists so influential on McCormick's thought. On May

9, 1904, in New York, J. P. Morgan & Co. received a United States Treasury warrant for $40 million. In Paris the next day, the last of a series of French companies which had failed at trying to cut a canal across the Central American isthmus handed over to lawyers for the Department of Justice all its documents of permission and interest, assigned to the United States of America. The papers were no mystery, but the story of the $40 million is not told yet. Morgan's bank, as disbursing agent, paid out in secret. If the intent was to keep down stress, it was misplaced. The manner in which the Panamanian revolution had come about in 1903, coupled with the hole-in-corner settling of claims on the French company, put the whole great feat under a cloud. Sixty years and more later, the cloud still hung there.

Mr. Roosevelt was jumpy and hypersensitive. It was a nonsensical tragedy that had felled McKinley and ruined the old order, but T. R. had never been a member of that club, anyhow. Now, if his first attack on grandeur had its shady aspects, he saw the remedy in a triumph at the polls, delivered not by the oligarchs, but by The People. By now, Henry Adams had been in Washington long enough to accept the reality without shock, if still with an unconcealed contempt. Here was no Rutherford Hayes uneasily counting the days until he could escape the White House for the obscurity of Spiegel's Grove, in Ohio, from which he had no business ever being called, anyhow. Here was "Theodore," the thoroughly understandable Harvard man [to Adams, it was meaningless that Hayes had a year and a half at Harvard law school], using all the power he could get and scheming for more in pursuit of lauds in books. Adams got everything into just one of his famous letters to the wife of Senator Cameron from Pennsylvania. Roosevelt was so worked up about politics, he said, that if someone remarked God is Great, he asked how that might affect the election. And to catch votes anywhere out West, "Theodore writes like a centipede."

Adams thought it silly. Between Wall Street, Bryan and Hearst, the Democrats were breaking up. Roosevelt should hold his tongue and just "buy Democrats to bolt." But could T. R. build his New Nationalism, holding his tongue? Impossible. Even so, it turned out that 1904 was a vintage year for bolters, nowhere more than in Chicago, which put on a caricature of the whole national exercise with exaggerations and curlicues unlike any other.

McCormick was only a first-year law student at Northwestern, but when the dust settled, he showed up as a genuine, elected member of the Chicago City Council, aged twenty-four, a man on his own at last. How he made his deal, he never told. All he said was that Fred A. Busse, a coal dealer turned to politics, offered to run him for alderman from the old 21st Ward on the North Side and he agreed. Busse, hardly remembered now in Chicago but important for even more things than drawing McCormick into public life, was a rough customer. He liked nothing better than to lead a candidate into a saloon and make him the butt of the barflies, just to show everybody who was running things. When McCormick went on the first of these adventures he was very nervous for fear Busse would, following custom, invite everybody to step up and "have a drink on this son of a bitch that followed me in here," in which case there would be nothing for the son of Katharine Medill to do but knock Busse down and forget about becoming a statesman. But, of course, Busse made it plain he was greatly honored to be escorting a member of the *Tribune* nobility and that everybody present should go home and tell his wife about it.

McCormick's mother, just then, was heavily engaged with her eldest son in the project to displace R. W. Patterson as editor. Almost every day a letter came, rich in maternal advice and festooned with encouragements.

In every way, Joseph Medill McCormick was a spectacular young man as of 1904. After graduating from Yale in 1900, he started on the *Tribune* at three dollars a week as a police reporter. The next year, he went out to the Orient as an investigator of Chinese and Filipino political violence. Next, in rapid order, he married Ruth Hanna, made an enemy of Robert W. Patterson and lost all his free capital trying to run the Cleveland *Leader*. But none of these matters inclined him one whit to cut his range of action. He became a power in the Progressive movement and in 1912 even showed an inclination to back Robert M. LaFollette against Theodore Roosevelt. Then he switched back to Roosevelt and was denounced by LaFollette as a traitor, which didn't hurt much for he was certainly one of T. R.'s most intimate advisors. In the midst of it all he was deposed from the *Tribune* by its board of directors and led away by his wife for the first of a long series of cures abroad. He was among the first of Middle Western notables exposed to the ministrations of Carl Gustav Jung, the best known of these being James Joyce's patroness, Edith Rockefeller McCormick. Whether Mrs. McCormick put her young in-law onto Jung or he directed her is not of record. In any case, neither appears to have gained much relief.

Joseph Medill Patterson was an even more pyrotechnic operator than Joseph Medill McCormick. Patterson got out of Yale in 1901. He, too, went to work on the *Tribune* as a police reporter, and he, too, made the Asian tour. In 1902, he married Alice Higinbotham, whose father was president of Marshall Field & Co. In 1903 Patterson went down to Springfield as a Republican member of the Illinois House of Representatives. There he made himself the delight of all by throwing an inkpot at the Speaker of the House in the course of what went into the journal of proceedings as a "discussion" of streetcar franchises. He ran to his father for support of his position, municipal ownership. There was a cruel row. Patterson, senior, not only declared the *Tribune* would never endorse any such socialist outrage, but let his son know that unless the young man calmed down he would be fired out of the organization that had given him a start. Patterson was horrified to learn that his election, far from being a personal triumph, had just been a simple deal made by his father. Not only was he without power. He had no excuse for pride, either.

So, in the year of the bolters, Patterson began a search for political identity that really never ended as long as he lived. In 1904, he switched to the Democrats who, in their time of troubles, at least elected the mayor of Chicago. Patterson, at age twenty-six, was appointed commissioner of public works and immediately set out to make the elders squirm. His first victim was his father-in-law. He hauled up Marshall Field & Co. in court on a charge of using city property in its operations. Then, to show he had no favorites, he laid into all the newspapers together for riotous behavior in their circulation wars. When the wranglers laughed at him, he went for them with fist and boot.

It was not long, naturally, until he blew up again, denounced the Democrats as trimmers, and joined the socialists. In the Presidential campaign of 1908 he was National Manager for Eugene V. Debs, his Grandfather Medill's old enemy. By 1910, Patterson was an established socialist pamphleteer and moneymaking author of doctrinaire books and plays; a dairy farmer of considerable success at all aspects except the economic, and one of the sights of Chicago, regularly seen at the opera in a hickory shirt, slightly drunk and smelling grandly of the barnyard. He was also quarreling with everybody except his cousin Robert, to whom he proposed that they heave out McCormick's brother and his own father and run the *Tribune* themselves. The idea didn't take, at first, but a seed was planted.

The old order in Chicago really never recaptured its poise after the Haymarket Riot of 1886, and by 1904 the degeneration of structured party discipline was near to total. Instead, there was a network of trades and loyalties derived from ethnic, religious, economic and political aspiration, without concern for official party labels. In every ward, sometimes in each block of a ward, accommodations were reached for local benefit.

If anybody understood the distinctions at all it was Charles E. Merriam, for many years professor of political science at the University of Chicago and author of an engaging, even though scholarly, literature on the mystery of the Chicago style in self-government. He classified the heretochs of that period who called themselves Democrats as drawn up into two distinct armies, the Republicans into three. The real, and invisible, government he defined as lying somewhere within the grip of special interests which had no party label. The official ballot on election day was nothing more than a sort of public ritual to sanctify a consensus arrived at beforehand. McCormick entered politics just as that arcane process was beginning to exhibit its power. He never, afterward, gave any sign of thinking it other than the whole way of the world.

The Democrat who became mayor in 1904 was Edward F. Dunne, a circuit court judge who had been a Free Silver supporter of Bryan in 1896 and now drew his main power from a promise to put the city of Chicago in the streetcar business. Even the dullest wardheeler could see the sense in it. Motormen's jobs could be peddled at a good profit. Whole neighborhoods would just sit up and beg, with votes and cash contributions, for track extensions and special service. But when the bolters' year was done, the wardheelers found that somehow authority had fallen into the insensitive, wide-gesturing hands of strangers.

Joseph Medill McCormick and Joseph Medill Patterson were

not the only Bright Young People of 1904. Some could vote, some not. Some were already known, and nearly every one, before they were done, would be the subject of literary fascination the country over. It was the rising time of such as Jane Addams, Janet Ayer Fairbank, Clarence Darrow, Vachel Lindsay, Raymond Robins, Carl Sandburg; also of two more particularly involved in this record, Harold Loy Ickes and William Hale Thompson. It was precisely in 1904 these latter two collided with McCormick from opposite directions. As the years wore on, each generated passion toward him, as he did toward each of them, that the all too simple word "hate" fails utterly to suggest.

Ickes was born, March 15, 1874, on a hardscrabble farm in the rough country of middle Pennsylvania from which such families as McCormicks had fled, after the Revolution, for Virginia. Like McCormick, Ickes had a lonely and depressed early life. At sixteen, he tried for a fresh start in the Middle West and found his true spiritual home on the campus of the University of Chicago. In his years as Franklin D. Roosevelt's Secretary of the Interior, Ickes assumed a special obligation to educate the general public on the sins of journalism and thought it useful to say that even he had once taken money from the Chicago *Tribune* as a college campus correspondent. To this, McCormick's rejoinder was that he could understand Ickes trying to claim such an honor but the auditor's records proved it a lie. By comparison with the average exchange between the two, that was feeble.

More usually, the *Tribune* would recall that Ickes first married a woman older than himself and of considerable means, and Ickes took this to suggest he had something shady in his financial past. After his second marriage, to a woman much younger than himself, he felt his masculinity wounded when the *Tribune* claimed he had been called "Dahlia" Ickes, as a fancier of these blossoms.

For his own part, Ickes liked nothing better than to sit up in the night, after a grueling Washington day at the public business, and write about McCormick in his *Secret Diary*, one of the most valuable and fascinating documents in all American political history. It is said to run near to six million words in all, but so far only a small fraction has been let into print out of consideration for persons living. If the comments on McCormick are any cue, it is a good thing. To Ickes, McCormick was an overgrown lummox of less than average intelligence and "a damn physical coward, to boot," who sat up in Tribune Tower "squirting sewage" at people he happened to dislike. When President Roosevelt neglected to have McCormick collared on a charge of treason just after Pearl Harbor, Ickes was puzzled and disappointed.

In 1904, Ickes had his law degree from the University of Chicago, a small foothold in Republican politics, a warm attachment for Charles E. Merriam, and a burning passion for Theodore Roosevelt, his first great national hero and, as he put it himself, the last successful candidate for President he ever supported until his lonely wanderings brought him to safe harbor with Roosevelt II. In the years between, he was frustrated and ineffectual, ridiculed by some as an incompetent living on his wife's money, admired by others as a champion of public justice and liked by many people who knew him in his personal role. Among these, one was McCormick's cousin, Eleanor Patterson. Ickes' *Secret Diary* suggests that after his first wife's death Mrs. Patterson flirted as if to invite him as her third husband. It is unquestioned that the two were close friends until they parted, in 1941, with bangs heard from one end of the United States to the other, which was taken by McCormick as one more proof that he was a shrewder judge of men than his cousins.

It gives an idea of how the Republican organization in Chicago was fractured, as of 1904, that Harold Ickes, Robert R. McCormick and William Hale Thompson could each find in it his own, particular point of departure into public significance.

Ickes allied with a faction headed by Charles S. Deneen, which Merriam has defined as appealing most to business, the middle class, to the press and to reformers in the outlying sections of the city. McCormick was in the hands of Busse, whose group never quite reached any special definition before he died.

The principal operator was Representative William E. Lorimer, who liked to be called "the blond boss." Merriam is quite direct in saying Lorimer's force was built out of patronage, graft, privilege, "and all sorts of political alliances of whatever character seemed useful at the moment." In 1904, Lorimer's bright young man of the moment was William Hale Thompson, born, of all places, on Beacon Street in Boston, and a fugitive from his family's honorable tradition of Phillips Exeter, Yale, old money and sound public service. It happened because Thompson, senior, married a Chicago girl and headed West to take advantage of the great boom after the Civil War. He never got back to Boston. But he drew his son's attention to the wonders of public life, in that he went down to Springfield and sat in the legislature as champion of laws to prevent cruelty to animals. He even rose to the rank of colonel on the staff of the Honorable Shelby M. Cullom during that far-darting Apollo's turn as governor. Unfortunately, his much-beloved son Billy, at age fifteen, ran out West and for several years was a cowboy in the wildest sort of country. For the rest of his life Thompson sought to bemuse the great city of Chicago by playing Cowboys and Indians on both sides of the battle at once. In the end, he came near to bankrupting the city. Except for McCormick he might very well have done so. All of which is elaborated on here in due time.

At the turn of the century, Thompson luxuriated in the newspapers as a football and water polo hero. The First Ward, in the heart of Chicago, was a frightful place. Bank robbers and holdup men bought sanctuary on a straight business basis. White slave kidnappers really did scout the railroad stations for victims. The criminal trade became so profitable it expanded into the 2nd Ward, which clung to some notions of respectability. So it was there the reform element and the main force of particularly free enterprise met to have things out. In early 1900 two harridans, who claimed their names were Ada and Minna Everleigh, opened an establishment advertised as "The Everleigh Club." They puffed it all through the Middle West in brochures as "the most elegant and costly brothel in the world." Thompson promptly announced himself as a Reform candidate for alderman in the 2nd Ward and the Municipal Voters' League, sure that such a famous athlete would also be a leader in public purity, turned the election his way.

It turned out that Alderman Thompson's idea of closing down such places was that on Election Day everybody should suspend business long enough to vote for him. Popular histories of Chicago have built the mythology of elegance at The Everleigh Club, which lasted eleven years, to the point that it is almost fair to say no other city in the United States, except perhaps Phoenix City, Alabama, or Reno, Nevada, ever so preened with pleasure at the thought of prostitution as evidence of civic progress.

McCormick made his entry into this arena of confusions and concealments as a member of the city council's special committee supposed to solve the vexing issue of municipal ownership for the streetcars. Dunne had been elected by "the best people" who had not let party stand in their way. But it was not long until discovery was made that there is a considerable distance between language and achievement in the process of governing. Nobody was more outraged than Edgar Lee Masters, more known today for his poetry than for his other career as a Chicago lawyer. Masters turned in a summation of Dunne's administration, at once funny and scathing political analysis, in his *The Tale of Chicago,* which demonstrates that he could put a hard, practical eye on real men and real events with just as much effect as he could evoke poetic imagery in the *Spoon River Anthology.*

Any exceptional fluttering of sandpipers along the shore is said to be a sure sign that something monumental is happening in the deep waters of the ocean. So do gyrations of the visionaries mark a sea-change in American political behavior. Masters cataloged the Chicagoans who now surrounded Dunne. He specified the single-taxers, eloquent infidels, ideologues, lecturers in back halls, "gap-toothed men and bucktoothed men" left over from the spasms of the Altgeld and Bryan days. It is easy to see individuals of this present record among his types. The lawyer with time on his hands to study the street railway laws: Harold Ickes. The radical Democrat in fedora hat, string tie and blue shirt: Joe Patterson. The dreamer in broad-rimmed hat, low collar and flowing tie: Raymond Robins. All of them "staring at the scene of Chicago's predicament," and all of them having Dunne's amiable and credulous attention. The result: "rich with imbecility." If achievement is the test, it was indeed. Nothing of immediate tangible benefit happened. There is another view: that the importance of 1904 in Chicago and elsewhere lay in the inspiration of commitment; the simple, vital discovery by the visionaries that government is an enterprise really available to them and at which they may occupy themselves, to the public good, but only if they can do more than just talk about it.

On the vision itself, of what government ought to be like, Masters and McCormick, for all that they had a habit of glowering at each other, were of remarkably parallel mind. Of course, by family tradition and in personal terms, Masters was attached to the legend of Stephen A. Douglas, as McCormick was bound to the Lincoln legend. But their writings reveal them. The poet and the editor, one adopted by latter-day literary rebels as their private property, and the other condemned by these same enthusiasts as the Archfiend's walking delegate, saw government in the Douglas version. After all elaboration is stripped away, it amounts to a set of broad general public aspirations executed according to local options; this as against the Lincoln vision of authoritative national commitment made effective through the work of a central agency. How McCormick chose between these views, as he matured in experience with public issues, can be seen in his fifty years of performance between his first office-holding of 1905 and his death in 1955.

It may be gathered from Masters that McCormick was lucky to begin with Busse as guide. Dunne's fripperies and fecklessness led Chicago next to choose Busse as mayor and Masters considered it the irony of life that such a piece of slag turned out to be "a rough diamond for Chicago." Busse was a man of property himself, so he had common enough cause with its interests, but he had no difficulty at facing down the idiotically selfish.

He settled the long streetcar battle with precise intelligence. The city wouldn't take over the companies. It would take only 55 percent of their earnings. Busse also nailed down the five-cent fare for the users. His formula stood until the automobile era made it pointless for anybody at all to debate who should own the trolleys.

The waterfront was a noxious morass. Chicago's most famous architect was Daniel Burnham, who had saved the World's Columbian Exposition of 1893 from becoming a standard Chicago mess of jerry-building. Burnham had also been first chairman of the Fine Arts Commission which fixed the architectural identity of Washington—at least so far—for the twentieth century. He also had ideas on what to do about the Lake Michigan shore. So Busse formed a Chicago plan commission, with Burnham as chief architect. And to the shock of his cronies among the Republican factions, he chose a Democrat, Charles H. Wacker, as chairman of the commission itself.

Just as the anarchists and visionaries of the Haymarket Riot time illustrate one side effect of Henry Adams' caravan in passage through Chicago, so does Wacker illustrate another. Wacker's father was a fugitive from consequences of the 1848 rising in Germany. To this day, the Chicago scene still bears its traces of these thousands. Their descendants, in twentieth-century America, have had ties that bound them to special meeting halls, eating places, forms of speech, lines of commerce, degrees of intermarriage. These have also left them vulnerable to charges of disloyalty and dubious faith with their fellow citizens, as the United States has twice found itself at war with a Germany that really had rejected them.

Wacker was the essence of the pragmatic Chicagoan, a slightly more elegant Busse. He evolved from grain trading, to brewing, to real estate, and became the president of the Chicago Heights Land Association. From 1909, until illness removed him in 1926, he commanded the Plan Commission and the best men of the city were proud to serve him. None jumped at the chance more eagerly than McCormick in his own turn, and the spectacle of the Lake Michigan waterfront of modern times is as much a monument to Wacker's square, stern, stubborn will as it is to Daniel Burnham's imagination. It is part of this record, too, that at the very center of it, where a channel threads from Lake Michigan away to the Southwest, there sits what some modern architects like to scorn as a monumental offense in "wedding cake Gothic," the Tribune Tower. From the top floor of this McCormick hurled his paper thunderbolts, but always with an anxious and knowledgeable eye on the water below. For all of which he owed the most, next to himself, to old, rough, roistering Fred A. Busse.

McCormick's 1903 letter from Panama to his parents in St. Petersburg has been offered here as evidence that there were energies and curiosities in his makeup that no niggling law practice would ever be able to stifle. Now, two years later, there was another letter to his parents in Paris, equally informative. He was famished for appreciation, he had problems keeping his manhood intact from his mother's connivances, but he was already showing himself competent at grasp of political calculation. Like the other letter, this one is undated, but quite evidently is of early 1905. Every sentence throws out a clue to McCormick's feeling, thought and outlook:

> Dear People:
>
> If you were surprised at the tenor of my telegram, you were at most no more surprised than I when the nomination [for presidency of the Chicago Sanitary Commission] was offered me.
>
> Last Thursday afternoon as I was sitting with the Committee on Local Transportation [in the city council] Roy O. West called me on the telephone and asked if I could go to the Republican headquarters.

I replied that I was too busy to leave but would go when the committee adjourned. He then said he and Busse would come and see me. I returned to the committee, thinking that they wished to discuss Lincoln Park appointments, and getting into an argument with the mayor [Dunne], forgot all about them.

Soon after, West and Busse called me out and told me that the county central committee could not agree to the nomination of any of the candidates and wished me to run. I thought the matter over and concluded that although it was questionable whether it was advisable from a selfish point of view, yet the duty was clear and not to be avoided.

As you know, under past administrations, the canal has been a harvest of graft. Now the legislature has changed the organization of the board, giving to the president the appointment of all committees, the appointment of all employees and the power of veto over all action of the trustees. In other words, it has centered all the power in the president. Such being the case, when the Republican Party offered me the nomination, asking no promises of me whatsoever, I could not consistently with my ideals refuse to accept it.

From a personal point of view, it is doubtful whether I benefitted myself by accepting the nomination. I am considered one of the leaders of the council. I have the respect of all the members and the friendship of most of them. My speech on the new Charter Convention [for Chicago] was said by many to be the best ever made in the chamber, which statement may be taken *cum grano sali*. It was further understood that I should become chairman of the Finance Committee when Bennett retired in 1907. In due time I could expect to be the logical candidate for mayor.

On the other hand my ward is Democratic now and becoming more so as the bums come across the river. I would have a hard fight for re-election, next Spring, and a terribly hard two years from then. As it is, I have about an even chance of election this Fall.

Dunn's majority of twenty-five thousand will be offset only in part by the country towns in the [Sanitary] District, leaving a majority of some ten thousand to be reversed by the campaign. Assuming that Winter, the Democratic nominee, and I should develop equal strength, a campaign more skillfully managed than that of last spring, aided by dissension among the Democrats, should turn the trick. I explain the personal side only as a matter of interest, as the principal [sic] was conclusive.

I feel deeply touched at your offer of twenty thousand dollars if I would join you in Paris, not because of the money offered but because of the affection it proved. Had it been delivered promptly, I should certainly have accepted the invitation and might have felt precluded by that from taking the nomination. By some mistake, it was delivered at Medill's house and mailed to him in Cleveland and did not reach me until after I had accepted the nomination and the publication of my acceptance.

It was delivered to me while I was in a conference with Busse, Reddick, Hamberg, West and one or two other politiciance [sic]. I put the matter before them, not mentioning the twent. thou., but saying I had received an urgent request to come over and wished to accept. They replied unanimously that to do so would probably prove fatal to my election and that of the whole ticket. The reasons given were threefold. First, a wide and unfavorable publicity. Second, it will take the entire summer to get a working knowledge of the issues in the campaign. Third, I must spend the summer making friends of the politicians and organizing for the campaign which will open in September.

Further, they urged upon me the fact that I must make the campaign for the whole ticket, judicial as well as sanitary, and that a defection on my part would affect not only me but the whole party in Cook County. So you see that a second time in twenty-four hours I had to put duty before self.

Why do not you come over for the month of November. After the election I intend to merely walk through my Council work for at least a month.

It is awful to think that we will not see each other for another year although, after that, I hope to be able to make my public duties obey me so that I can take care of my family duties and pleasures.

In conclusion I will remark that, if elected, I will hold office for five years and can expect at the expiration of that time to be one of the foremost public men of the Middle West.

Your affectionate son,
Rutherford

McCormick's widow has interpreted the offer of twenty thousand dollars as she understood it from McCormick himself as a gift conditional on his giving up Chicago to stay abroad with his parents. The elder Mrs. McCormick was, after all, a thoroughly experienced Chicagoan. Her eldest son was now the rising star of the *Tribune* and it was on him that everything depended. Yet, here was Bertie stumbling around among the gray wolves at City Hall, menacing the whole family's reputation in his ignorance.

Seen with this in mind, one would like to know a good deal more about that rigmarole of how the summons, with bribe attached, was misdirected for the crucial few days within which commitments were made that could not now, with honor, be repudiated. The elaboration of names, moments and logical contentions, all must be read as a sort of plea to be excused from answering a *subpoena duces tecum* issued by dread authority, against which any appeal is a grave risk.

But it is also clear as day that by 1905 McCormick had the bit in his teeth. All that talk about indifference to self and the urgent necessity of the Republican Party is evidence that McCormick lacked style at unctuous language. But it is also evidence of his will to power. Furthermore, he was entirely correct in estimating the chance that the job opening before him could help him become "one of the foremost public men of the Middle West."

In many respects, McCormick's next five years were the best of his life. Certainly, they were important in the life of Chicago. All the more poignant, therefore, that he ever came to think of government more as enemy than as friend.

He had gifts, instincts and personal connections with Franklin D. Roosevelt that might very well have put him in the chair actually occupied by Harold Ickes, as Secretary of the Interior and director of the Public Works Administration. In 1905, those gifts and instincts were dominant in his actions, and the end result was a gain for the public good.

The Sanitary Commission, which introduced him to the idea of building things and showed him he could command men, had an assignment that was formally begun in 1892, but really dated from the winter of 1673, when French explorers discovered how the Indians of the Mississippi river system and those of the Great Lakes came together at a portage separating the two great waterways by less than half a mile.

Chicago is Chicago because of that geographic fact. It is the point at which the east-west axis of travel through the Great Lakes-St. Lawrence system intersects with the Mississippi's north-south axis. Because these water systems come closest together there, Chicago is a great seaport in the heart of a continent. It is also the natural aiming point for airlines, railroads and highways, so that Chicago's fundamental business is receiving, sorting and rerouting persons, animals and objects for a national and a global market. Chicago as pivot is determined further by the pattern in which the people of the United States have distributed themselves around it. Since 1890, the statistical "center of population" has never been more than 300 miles from Chicago. At the taking of the decennial national census in 1960, the spot, if anybody would like to know, was marked as 38° 37′ 57″ North, and 88° 52′ 23″ West, which is four miles east of Salem, in Marion County, Illinois. That would put it almost due south of Chicago by something on the order of 225 miles.

Any visitor to Chicago can sense that its presence must be the consequence of some great dramatic fact of nature. The very spectacle of Lake Michigan itself, even without knowledge of the two great continental water systems connected by the Sanitary and Ship Canal, would be sign enough. But if the visitor will start at the Tribune Tower and follow the water channel at its foot, he will discover the true governor on which the somewhat more than 6,795,000 people of the Chicago industrial complex depend for their growth, their health, for their very life.

In a short distance the channel divides. One branch leads northward, parallel to the lake shore, to lose itself in the parklands back of Waukegan near the Illinois-Wisconsin state line. The other curves past steel mills, freight yards, warehouses and machinery plants, the world of South Chicago. The whole is called "the Chicago River," probably the only natural watercourse in the world that men have worked over so that it hardly runs at all, and when it does, begins by running backward, then turns entirely away from itself to run off into a stream behind it, without ever being allowed to flow in a state of nature from origin to exit in the lake. Every drop of water that Chicago drinks must come from Lake Michigan. So, too, every drop to empower its industrial plant. The return is all into the governed Chicago River flowaway to the Southwest instead of Lake Michigan, as it used to be. The difference, in one among many consequences, is the rate of death from typhoid fever. And what makes all this work is a complex arrangement of machinery and law which meters the water of the lake into the Chicago River to back up a man-made tide in the North Branch, then start a flow to a point, roughly ten miles west of Tribune Tower, at which the head of the South Branch turns into the canal on which McCormick learned what sort of man he could be.

The South Branch, in primordial times, formed on the east slope of a low ridge that starts up gently about five miles west of Tribune Tower and five miles farther on, drops sharply to the Des Plaines river. The headwater for the South Branch at its nearest point to the Des Plaines is marked today by a small park. The streams are about a half-mile apart, and it is evident their separation was a geographic near miss.

The naturally squashy prairie, the erosion from eons of rainfall on the light soils of the ridge and the dragging of the Indians' canoes across the portage, reduced the original barrier between the whole Great Lakes-St. Lawrence complex and that of the Mississippi to a sort of jellied plug, all too temptingly feeble. Behind the low ridge, the land falls well below the level of Lake Michigan, so that the very earliest of the French explorers saw at once the possibilities of it. So has everybody since. Cut that plug and the waters of the lake are bound to rush backward into the Des Plaines and on to the Gulf of Mexico with, it hardly need be said, consequences. From the times of the French until 1892, one group of venturers after another had hacked away at it. Then was begun one of the great feats of North American engineering, a gated water channel that runs from the foot of Tribune Tower some thirty-five miles in a curving path to merge with the Des Plaines river at Lockport, just above Joliet, Illinois. The point was chosen because it is the head of navigation for river traffic, thirty-four feet below the level of Lake Michigan. Waters converging on Lockport rush so that it is a natural site for the generation of hydroelectricity.

By the time McCormick was put in charge of the Sanitary and Ship Canal, the main channel had been dug. Plans were being discussed that would open up more of South Chicago with feeder channels running between the lake and the main canal. There was also demand for the generation of electricity at Lockport. It hardly need be said that every industrial, mercantile, political and social enterprise in the Middle West felt an interest in the details of how these should go. It hardly need be said, either, that every city and every shipper in the Great Lakes-St. Lawrence region had a passionate concern to see that the gates at Lake Michigan should not be left ajar. It came down to this, and it remains the same today: the more water out of the lake, the better for Chicago. But the more water out of the lake, the worse for Milwaukee, not to mention

Detroit, Cleveland, Buffalo and everywhere in between. If the level of the Great Lakes should drop enough, what would happen at Niagara Falls?

More than once, in the years since the building of the Chicago Sanitary and Ship Canal, the halls of the Supreme Court have rung with demands for justice. Congress has been laid under siege. Presidents have been exhorted and cajoled. McCormick, through formal study and field effort, became one of the best-informed men of his time on the problems of the Great Lakes-Mississippi water relationship, and in no other aspect was his editorship on the *Tribune* more valuable to Chicago. This fact elevates one of the oddities of McCormick's life. In Canada, he proved he could adapt gracefully to things as he found them. And the knowledge he had from his canal assignment proved beyond all doubt that no local option can ever hope to stand against broader interests. Yet, in the climactic years of his life and in matters involving Chicago, McCormick abandoned all power to adapt and threw himself into the blind resistance of the hooked fish. And to the same end.

But in 1905, he was entirely another sort of man, as he discovered that he did not have to be the unknown, unwanted younger brother of the maternally designated family star, nor a political hack, either. To enlarge the main canal and build the industrial feeder channels he avoided wardheelers and in-laws. He hired technicians whose careers in later life are a tribute to his judgment and a vindication of his determination to, as he put it in his memoirs, "violate political ethics" by putting ability ahead of orthodoxy. One such technician was Edward J. Kelly, an obscure engineer who battered his way up through the maze to become Chicago's mayor and boss of its Democratic power system in the days of Franklin D. Roosevelt.

Harold Ickes' *Secret Diary* is heavily inscribed with evidence of shock and frustration that he could never get Mr. Roosevelt to react properly to demonstrations that McCormick and Kelly were hand in glove at the running of Chicago's municipal works. Mr. Ickes and University of Chicago purists bargained with other Chicago publishers, sought alliances with aspiring Chicago politicians, tried to alarm Mr. Roosevelt through messages by way of personages from other parts of the country, but all in vain. McCormick and Kelly carried on a sort of Chinese campaign against each other, in which menaces consisted of loud noise, horrid faces and violent flapping of particolored ensigns. But no bones were ever broken. Mr. Roosevelt saw to it that Kelly got the necessary millions in public works funds to do Chicago enormous good, with the name of Edward J. Kelly, Mayor, on all appropriate plaques. And Kelly listened to McCormick's quiet, sensible suggestions for such major improvements along the lake front as the Outer Drive and the building up of land for valuable constructions of buildings which now even overshadow the Tribune Tower itself. It was all very Chicago, as, indeed, was the sigh of Janet Ayer Fairbank during the 1944 Democratic Convention:

"I just can't make Bert McCormick listen. He gets into these deals with Ed Kelly and he loses, every time. But he keeps on making them."

Whatever deal it was the delightful lady reformer objected to at the moment she did not say, but her complaint was traditional. In Chicago's politics the improbable is the usual and the inexplicable is the one that works. At bottom, the answer really seems as simple as this: McCormick, in the vigor of youth, met Kelly, who had the one quality McCormick admired above all others, a hard competency at driving through a specific task to produce a thing men could see and use. When they were young, they had fun together. Keeping in touch was a way of remaining loyal to their own past.

Given all the opportunities it had to go sour, their friendship, or whatever it ought to be called, is a demonstration that McCormick had a more complicated nature than simplistic political critics ever dreamed. For the city of Chicago, there was profit in it, too. Kelly was a roughneck, to be sure, and the most domineering sort of partisan political boss. But he was an excellent mayor. It could not have caused him any too much anguish that McCormick used the *Tribune* so that the worst of Kelly's associates feared being caught at stealing too much. Such a menace was some help toward preserving Kelly's own honorable record. It may even be said, without utterly shattering truth, that the combination resulted in the taxpayers almost getting their money's worth, on occasion, perhaps for the first time since Fred A. Busse's equally roughcut day.

McCormick's venture with the Sanitary Commission not only brought him into collision with patronage managers, but also with one of the most ravenous financial manipulators of the early twentieth century. Robert Todd Lincoln, from his figurehead position with the *Tribune* law firm, went to the presidency of the Pullman Company, and then took an interest in the important new business of selling electricity. He became part owner of the Chicago Edison Company. On a trip to the fountain of Edisonian wisdom at Menlo Park, New Jersey, he discovered a sour, intense, English-born clerk who impressed him as exactly the man to liven things back home. Samuel Insull came to Chicago in 1891. By the time McCormick got into public life, Insull was already one of the city's most serious dangers to the unwary.

Electric generators were indicated at Lockport, the downriver terminal of the Sanitary and Ship Canal, but it was not altogether clear in law just what the rights of claimers to the privilege to build and operate might be. McCormick, who was carrying on his law study on the side, settled down to a historical analysis of riparian and other rights. We have his own testimony that it was this investigation which waked him to the fascinations of American history. In 1945, he published *The American Revolution and Its Influence on World Civilization.* In the Foreword he wrote:

> At school I was given a good course in ancient Greek history, in Roman history up to the accession of Caesar Augustus, and in English history which carried with it a large part of the history of France. In college there was an excellent course on modern European history down to the death of Bismarck. Both in school and in college I received considerable instruction in French and English literature, which complemented the historical studies, but of American history and of American literature in school and college there was not one page.
>
> It was after I graduated from college that I heard of the expedition of George Rogers Clark in a political speech, and at about the same time read the Ordinance of 1787 in connection with a dispute over the navigability of the Des Plaines River.

As his books and broadcasts show, he never forgot the insights into development of the American spirit that reading gave him. And it may be added that Insull never forgot, and never forgave, some insights by McCormick which were also byproducts of that early investigation into the fundamentals of public service.

To solve the problem of who should run the power plants at Lockport, McCormick not only read up on history and law. He took a trio of friends and a rowboat and explored the watercourse. He did an elaborate study of hydroelectric power costs and fixed a rate at which he offered to sell the power, as a Canal Commission by-product, directly to the city of Chicago for its street lighting system.

Insull thought the best way to get this power under a contract of his own was by way of the state legislature. McCormick dynamited him, and another of Chicago's outlandish political hate-fests was on. It lasted thirty years. Insull became a mighty scooper-up of other people's money in the building of a corporate system which, in 1928, was valued at four billion of that period's gold dollars. Few men of business, politics or even of crime have ever been as whole-heartedly disliked. It was Edgar Lee Masters who described Insull as having "a barracuda curl to his lip." He arrived at his office not later than 7:30 each morning, even after forty years of single-minded slaving. He was never known to smile at an employe. Arthur Meeker, as mild and genial a historian as Chicago's Gold Coast ever produced, noted with loathing that Insull was equally surly to tenants and employes of a Lake Front apartment house in which the great money hog occasionally reposed. Whether Insull was an unappreciated genius at putting together electric utilities or just a manipulator who got away with monstrous abuse of public trust is an issue which has been debated in Chicago for now more than half a century. One thing is certain. He made a mistake when he tried to browbeat Robert R. McCormick. And when, at last, he ran snarling for cover in the islands of the Aegean Sea after the crash of 1929, he accused McCormick of using the *Tribune* to persecute him.

It is difficult to say. Certainly the *Tribune* had never swallowed Insull's version of himself. And when the crash of his holding company system carried away great portions of savings and speculations in the Middle West, the *Tribune* was merciless in calling him to account. In reviewing his early collision with Insull, McCormick had this to say in 1952:

> . . . Insull was indicted under the charge of defrauding his stockholders. He thought I was responsible. I was not. He was a political corruptionist, but I never thought he was dishonest to his associates.

It is curious distinction. In any case, it had no noticeable effect toward improving Insull's reputation, if it was so meant.

As for McCormick, aside from colliding with political corruptionists, discovering talented young engineers, exploring the Des Plaines river and generally getting a taste of the high life, he plugged away at his law books until he graduated in 1906. Two years later he passed the bar examinations. But in 1910, as his first term on the Canal Commission expired, the Middle West was caught up in a great general revulsion against the label "Republican" for reasons generated again in distant Washington, reasons which also had important effects on McCormick's next career.

He ran for re-election, was defeated, and thought he would go into law practice. As it turned out, he had hardly got his office organized before he was dragged out of it in the climax of that long-building battle for the *Tribune*'s control.

CHAPTER SEVEN ★★★ Chicago journalism, in 1910, was dizzy with excitement about itself. The caravan of immigrants had done well for the newspapers. Population was still shooting up and citizens liked variety in their reading matter. The hard-cider political style of Joseph Medill's day was long gone, but in its place there was the melodrama of everyday life. Medill's grandsons, who became expert in the uses of this new theme, were there to see it form: the doctrine that what one man does to one woman, or better yet, what one woman does to one man, will sell more newspapers than any number of floods in China.

There were plenty of readers, plenty of newspapers, and there was an open question which one could claim to be on top of the heap. The *Tribune* certainly had the most dignified history, the longest taproot, and it dominated the morning field. But it did not dominate Chicago, by long odds. One difficulty was that over the years it had trained too many excellent men who had struck out on their own. The leading case was Melville E. Stone, son of a downstate Methodist preacher. Stone started on the *Tribune* in 1860 as a carrier boy, aged twelve. Four years later, he made it up to reporter. In 1874, when he was twenty-six years old, he talked an English remittance man into putting up five thousand dollars to start an evening paper, the Chicago *Daily News*. To Stone, the issue of the Gilded Age was more what men and women did to each other and less how they should think. His paper was an instant success. Stone stuck to editing and let the business management out to a proved Chicago realist, Victor E. Lawson, who was not long in crowding the *Tribune* with a morning edition of the *News*. Stone astonished Chicago in 1888 by declaring, at age forty, that journalism had now reached such complexity and erudition that one of his limited education was no longer fit to edit so important a newspaper as the *News*. He retired. Nobody was ever more hopelessly in error. In 1893, the Associated Press, which had been caught in a great scandal, called him back to be its general manager. He stayed on that job until 1921, and for the five years left to his life thereafter, served as a sort of senior counselor to its board of directors. It was in his time the Associated Press adopted the rules and policies which, in 1941, would be McCormick's own weapons in his back-to-the-wall fight against the Government of the United States, most of his fellow publishers and even a majority of the board of directors of the Associated Press itself, on which he then had held a seat since 1927. And Melville Stone's Chicago *News,* having passed through many hands would be a party to McCormick's grinding down.

As a creative journalist, Stone made the *News* a remarkably interesting body of reading matter for anybody and a source book on urban manners for the farmer come to town. He heard of a poetaster down in Indianapolis, James Whitcomb Riley, who had the corn planters of three states drowning their families in tears as they read out his lamplight lyrics on rural delight that young and old, alike, were that very minute plotting to flee by the next milk train. And that is how Little Orphant [sic] Annie came to Chicago's house to stay. She may be seen there, yet, in a *Tribune* cartoon serial nobody could possibly relate in logic to the original. From Denver, Stone rescued another, not so roly-poly, versifier and so Chicago was flooded with eyewater on being exposed to Eugene Field's *miserari* for Little Boy Blue, his little toy dog all covered with dust and his little tin soldier red with rust. But it was by no means all sniffles.

George Ade produced his "Fables In Slang." Finley Peter Dunne gave American letters "Mister Dooley." Nobody can read either today and dismiss Melville Stone's Middle West as all yap. For if the authors could project irony and wit even beyond the sardonic, what is to be said about their readers? No daily journalistic commentators ever had a more devoted audience, nor was it small, either. Something about that audience can be learned through a comparison of editorial judgment in their day with the common trend in newspapers of the mid-twentieth century. No modern newspaper supposes its readers to have the intellectual energy for enjoyment of the word play, not to mention the mordant insights, that qualify Mister Dooley and the Fables as true source material for any scholarly investigation into the best of American comic writing.

McCormick was certainly one editor who believed the cleaver put the rapier out of business in Chicago. In New York, Patterson made it seem that he felt the same way. Only the most careful analyst will discover that Patterson's apparent meat axe was, in fact, a far more peculiar weapon. Just what it was yet waits his sufficiently alert and competent biographer. Each man, for his thorough grasp of the idea that newspapers should not be just thrown together but firmly edited for a model reader in the mind's eye, owed something to the instinctual craftmanship of Melville Stone. It was the competition forced by the *News* that did much to help the *Tribune* free itself from preoccupation with partisan politics of the old regime.

Stone could find not only clever essayists and masters of rhythmical sobbing. Men of talents all across the board were drawn to the *News*. Guy Carleton went on to edit *Life* in its incarnation as a magazine of wit and humor. Clarence Dresser, who sold his "the public be damned" interview with Commodore Vanderbilt to the *Tribune* when the *News* declined it is a magnate's lapse that ought not to be exploited, became a writer of popular songs. And there was George Harvey, whose role in this account comes later. Here, let it be noted only that Harvey, like Stephen A. Douglas, was a fugitive from the bony hills of Vermont, and like Douglas, was inflated by the opulence of the prairie to think himself a great master of affairs.

Stone's *News* also was a starting point for some of journalism's finest talents at political cartooning. There was Thomas E. Powers, whose sense of fun is portrayed in this book with an early sketch on Joseph Medill as a Chicago booster. Powers grew to be W. R. Hearst's most feared and yet somehow not offensive graphic commentator. His eye was merciless, but he did not give false witness. And there was John T. McCutcheon, who went over to the *Tribune* in 1903 and until 1949 played his pawky, nineteenth-century sense of humor across the scene of American political pietism. McCutcheon was utterly lacking in the power to wound anybody. Not even such certified enemies of society as the German Kaiser, not even Hitler, nor even Stalin, could be brought off without some sign of human faculty. In the years of the New Deal it was the official duty of every *Tribune* functionary to strike the pose of Mr. Christian challenging Apollyon across the way. But McCutcheon's attempts to convey horrification somehow always turned out to be another window for Chicago on its past. His gentle mixture of corn shucks, bombazine, bent-pin fishhooks and "slippery ellum" whistles lasted to the hour of the hydrogen bomb. Then it was all gone at once. But one of McCormick's kindlier, and wiser, decisions had been to let his old friend play it out unhindered. Modern inspectors of the *Tribune*'s running war with political trends, who may be puzzled to discover in McCutcheon a single strain of inconsistency among the paper's stridencies, may just put him down as a sign that even McCormick could be weak before an unremittingly genial and compelling talent. But not more than once.

On the editorial page, this time of transition had its distinct signs, too. The *News* was just as much alarmed at the anarchists and the socialists, just as much demanding the iron hand with Haymarket Riot criminals, as the *Tribune*. But on the *Tribune,* Robert W. Patterson attacked his problems in language comparing favorably with heresy findings by the Chicago Presbyterian Synod, which had a great deal of that sort of thing to worry about in the Gilded Age. Stone, with his instinct for the light and feathery and an inability to resist Eugene Field's raffishness, set *News* commentaries to a tone less dominated by sulphur and brimstone.

It is not part of this record to explore another of the transitional journals, the Chicago *Times,* and its magnificent fantast, Wilbur F. Storey, but merely to indicate that as Chicago came into the twentieth century it had more to be thankful for in its journalism than not. Things could have been a good deal worse. And in the opinion of many a student of the city's affairs, very shortly they were.

The signal for the great change is usually given as:

"And then came Hearst."

In 1900, Chicago was jolted with the grand opening of Hearst's evening *American.* That had hardly been absorbed before the morning *Examiner* came spinning off the same presses. And so there followed what has come to be dramatized by people who should know better as "the Chicago newspaper war," supposedly the start of organized gangsterism, as told in song and story around the world. This is, of course, just another Chicago decoration of drab fact to impress natives and visitors alike that here the days and nights are filled with unusual magic. It is certainly true that when selling newspapers on the streets of Chicago involved intense competition, gangs quite inevitably got into it, but in Chicago, as in London, Rome, New York or Peking, street gangs are as old as the city itself.

McCormick once, in a private conversation, blamed Lawson for letting things go too far. At the turn of the century, he said, the *News,* printing both morning and evening papers, made the ground rules. There was a great brass bell in the alley back of the *News* plant and not until Lawson had come out and rung it could any vendor switch over from evening to morning papers, if he wished to handle any of Lawson's products again. This was all very well until Hearst learned of it and directed his people that no small-bore Chicagoan whatsoever should limit their activities. No matter which publisher was first to lose his head, the ordinary quarreling and fistfights which were normal exercise among the street salesmen did degenerate into serious cuttings, shootings and massed forays of louts hired to help break up restraints of trade without the niceties of the Sherman Anti-Trust Act.

But it was all low-level piecework, hardly the sort of thing to interest an ambitious, first-chop gunman. To begin with, the pay could not compare with what any competent journeyman could do on his own, at minimum risk, among the undefended cigar stores. Why go against equally armed professionals, when there are easier ways to make a living? And, finally, in the circulation combats there was no way for soldiers of fortune to wind up with the main swag, an aspect just as interesting to an Alphonse Capone as to any publisher. Once some tried it against the *Tribune.* They shot up a guard, got some publicity and a few thousand dollars. They also got long prison terms in the end. It was not among these the great Chicago newspaper war was so real. Even the toughest gunmen cannot fan out through town and force people to buy papers they find dull. But it is true enough that in the editorial rooms there developed a style forever preserved in *The Front Page,* by Ben Hecht and Charles MacArthur. Ignorant unbelievers may delight in this as a comic fantasy, but not anybody of even the mildest personal experience with the men and the period. To all who ever knew Chicago's journalism of the vintage years *The Front Page* is a pure and muted statement of the literal truth about men and events exactly as they were. Or so, to his dying day, the last survivor will eternally believe, nor be guiltier of exaggeration than veterans of any other wars.

It was a bruising half-century. In 1900, Chicago had twelve daily papers. By 1910 the number was eight. By 1965, there were just four, of which the *Tribune* company owned two. Its sole opposition, organized by the grandson of Marshall Field, ran the others. Nobody disturbed the peace, morning, evening or any time at all.

McCormick was drawn into the battle, so he always said, by misadventure. He went to the Chicago Athletic Club one day in 1909 and found the *Tribune* treasurer signing checks in the steam room. He reported to R. W. Patterson, who promptly made McCormick treasurer, but neglected to add a salary. Patterson was downhearted with the whole thing. Neither Medill sister any longer pretended interest in Chicago. Mrs. Patterson had McKim, Mead & White build her a house at Fifteen Dupont Circle in Washington, which got her favorable mention in dispatches by Henry Adams, the capital's arbiter in matters of taste and beauty. Adams not only admired the house, but also made a point of showing attention to "my friend, Nelly" at T. R. Roosevelt's dinner table. Mrs. McCormick had her house at 3000 Massachusetts Avenue done by John Russell Pope. Adams seems to have taken a dislike to her and so all his reports were cutting. For that matter, the sisters entertained all of fashionable Washington by cutting at each other. Mrs. Patterson held that her sister couldn't get a place among the proper people and so had gone "out in the sticks," where she would be murdered one night in her bed. Mrs. McCormick said that everybody knew Dupont Circle was a swamp at the wrong end of town and her sister would come down with malaria soon.

In Chicago, the board of directors met once a month to measure up the credits against the debits. The cash surplus was paid out immediately as a dividend. R. W. Patterson became so morose he sold his ten shares of stock to McCormick on the basis of Medill's evaluation of the *Tribune* in 1894, which was six million dollars.

As for McCormick, except for landing some of the paper's law business and acting as unpaid treasurer, he stayed out of it, until:

> One day in March, 1911, the chief telephone operator, Anna Garrow, rang up and said that Mr. R. W. Patterson had just died. This was a great surprise to me as I had seen him in Washington a few days before, apparently well, when he expressed a desire that I go to work actively in the *Tribune*. I went down to his office to obtain more information and, to my surprise, found there Mr. William G. Beale, Mr. Alfred Cowles, Mr. Horace White, Mr. Azariah T. Galt, the trustee for the Bross estate, and one or two of the very small stockholders. They had come together to accept a proposition from Mr. Victor Lawson to buy the *Tribune,* with a new building and machinery, for ten million dollars. If Mr. Patterson had lived a day or two longer, the sale would have taken place.

It is curious that McCormick could make any error on such a momentous event in the affairs of the *Tribune* and his own life. The meeting happened, all right. But not in 1911.

In February, 1910, R. W. Patterson notified his wife that the *Tribune* was in crisis. W. G. Beale had refused any longer to serve as a director unless Medill McCormick were taken away and Patterson, too, wished only to get out of it all. With Hearst pressing from one side, Lawson from the other, and the lesser competition burrowing where it could, the elders of the *Tribune* all lost heart. Then, on April 1, 1910, Patterson's mother, widow of the venerated Presbyterian pastor, died in Chicago. Patterson was in Philadelphia. None of his family seems ever to have known exactly what took him there or the details of events following, but on that same day, in that city off his usual path, Patterson died, too. The joint funeral for mother and son was reported in all Chicago papers as one of the most impressive in the city's history. Even so, there remained the *Tribune*'s pending dissolution.

McCormick argued for time. The *Tribune* had an excellent staff below the level of its owners. The business manager was William H. Field, the operating editor was James Keeley and the circulation manager was Max Annenberg. The directors agreed to delay on condition that McCormick take an active hand in the paper's affairs, and he did so, his first act being to tell Lawson that the sale was off. As he later described it, he shook in his boots as he broke the news to the most formidable power in Chicago's journalism. Lawson was furious and promised to run the *Tribune* out of business, but wound up with an increased offer. McCormick asked for time to take this to his mother, aunt and other representatives of principal holdings, by then off to Europe for the summer. He was already determined against selling, but wanted breathing space for the working force to settle down.

Instead of hawking the *Tribune* around the Continent, he went up to Berlin to study the new sewage plant. In England, he took in the Manchester ship canal, the managers of which had won suits for damages in libel. He learned the canal was operated not as an arm of government but as if it were a private corporation, a distinction he remembered later when an associate of His Honor, Mayor William Hale Thompson, sued the *Tribune* for $10 million in damages on behalf of the city of Chicago, claiming its municipal reputation had been libeled, and citing the Manchester Ship Canal Case as a precedent. McCormick's formidable memory thereupon paid dividends in more than one fashion. The *Tribune* was able to establish the doctrine in U.S. practice that governments, as such, cannot charge libel. This point proved its importance many times in 1954 and later as the country struggled with the consequences of racism in tax-paid education.

On his return to Chicago, McCormick broke the bad news to Lawson, who promptly attacked with a cut in price for the morning edition to one cent. McCormick's version of the consequence is primly given:

"Max Annenberg, later assisted by his brother-in-law, Louis Rose, proved to be much the best circulation manager in town. It was the *Tribune* that gained. . . ."

So much for gutters running with blood. If there were any doubt of Annenberg's real ability, he certainly demonstrated it in New York when he went on there with J. M. Patterson. And as for the *Tribune,* it soon steadied, once the top settled down. McCormick was made president in 1911, but still got neither salary nor a directorship.

At first, he was slow to meddle in editorial matters, but he did make one immediate and significant change. He put a stop to puffs for the Commonwealth Edison Company, centerpiece of Samuel Insull's power network. Ever after, McCormick was fierce in refusal of the news columns to entrepreneurs on the make. He took it as an important duty to promote the general welfare of industry and the stimulation of new enterprise, but he was strict in prohibition of favoritism. Of course, he was never unique in this, but whereas editors commonly let it be known they acted from highest journalistic principles, McCormick liked to be off-handed: "Why give away free what they pay for with advertising?"

He liked to say that Field "invented the science of newspaper advertising as we know it." There is something to it. The *Tribune* set up staffs to help merchants write their copy, provided market research teams, taught classes in window-display, the budgeting of advertising appropriations and did real service in bringing order to the random clamor of practice that had expanded, day by day, without much unifying purpose. From the *Tribune* workshops emerged concepts now taken as commonplace.

For himself, McCormick claimed the idea of "promotion," that is, the merchandising of the paper itself, both in its own columns and in direct circulation-selling schemes. Men who sought to rise on the *Tribune* learned expertise at organizing athletic contests, musical extravaganzas, parades and patriotic celebrations.

In direct circulation promotion, the *Tribune* developed a highly sophisticated system of give-aways with everything from kitchenware to insurance policies. But it was not all done in one single, great scientific marketing leap forward. Hearst was no amateur at such things himself, and in one such monumental collision the *Tribune* blundered into a city-wide contest of all the papers to see which could behave most foolishly. And it managed to win, or lose, with "Cheer Checks," a cash give-away that, in eight days of public riot, cost $53,050. All at once, the stunned publishers were stricken with conscience at the thought they might be violating the lottery laws and climbed down, each blaming the other for losing his head.

In all these excitements, McCormick delighted in direct, personal participation. One fondly treasured *Tribune* memory concerns a competition for subscribers in which rewards for merit included Christmas toys. McCormick liked to approve every detail, so there came a moment when he seized the phone and demanded, "Where are the dolls?" Came the answer from someone, mercifully never named: "Out eatin'."

An Insull might have taken that as insufferable impudence. Such an idea would not have occurred to McCormick. It was simply one authentic voice of Chicago in answer to another.

Smoothing out the editorial operation was a ticklish business. In the years of Medill McCormick's unsteadiness and Robert W. Patterson's decline, Keeley had come to dominate. Keeley was an Englishman of little education but superb journalistic competency. It was typical of his instinct and his gall that when the *Tribune* beat the world with news of Dewey's victory in the Battle of Manila Bay, Keeley himself called President McKinley out of bed to tell what the Commodore had been holding for his own good time. Keeley, too, was author of the *Tribune*'s claim to be "The World's Greatest Newspaper," and flaunted it well before McCormick ever got onto the job. He also enjoyed such diversions as his well-remembered campaign for "A Safe and Sane Fourth of July." Keeley hated firecrackers. He was a great driver of men, imperious as Insull in disposition and, like Insull, whom he admired, jealous of recognition.

He had been careful to cultivate the Medill sisters. He saw that their tastes were reflected in the society columns and consulted them earnestly on world affairs. They not only sent him plenty of genuine news tips picked up around the capitals, but also turned in letters to the "Voice of the People" on good manners, cooking recipes, cute sayings of children and great issues of the day. Some were signed "A Friend" or "Observer." Occasionally, they used their initials. Mrs. Patterson liked to paste these in her scrapbook with appropriate footnotes to elaborate her own thoughts and criticize her sister's.

But when the board of directors elected both McCormick and Joseph M. Patterson in 1912, Keeley would have been obtuse, indeed, if he had not seen the meaning. Immediately, he began to formulate a grand design involving T. R. Roosevelt. A bureaucratic quarrel in Washington, here described in due course, must be put down as of primary importance in deflecting him from his purpose, not to mention that in McCormick and Patterson he was up against two young men whose inexperience was no real index to their competency.

A survey of McCormick's total career in journalism must credit him with two achievements of enduring importance, started in the period 1910–14, when Keeley thought to take over the *Tribune*.

The first was that personal adventure on the north shore of the St. Lawrence river in Canada. There, between 1912 and 1955, McCormick led the construction of a great paper-making, power-generating, mining and shipping development which not only made the *Tribune* company secure at its base, but also initiated a complete change in the economy of the region. The second was in persuading Joseph M. Patterson to return to the *Tribune*. If it can be said McCormick proved the Tribune Company's master of business and financial management, it is equally true that Patterson proved to be its master dollar earner at the vending of ideas and interest by words, by pictures and by drawings.

Patterson and McCormick, in the working out, achieved a personal relationship which survived in remarkable harmony and with conspicuous success, against every superficial expectation. In externals, they showed little in common. McCormick's public pose was oracular, dour and unsmiling, correct but aloof. His concern for appearances could put the Washington bureau of the *Tribune* into urgent investigation to be sure his portrait as a colonel of artillery would be all right with a cannon in the background, which suggested action in the field, considering that the braid on the sleeve signified he was, in fact, assigned to staff duty. Patterson, on the contrary, was genuinely slouchy, and likely to disappear on pub crawls. He was an impossible public speaker, though he could, without ever losing his sense of command, loaf or belly-laugh with any casual companion. McCormick knew editorial operations intellectually, and could tell precisely whether he was getting what he wanted; but emotionally, he was at his best in the financial and physical development of the complex instrument the Tribune Company came to be. Patterson's heart, as much as his head, was bound to the ideational consequence of all the milling, shipping and printing works. His most intimate tie in the system beyond the editorial room was with the circulation people, to whose intuitive wisdom about the crotchets of their customers he paid close attention. It was his pleasure to translate their undisciplined perceptions into vendible goods. As an inventor of comic-strip ideas, discoverer of changing tastes in public fancy for serials, Sunday features and as a judge of news, Patterson proved himself the superior of every rival in Chicago and in New York. Hearst's defeat in both cities stands in evidence on the point that if circulation is what makes newspapers, and so far nobody has a better test, Patterson knew more about how to get it than any other man of his time.

It would be wholly wrong, however, to see Patterson merely as a gifted merchant of popular entertainment in print. All his life he was in deadly earnest, seeking from experience some meaning he could convey to others. At the exposition of complex ideas in simple language, he became so effective that when he supported Franklin D. Roosevelt between 1933 and 1941, the President considered Patterson his most prized popular teacher of reasons for the New Deal and its pursuits. And when Patterson turned against Mr. Roosevelt on the matter of foreign policy in 1941, his editorials, far more than the *Tribune*'s, cut the President to the quick.

A modern reading of Patterson's effort to understand human feeling leaves the investigator to ponder what might have happened if the socialist romantics of the Debs period had been even moderately sensible. Here was a young man of education, passion and promise, drawn to their logic, philosophy or whatever they thought it was. If he did not yet have much money in his own right, he knew where it was kept and he had access to the keepers. At the minimum, he was certainly useful as a recruiting agent among the enemy, from whom it was evident defectors could be had.

As a social propagandist, he proved his competency several times. He worked over Marshall Field & Co. in *Collier's,* the muckrakers' house organ, and in books and plays he projected the demand for justice in the best socialist terms. More importantly, he did it in a style such that customers paid to get his thought. Perhaps that was his sin.

But it was part of the dogma of social uplift then, as so often, that to be of the nobility it was best to be unwashed. The uniform of the day required a cloth cap and many commentators reported they found the odor of sanctity noticeable, and not only in a closed room. Patterson did his best to pass for a roughneck. He scandalized his wife and relatives with outlandish dress and put in regular stints fighting in bars, to prove virtue in political thought. But he could never escape the disgraceful fact that if he slept on a park bench it was for his own reasons and not because he hadn't anywhere else to go. And so, instead of maneuvering him into their affairs deeper to bring recruits of money and talent, the thinking men of socialism cut him adrift.

It was lucky for McCormick, anyhow.

In 1908, after delegating William Howard Taft to hold the Presidency for a while, Mr. Roosevelt turned on Darkest Africa. There, he laid waste to lions, giraffes, hippopotami. And elephants. From Africa he marched on Europe to lecture the Kaiser, reprimand the Pope, clarify thinking at Oxford and the Sorbonne, pick up his Nobel Prize for peace and terrify the United States embassy in London, which got the notion that he intended to appear at the funeral of Edward VII in the Rough Rider costume he had worn so long ago in battle. In fact, he turned out in entirely conventional civil dress and projected somehow at one time both a solemn dignity and a beaming pleasure at being the most interesting of all the kings, living or dead, anywhere to be seen.

But for all his appearance of enjoyment, Mr. Roosevelt was furious. When he emerged from the jungle he was met on the White Nile by his old friend Gifford Pinchot, who had a tale of horror to tell. It is dim in the public memory now, but there have been few bureaucratic collisions in the history of the Republic ever to blow up into a scandal with as many consequences as Pinchot's assault upon Secretary of the Interior Richard A. Ballinger. This not only provided the focus for an all-out attack by Progressives on the Taft administration, but dragged on until Ickes, in 1940, published a final "Official Finding," itself one of the most peculiar expressions of judgment ever issued by an agent of the federal establishment. The controlling points of that long-delayed verdict were:

1. That when Ickes became Secretary of the Interior in 1933, he felt the awful uproar of 1909–11 had shown Ballinger a conspirator with private interests to defraud the United States of valuable forest lands.

2. That exhaustive investigation of the evidence now proved this false. Ballinger was "an American Dreyfus," and victim of a conspiracy in which Ickes himself had played a serious, if unwitting, part.

3. Of his old opponent, even then still sniping at the Interior bureaucracy, Ickes wrote: "Without Pinchot, there probably would have been no Ballinger 'scandal.' And even if there had been, without Pinchot, this disturbing episode in our national history long since would have been forgotten."

It is not possible here to pursue the complex details of what was, at bottom, a simple struggle for power between the Agriculture Department and Interior, which had other generalized duties with respect to conservation of natural resources. Ickes' 1940 Official Finding was just one more round in that bureaucratic war, however much it may be said that it was also an eruption of conscience long after great harm done. The one facet crucial to this annal was the bearing of the Ballinger case on the life and fortune of McCormick.

Analysts of Theodore Roosevelt's career are of one mind, that he resented the thought of surrendering the Presidency in 1908 and certainly had no intention of ever fading away. He agreed, before leaving for Africa, to do articles for *The Outlook* and for *Scribner's* and contracted for books on his jungle adventures, as well. Mr. Taft might be President of the United States, all right, but the all-seeing eye would still be on him. Taft sinned. Not only did he prove to be a man of stubborn honor in refusing to sit idly by as Pinchot worked to ruin Ballinger, but he even showed it was possible to get along intelligently with the oligarchs of the Senate. In matters of antitrust he was more strict at enforcement than Roosevelt had been, but not one-half so noisy. He took the position that government was administration, not explosions.

The rest is all too simply told. Theodore Roosevelt made a shambles of the Republican National Convention of 1912 and led the excited Progressives out to stand at Armageddon in their famous battle for the Lord. What the country got out of it was Woodrow Wilson. What McCormick got out of it is plainly indicated in one single flash. He was a delegate at the convention and when the proceedings degenerated to their lowest, rose to put in the name of Howard F. Gillette for Vice President. When asked to identify the gentleman, he gave out:

"He's a friend of mine."

Nor does the record of the convention tell any more about it, except that when the votes were cast, one for Howard F. Gillette, whoever he was, embedded itself in the permanent file of American political folkways.

One more among the many whose hopes were destroyed by the Republican St. Bartholomew's Day of 1912 was James F. Keeley. It had been his idea to head off the McCormick-Patterson combination by the very appealing thought of Theodore Roosevelt for editor of the *Tribune.*

McCormick's version of this project was that he and Patterson overruled it by themselves, but at the time they were in no such firm position of command. If Keeley had been able to get Roosevelt, the Medill sisters and the elders on the board into discussion, he might very well have brought it off and for the rest of his life enjoyed himself as executive officer in a journalistic adventure of unimaginable consequences.

The verdict of the historians on Theodore Roosevelt is that he was the President who shifted the Republic's world view from the passive to the active mood. His "Roosevelt corollary" to the Monroe Doctrine brought Europeans back to meddling in Latin America. His own intervention in the Russo-Japanese war invited the next man to think such things part of the duty for any Chief Executive. In Europe, in Africa, in Asia and all around the world, Roosevelt left the mark of something he called "the New Nationalism." Henry Adams' reaction to this performance was to write Mrs. Cameron he would soon be dying, thank God, and out of all such drolleries. In fact, Adams lived on to March 26, 1918, happily engaged, in his own peculiar way, with a world that had forgotten the eighteenth century's very existence. Just a month before he died, he wrote a friend in London of watching British airplanes sail up and down at all hours before his window onto Washington.

The thought of Theodore Roosevelt in charge of the *Tribune* when war broke out again in 1914 is one to conjure with, but all that happened was another misfire. So Keeley began to plan another sort of retaliation, as McCormick concentrated on how to meet Hearst's enormous advantage of buying newsprint in bulk below the going price. At the time, no American publisher believed it possible to succeed at a vertically integrated system. Even Hearst, though he often threatened, had not dared to start up his own mill, nor did he ever.

The *Tribune*'s charter of 1861 included a clause which would allow it to manufacture paper. McCormick felt that he had proved on the Sanitary Commission that he had the kind of judgment wanted. He asked the board of directors for a million dollars' credit to prove himself, but he couldn't get it until his mother put her personal interest forward as security. An excellent account of the consequence may be found in Carl Wiegman's *Trees to News.* Here it can best be indicated by an excerpt from an address by Arthur A. Schmon, head of the *Tribune* paper-making enterprise, at the 1962 annual meeting of the Newcomen Society of North America in Montreal.

Schmon was himself an interesting example of McCormick's way with men. He was a native of Newark, New Jersey. On graduation from Princeton in 1917 he was soon in the army and there got to know McCormick, who said casually to look him up after the war. Schmon knew nothing of paper-making and started humbly enough in the then still wide-open adventure in the wilds, but proved himself a master of the whole process. And, five years after McCormick's death, he became a Canadian citizen, in reversal of a practice Canadian nationalists have cursed as a blight on their country's self-development.

Schmon's summary description of the enterprise he headed was:

> This [1962] is the twenty-fifth anniversary of the Quebec North Shore Paper Company newsprint mill at Baie Comeau, the first major industrial undertaking on the north shore of the Lower St. Lawrence, and 1963 will be the fiftieth anniversary of startup at the parent Canadian Company, the Ontario Paper Company at Thorold, Canada, the first paper mill built in Canada by American capital after the tariffs were removed in 1911, permitting Canadian newsprint to enter the United States duty free.
>
> Today, our two mills produce about 400,000 tons of newsprint annually; this represents more than two-thirds of Russia's entire newsprint production for 1962. We are the eighth largest producer in Canada, and we are beginning an expansion at Baie Comeau that will add about 90,000 tons a year to our capacity. We lease timber limits in Ontario and Quebec, where we cut, drive and process pulpwood for our mills. We make almost a million gallons of alcohol each year, and can produce enough vanillin to flavor all the ice cream eaten in Canada and the United States in one year. We have the controlling interest in a power plant on the Manicougan River and own another on the Outardes River, both near Baie Comeau. We also have an interest in an aluminum smelter at Baie Comeau. We have a fleet of eight ships and charter others to move our raw materials and finished products.

More than 4,800 people in Canada and 12,000 in the United States were employed in the business of the Tribune Company, as of 1962.

McCormick had not been far wrong, it would appear, in thinking that he had, as he put it, "a general instinct for machinery."

CHAPTER EIGHT ★★★ Innocent as the next man of any idea where it was all heading, McCormick put in the years between 1910 and 1914 learning the publisher's trade. He was fortunate to have an engineer with the true Frank Merriwell spirit as his guide into the paper-making adventure. The *Tribune*'s business manager, William H. Field, went to Canada on a fishing trip and there met Warren Curtis, Jr., whose family owned a paper mill at Corinth, New York.

The result was a handsome match. McCormick was tall, solemn and to the point. Curtis was short, fat and garrulous. McCormick never in his life let go money without first laying out a provable budget. And he built an accounting system into the *Tribune* that became a legendary terror among evil-doers. Curtis thought that when he had the price of wood and sulphite and a final cost of paper he had done his homework. But his reach at the possibilities of engineering is fairly illustrated by the Wiegman history of the project. For the *Tribune*'s first mill he demanded electric generators no American company would attempt. Finally, a Swedish company was persuaded to try them. Forty years later they were still running the mill with unparalleled efficiency.

By 1914, the *Tribune* was in the paper-making business on a solid basis and had its own shipping company, as well. Woodrow Wilson was in the White House. One of Mr. Wilson's thoughts was to send the United States Marines to Vera Cruz, with effects that left 19 Americans and 126 Mexicans dead, 71 Americans and 95 Mexicans wounded. Some argued that he had done this because he was seduced by the benign, whiskered appearance of one warlord, Venustiano Carranza, and revolted by the less attractive appearance of Carranza's opponent, Victoriano Huerta. There are many other theories, ranging from malignant influences of American oil entrepreneurs, to the bullying of jingoist publishers, to plotting by Wilhelm II in Germany meant to entangle the United States in a war with Japan. Wilson's own version was that "we have gone down to Mexico to serve mankind, if we can find out a way. We do not want to fight the Mexicans. We want to serve the Mexicans if we can."

Joseph M. Patterson went down for the *Tribune* to report on this ambition in the working out. McCormick went up to Canada on a hunt for timber lands. By rail and then by sleigh, he and Curtis made their way into the remote country of the Ha Ha Bay on the Saguenay river, some two hundred miles north of Quebec. Curtis became exhausted and McCormick sent for a doctor, who happened to bring along a Quebec newspaper. Many a time, as newly elevated executives trembled for sins they had never dreamed of, McCormick liked to recite the lesson in it all. When he left Chicago, he made the mistake of not insuring that he could check up every day, one way or another. It had not occurred to him that Mr. Keeley would abandon his command post on watch against the demonries of such as W. R. Hearst and Victor Lawson without, at least, conventional notice. But after taking the doctor in to Curtis, McCormick settled down to scan the Quebec paper. Entirely by chance he hit on an obscure note to the effect that on May 8, 1914, James F. Keeley had quit the Chicago *Tribune* to bring out his own paper. McCormick spent a fearful forty-eight hours jumping from one train to another on the way home.

Victor Lawson, it appeared, was at the bottom of it all. His morning paper had never worked out. Lawson had tried to unload it on Keeley as early as 1909, but there had been a change in circumstances since then. It is sometimes said that Samuel Insull helped form the syndicate that took up both Lawson's paper and another faltering effort, the *Inter-Ocean.* The combination called itself the *Chicago Record* and Mr. Lawson pronounced that with Keeley in command it could not but triumph. Within two years

McCormick cornered Keeley in a scramble for newsprint and in two years more it was all over.

There was some staff raiding. Keeley took away the head of the *Tribune*'s Washington bureau, John Callan O'Laughlin, one of Theodore Roosevelt's favorite balloon raisers. McCormick got James O'Donnell Bennett, his idea of "perhaps the best newspaper writer who ever lived." Like John T. McCutcheon, Bennett was a figure of transition in the shift from the sort of homey talents Melville Stone liked to cultivate on the *News* to the massive, organized striking forces with which McCormick came to arm the *Tribune*.

Bennett was a stylist with the same completeness as McCutcheon, but of a more sophisticated usage. During the 1914–18 war he was chief of *Tribune* writers abroad and developed an imposing presence that came through in his copy, which yet he managed to keep as light and airy as if he had done it at leisure in his library at home. It may be this derived from his fix against typewriters, for he continued to the dogged last in 1940 turning out his copy in longhand. And again, McCormick, who usually had no patience with any affectation that worked against his intricately organized production system, saw to it that Bennett's copy was treated with reverential care.

In his reading up of the *Tribune*'s back files, Bennett discovered that Joseph Medill, in his old printer's impatience with the tedium of long words, had done some pioneer experiments toward something McCormick now seized on as "improved spelling." It is doubtful that either McCormick or Bennett ever heard of Thorstein Veblen's proposition that English orthography satisfies all the requirements of the canons of reputability under the law of conspicuous waste, or George Bernard Shaw's accusation that the English have no respect for their language and spell it so abominably no man can teach himself what it sounds like. But for all their preachments, both those masters took care to tot up their merchandise for sale in complete submission to the canon. Not so, McCormick. He counted up the letters and saw at once that "frate" made an unmistakable sound, saved wear and tear on the linotype machines, took up less space per column inch and was a great relief in the hard art of headline writing. And it was so ordered. Outraged schoolmarms denounced the *Tribune* for yet another sin. How could they teach children correct English when every day they saw in the *Tribune* such horrors as "grafic," "thoro," and "biografy"? But not until McCormick died did they get anywhere. His successors surrendered on the main front, even though they kept a scattering few "improvements" here and there that even schoolmarms now find convenient.

Bennett started a complete *Tribune* style book which McCormick, with reason, considered invaluable to unify practice among stablesful of varied writers. He adopted it for his books and letters, though he never was able to enforce it any too well with his head secretary, Miss Genevieve Burke, and searched the paper every day against sinners. When he took over the Washington *Times-Herald* in 1949 he was mightily pleased to find a modification of the style book in effect and lost little time in having the whole paper made over on the *Tribune* model. But in Washington, for several reasons, the effect was unfortunate.

McCormick lost two other rounds in his ambition to improve English spelling style. Advertisers claimed the right to use their paid space conventionally. And while McCormick developed some very strict rules on taste, typography and the selling content of advertising, which he enforced with conspicuous success, he lost on the spelling issue. Nor could he interest very much that otherwise lifelong fan of the utilitarian, J. M. Patterson, who agreed with advertisers that "improved spelling" tended to distract from focus on ideational arguments. And Patterson, beyond all, liked to win the argument.

At any rate, McCormick had every right to be proud of his work with Bennett. His own command of words always bothered him and he was galled by the memory of his Groton master's red ink, for which he took revenge in a number of ways. One was to spit at the high-flown. This even led him, on one early occasion, to put down Thomas Jefferson as "just a word man," and it was a good long time, too, before he announced the philosopher-President as his own guiding genius at discovering dangers inherent in government. But McCormick could quite justly say that he knew how a newspaper should be put together, not only in the mechanical sense, at which he was a total technical master, but as a uniform body of reading matter. Those who have denounced the *Tribune* over the years for being wrongheaded, cruel to anybody it happens to dislike and deliberately misleading at interpretation of events, are a number without end. This, after all, is standard indictment of any newspaper if one happens to disagree. But nobody denies that *Tribune* prose flows neatly from page to page without condescending mannerisms. When Patterson went on to New York to found the *News* he summed up the whole doctrine with a famous advertising promotion which invited merchants to "tell it to Sweeney and the Stuyvesants will understand." If it can be said that Patterson turned out to be the most powerful single writer ever turned up by the *Tribune,* it must be added that McCormick found, in Bennett, his best machine for teaching the work force as a whole how it should perform.

Keeley's jump, therefore, did the *Tribune* no harm. If anything, it was just what McCormick needed to settle the proposition of command. In his later years, to make sure no subordinate suffered illusions of unique importance, he liked to say the money Keeley wanted to lay out on Theodore Roosevelt went to buy Rudolph Dirk's *Katzenjammer Kids,* a reduction of race-comedy to cartooning, with Teutons the butt. The whole country rocked with belly-laughter and the Germanic immigrants, perhaps not always getting the whole point, took it amiably. But it had not long to go.

As a matter of fact, 1914 caught McCormick himself in a sort of *katzenjammer* that has been ever since a problem for *Tribune* historians. Quite naturally, his aunt, Mrs. Patterson, blamed the whole thing on Mrs. McCormick's refusal to rusticate in Chicago, and give her son a proper residence from which to find himself a wife.

After Yale, with no home of his own in Chicago, McCormick went to stay with a cousin-german, Edward S. Adams, whose parents had been early settlers in the McCormickville enclave on Rush Street. Adams' mother was a sister of Cyrus, William and Leander, the builders of the Virginia reaper works. His father was a wholesale grocer. Adams himself had a formal title as a sort of trader in stocks, but in Chicago, generally, he had more of a reputation as an opponent of the distilleries. He seemed to be trying to deny their product to the general public by drinking it all up, himself.

And now, for a confused mixture of fact and conjecture which has plagued the curiosity of Chicago's upper society ever since as to some details of the relations between the cousins, we may thank both the gallantry of McCormick and the political methods of William Hale Thompson.

The sum of it is that Adams' wife got a divorce and married McCormick. When Thompson became mayor he sought to use the circumstances to degrade McCormick in the public esteem. But it was beyond Thompson's comprehension of what people are like, to grasp what had really happened. If he had, he might very well have shattered McCormick's internal mechanism of survival. The real contest was not between McCormick and Adams. It was, again, McCormick in defiance of his mother.

Amie deHoule Irwin Adams was what used to be called in the old American military establishment "an Army brat." Her father was Bernard John Dowling Irwin, a regimental surgeon in the Civil and Indian wars. He won the first Medal of Honor ever given, for "distinguished gallantry in action" against the Chiricahua Indians near Apache Pass, Arizona, in February, 1861, and retired a brigadier. Her brother, Major General George Leroy Irwin, graduated from West Point in 1889 and became a master of artillery. Perhaps impressed by him, McCormick was loyal to the same branch when he, too, took the field. In the First World War, the second General Irwin won many honors, including the French Legion of Honor, the Croix de Guerre and the American Distinguished Service Medal. His highest assignment was the command of Panama Canal fortifications.

The elder Irwins settled in Chicago at the time of the World Columbian Exposition and were immediately welcomed into the inner circle. The military life, which members of their family have pursued ever since, does not lend itself to the accumulation of great riches, but it has other consolations of which their daughter, Amie, was an excellent exemplar. She had flawless French, she was a superb horsewoman, and she was a more-than-amateur painter in oils. One of her works, now in an upstairs bedroom of the house McCormick left as a museum of his interests, is a portrait of a young woman, done with sunny charm. The sitter was one of the striking beauties of the DuPage Hunt, and for all their difference in years, an intimate of the artist. Later, the young woman became the second Mrs. McCormick.

Edward Adams and Amie Irwin married in Chicago on April 10, 1895. The groom's age was put down as thirty-five, hers as twenty-three. When McCormick came to stay, after 1903, he found a cheerless house with little money and no children. By all accounts, Adams was of difficult temper and few people sought his company. Mrs. Adams was certainly well past any girlish illusions, but had a high, jolly humor and a sympathetic ear for McCormick's own tendencies to fits of gloom about his role as less than a mother's darling. The evidence is, also, that she was entirely a private person, disinclined to meddle in his attitudes on public policy, so that even in the years of unusual adventure that lay ahead, she stuck firmly to the rule of "seeing one's friends and one friends, only" in all things except managing McCormick's houses and entertaining his business and political visitors, on demand, with total grace. There is no record that she ever once tried to influence his judgment on *Tribune* affairs.

On February 20, 1914, Mrs. Adams sued for divorce in the chancery division of the Cook County Superior Court, charging that she had reached the limit of tolerance for drunken abuse. In light of suggestions developed in Mayor Thompson's later conflicts with McCormick, it is unfortunate that documentation is so sparse. The silences of Chicago newspapers, and unaccountably missing court records, have invited more conjecture than, perhaps, a complete account might have supported.

Enough remains, however, to make the outline plain. On March 5, 1914, Mrs. Adams and her sister's husband appeared before Judge Denis E. Sullivan of the Illinois Superior Court for Cook County and portrayed Adams as a drunkard verging toward incompetency. He did not so much as have an attorney present, much less resist the petition for divorce, granted the very next day under a limitation of Illinois law that neither party could remarry within 365 days, unless to each other.

But then, for some reason not now of record, Adams decided to fight. He entered suit to quash the divorce and asked $100,000 in damages from McCormick. In turn, McCormick sued Adams, claiming loans of money past due. Within the McCormick and Patterson families, apprehension grew to the edge of panic. Both the younger Pattersons had done their bit to liven public interest, one by his socialist rebellion and the other in her adventure with the noble Polish horse fancier. Medill McCormick had several times come close to alarming notoriety with his political and other intense enthusiasms. And now, of all things, solemn Bertie, never before in all his thirty-four bachelor years the subject of any sort of shocker, was headed for court. Sooner or later, the *Tribune* would have to print something or look utterly absurd. The New York and Milwaukee papers were being handed around privately at the Chicago Club and the Onwentsia, where McCormick worked at his polo and his skill for taking the jumps in pursuit of the fox. Once Adams got on the witness stand it was unimaginable that Hearst or Lawson, not to mention Keeley, would be gentlemen about a competitor's little personal difficulties.

But then the roof of the world came down.

Half a world away from Chicago a fugitive from the Tsar's police lost himself among the street mob of Vienna and wondered at the foolishness of mankind. Here was war and here were shoemakers' apprentices cheering it. What idea moved them? Surely not the national idea. The empire of Francis Joseph was the very negation of a national idea. No, the mob that rushed to war was only demonstrating how grinding and terrible it found peace. And because of that, this war would bring a wind to shake the world. At first, of course, all plans for social change would be submerged in the chaos the state would use to strengthen its grip on society. But this would only be a postponement, a moratorium. The note would be extended for a while, but in the end it would be paid.

Thus, Leon Trotsky, who ran on ahead of the Tsar's police to Paris; to New York, there inspired by the gum-chewers on the subway to do one of his most corrosive papers; and then to double back to the streets of that St. Petersburg Robert S. McCormick had seen in 1905 running with the blood of Father Gapon's credulous flock. And on to great triumphs and great humiliations until, at last, the pickaxe in Mexico City obeyed the will of that implacable judge of men in the Kremlin, who himself died in his own bed, in his own time, hurried off by nobody.

Half a world away from Vienna, the Chicago *Tribune* matched Trotsky with an editorial on August 2, 1914, entitled "The Twilight of the Kings." This has been quoted and reprinted more than anything else in the paper's history, even more than the "Cheer Up" editorial after the great Chicago fire. For once, the *Tribune* deviated from its customary flat, forthright style of exposition, to sound an elegiac note:

> Before establishing hell on earth, the pietistic kings commend their subjects to God. Seek the Lord's sanction for the devil's work. . . .
>
> This is the twilight of the kings. Western Europe of the people may be caught in this debacle, but never again. Eastern Europe of the kings will be remade and in the name of God shall not give grace to a hundred square miles of broken bodies.
>
> If Divinity enters here it comes with a sword to deliver the people from the sword.
>
> It is the twilight of the kings. The republic marches East in Europe.

Half a century later it was possible for the case to be argued that anyhow the *Tribune* in 1914 was no worse a prophet than Trotsky. The kings did go. The state power did pass through the hands of the shoemakers' apprentices, as the great wind shook the world. But in the end, the state, as such, was still there and stronger than ever. The guard had changed its uniform but not its assignment, a fact which grew to be the frustration of McCormick's life. For as it turned out, the guard, for all its mighty increase in power, was somehow taken by the shoemakers' apprentices as a friend of theirs, and in no way did McCormick, in his years of most intense effort, consider the state power any friend of his. He thought it an engine of universal oppression and the monarchs of old Europe, the world that died in 1914, puny by comparison. His question was: if war had been mocked as the sport of kings before, what was it now among the great formations of state power that called themselves "democratic," and "socialist" and "people's republic"?

According to his own testimony, the great catastrophe of 1914 took McCormick entirely by surprise. At that point he had little connection with things military and even less time to give. The Canadian venture was ripening into the solid and profitable foundation for the Tribune Company that it has been ever since. He and Patterson were negotiating to buy up the New York *Herald* from James Gordon Bennett, who no longer had the kind of zest that had sent Stanley to Africa for Dr. Livingstone. And there was the problem of Edward S. Adams.

On this last, McCormick's mother took charge.

The Tsar's ambassador to the United States was George Bakhmeteff, a wry and wholly Westernized member of the cozy world of diplomatic crossposting in which everybody knew everybody and friendly favors were possible. Moreover, Mme. Bakhmeteff, a member of an old and distinguished American family long established in Washington, was one of Mrs. McCormick's best friends.

In his memoirs, McCormick makes it appear that he worked it all out himself, directly with Bakhmeteff, man-to-man. But it is not so. His book *With the Russian Army,* published in 1915, innocently gave it all away long years before. McCormick, there, wrote in the introduction that when the United States got into war with Spain, he was considered too young to get in it and that his parents had again refused him permission to visit the front in the war between Russia and Japan. Then he had got into business and was so absorbed in this when the shooting started in 1914 the idea of touring the front never occurred to him. It was all a consequence of "the energy of my mother, who planned for me the experiences she had forbidden ten years before."

Mrs. McCormick, it is shown in a letter from Bakhmeteff, arranged an invitation for her son to visit Russia which, as "a unique exception," would let him tour the front not as a newspaper correspondent but as a "distinguished foreigner" personally known to the Grand Duke Nicholas Nicolaievitch, commanding the whole Russian land war.

McCormick reprinted the whole letter in his 1915 book and put it down as "a distinct shock to me." Before he was home again plenty of other people felt distinct shocks, too, not the least his mother, as the air around her vibrated to a long and mighty silver cord snapped in the most unexpected circumstances.

McCormick had himself appointed a colonel in the Illinois National Guard. He said the Russians took this to indicate he was of very superior importance, indeed. In the imperial order of life, guards officers ranked far above ordinary soldiers and McCormick was not only in the guards, but on the staff of a Governor. In Russia, a guards officer on the Tsar's household staff ranked next to royalty, so McCormick was duly organized as a "distinguished foreigner."

In New York, he consulted Richard Harding Davis, the highest authority on adventure, who advised that every day he should write a story, no matter how trivial or seemingly unimportant. This would not only keep a man in the field on his toes, but there was also the added importance that things not so meaningful to one on the scene might very well have greater significance to an editor back home with many separate items to compare. This was sound technical advice, and McCormick saw to it that *Tribune* writers, ever after, not only cabled breaking news, but sent in letters, always handy to liven up the inside pages and build importance into the Sunday feature sections. McCormick scanned every column, every day. If any man's byline were long missing, a telegram could be expected with some such electrifier as "Are you dead, or drunk?" One of his favorites was: "You are out there to report news, not to write ancient history." His premise was that news is always around for the man who has the drive to hunt it up, and notwithstanding anguish among some who preferred to wait for it to come up in the Ritz Bar and find them, *Tribune* men learned to hunt, or else. This led to some aggrieved memoirs among the casualties.

Following his briefing by Davis, McCormick sailed on February 10, 1915, and arrived at Liverpool the 18th, just as the Germans declared their submarine blockade of the North Atlantic. On the way over he entertained himself among the ladies. He dined with Mary Garden and one of the Mrs. Vanderbilts. Also on board was Mrs. Walter Farwell of Lake Forest, now no longer the austere Presbyterian retreat founded by the Reverend Dr. Patterson, but Chicago's answer to Bar Harbor. Mrs. Farwell had London connections and McCormick had access to Lord Northcliffe, first among equals on Fleet Street, the center of English journalism. In consequence, he was taken to lunch with the Prime Minister, Herbert Henry Asquith.

McCormick came away thinking of Asquith in terms of the Abraham Lincoln he had learned to understand from his Grandfather Medill, "the patient, comprehending politician, who bore on the force of his personality the strains of jealousies, hatreds and distrusts which threatened to wreck the machinery of government."

But sympathy did not stop him short of candor. He told Asquith "the small element known as 'society' was very strongly pro-Ally; that the element of German ancestry, and particularly that of German birth, was naturally pro-German"; but the bulk of the nation was inclined to be critical of all the nations involved in the war.

Asquith professed to be greatly surprised. He went into his standard speech about Home Rule in Ireland, religious adjustments in Wales, public welfare laws in the whole United Kingdom and the general putting down of the aristocracy, as reasons why the British

Empire was entitled to what McCormick described as "the whole-souled support of the American republic against the German military monarch." At that moment, Cecil Spring-Rice was in Washington as Britain's ambassador, burrowing away toward one of the supreme personal feats in the history of British or any other professional diplomacy, but Asquith, who in 1911 had thought Spring-Rice "hysterical" on the German problem, now made a further mistake. He had neglected to call Spring-Rice in for coaching on American politics and so he thought estimates by a not very significant journalist from the province of Chicago had little weight.

McCormick estimated the total British position to be that, "if the war turns out well for his country, Mr. Asquith's name will become immortal. If it turns out ill, there will be no more democratic government in Europe for several centuries." This essay at divination may be put down as suffering from several overs and shorts, for even as he and Asquith talked eminent Britons were taking steps to put the right honorable gentleman on the skids. One, quite openly bent on destroying Asquith's version of the traditional wartime coalition, was Mr. David Lloyd George, another of those rather tatty word men low in McCormick's estimation just then and so not interesting to him. Another, who didn't mean to harm Asquith but did, was Mr. Winston Spencer Churchill, First Lord of the Admiralty, to whom McCormick was immediately drawn. He estimated Churchill, in his 1915 book, as the second most aggressive man of his acquaintance, the first being the Russian grand duke he was then on the way to meet, and thought that with proper education Churchill would have made a great admiral or general.

The memoirs of several long-suffering practitioners officially exposed to books on the military art testify that Mr. Churchill himself felt no such limitation, then or later. So, too, McCormick. For 1915 marks the beginning of a copious literature in the *Tribune* and elsewhere on everything from the proper design for bayonets to the form and execution of grand strategy.

In 1942, the President of the United States and his closest military advisors were distracted from their labors when one of McCormick's letters to a critic got out in which he listed a few of his contributions to the sciences of war. One simply said: "I introduced machine guns into the army."

As a matter of fact, McCormick, like Churchill, was not so deficient a real military analyst as critics liked to make out, though he never got a chance to exercise his knowledge in public office; for which, no doubt, many a general of his time was thankful. This lack of authority in no way inhibited him, though, as a free-style advisor to any he thought would profit from his judgments. He not only wrote directly to chiefs of staff, published articles in the *Tribune* and lectured to the army and navy war colleges, he also worked up a thoroughly sound study of the Civil War campaigns.

The first of these, *Ulysses S. Grant,* was brought out in 1934 at a time when literature on the Civil War still in large measure deferred to the idea of Robert E. Lee as the greatest of all American captains. McCormick's introduction is a concise attack.

Lincoln, he held, had been allowed to fill the horizon so that the true character of Grant as democratic hero had been ignored. More than that, those who loved a lord had gone out of their way to elevate Lee beyond his true military worth to the point that "we find an active if undesirable part of our population, including a few military men, accepting and repeating without question European slanders of an American hero." It would be the just punishment of Grant's traducers that McCormick would show how "the hereditary soldiers and the soldiers laboring under the hereditary tradition have maligned him."

The body of the work, taken together with the second volume *The War Without Grant,* 1950, presented McCormick's case in solid military scholarship that proves he could, when he chose, turn in a study deserving the respect of anybody. Of course, it would be asking more than he could give to expect that he would leave aside polemic, for history was to McCormick always a sort of legal brief put together to win a case. But in Grant he did have a client, so to speak, deserving a day in court as of 1934, and McCormick did win credits among technical historians for his argument.

When others ridiculed him as "Colonel McCosmic," as they did after his disastrous claim to have introduced machine guns to the American military establishment, McCormick could read over his clippings on the Civil War study for some sort of consolation, if he needed it. Which is doubtful. Furthermore, he had a better case on the machine-gun matter than some thought, and this will be demonstrated in its proper place here.

No doubt it would be unfair to complain against McCormick's

mother for pitching him, unawares, out of commercial pursuits in 1915 and into the confidences of the Grand Duke Nicholas Nicolaievitch, who certainly was a great-hearted field soldier, if a most unlucky one. In time, McCormick would have made it on his own. But detailed accounts of maneuver, camp- and fort-building in the 1915 book are proof positive that by the time the adventure was up, McCormick had found his life's avocation. The plain, practical man of affairs who had mastered the workings of the Chicago Sanitary and Ship Canal and set the Tribune Company to developing the North Shore of the St. Lawrence could do much toward smoothing out the problems of war. His exchanges with General of the Army George Catlett Marshall both before and after Pearl Harbor testify that he never let any differences on other matters stay him from volunteering, in the national interest, from his free-flowing fountain of ideas on how to run the army.

While he was in London, McCormick got a briefing from Edward Grey, the foreign minister, on the elements of Balkan diplomacy; a set of combinations to give pause even to a master graduate from the ward politics of Chicago. Then, he made a midnight passage across the Channel to see an old friend of his father's, the French foreign minister, Theophile Delcassé, who had a reputation, soon to be exploded, as the experts' expert on the Balkans. The French were as difficult as ever about doing something for nothing. So McCormick, because he was eager to see the shooting war, did something for which he was ever after apologetic. He sent back to the *Tribune* dispatches reeking with bureaucrats' ideas of how to win sympathy: nuns impaled on bayonets, churches made into stables, libraries burned for the sake of sheer frightfulness. Such items were calculated, in the words of one famous English inventor, to make the Americans think Punxsutawney, Pennsylvania, would be next. But at least it fetched Delcassé's writ to admit McCormick to the front before Arras. His running diary cuts the great experience down to a confession that he got within forty yards of the German line but didn't see any Germans, that he had a fine lunch with a general who wouldn't let him see any guns and wasn't shot at, personally, though shells fell on the town near enough for him to feel the jolt. The people of Arras struck him as miserable. On the way back he finally saw some Germans, two prisoners under escort to the rear being laid out by a French colonel for failure to salute. And he got arrested. He was traveling under the patronage of the French foreign minister, but those wonders of the world, the French who check documents, found it difficult to reconcile his passport designation as a newspaper correspondent with his alternate set of papers to the effect that he was a "distinguished person." He finally decided his first adventure under fire was just funny and took off to see if he could meet Sir John French, the field marshal commanding the British Expeditionary Forces.

He collided with a guardian at the door, no doubt one of those storied British sergeants major, and had a row. As he liked to tell it later, his early education in England had taught him "how to browbeat the lower classes," but when an officer came out to see what was the matter, he remembered he had a letter of introduction. And so he had dinner with the field marshal and his staff. It is a pity no details are of record, for it must have been an interesting evening. McCormick's book elaborates at length on the field marshal's virtues in a fashion far kinder than usual among British military writers. In turn, French put McCormick in care of an important member of his staff, Colonel, Lord Brooke, son of the Earl of Warwick. He was taken up to the front at Ypres. A Major Charles Grant of the Coldstream Guard was told off to show him some action, of which there was more than a plenty at Ypres. That settles any doubt about whether French was making a serious effort to reach McCormick. Gentlemen of the Coldstream did not usher undesirables.

When the shells began to burst around their observation post, McCormick was all ready to take cover, but Major Grant continued his lecture on firing points as if he were in a classroom. McCormick's fear was such that he found it difficult not to ask they leave. He then took to ruminating on the whole problem of courage, a subject that bothered him for the rest of his life. Nobody had instructed him in it when he was a child, a mistake he hoped parents would note and correct. Courage may vary in the individual but with proper attention it can be improved, "like piano playing and polite conversation," and in a man courage is a more desirable accomplishment than either. And as for the British army, "I left it very much in its debt, uplifted by the association of men who sacrifice themselves for country. I had been the associate of very gallant gentlemen."

McCormick's 1915 journal simply records that he took off from Ypres for the Grand Duke, traveling by way of Athens, Salonica, Nish, Sofia and Bucharest, collecting along the way notes on "people and personages of those turbulent States, whose activities brought on—although, of course, they did not cause—the great war." But the most interesting thing he did in 1915 he never mentioned anywhere in his contemporary report. When finally he got around to the subject in 1952, he gave an elaboration that let slip the details of his performance as a secret agent. But, even then, on the most romantic part, all he had to say was: "I was married in London to Mrs. Amy [sic] Irwin Adams and took the steamer *Kaisar-i-Hind* to Malta."

A better account appears in *The New York Times* for March 11, 1915. Now that the *Times* operates as "the newspaper of record" for high school civics classes and chancelleries of world powers, it tends to stand somewhat aloof from the full, rich details of what goes on at the one-to-one level among people below, possibly, the rank of foreign minister. In 1915, its view of instant history allowed it to run through the McCormick-Adams relationship in somewhat lively fashion. It noted that the *Tribune*'s editor had left Chicago in a hurry, giving it out that he was off to Petrograd and the war. When Mrs. Adams sailed on a following ship, "it was gossiped that a marriage between McCormick and Mrs. Adams would follow." And so that had, on March 10, 1915, in the registry office of St. George's Church, Hanover Square, London. The date was exactly in keeping with the Illinois law which prohibited marriage for one year following the decree of divorce.

Like Theodore Roosevelt, McCormick thought it a good idea to marry without a lot of fuss. London took care of that. But there was no handy Cecil Spring-Rice for best man. No doubt the registry records could say who made up the wedding party, but McCormick never did. If he wasn't gabby about it, he stood alone in all of fashionable Chicago, not to say within his own family circle. His mother had several things to say—and she said them several times in the course of several years. They have come down second and third hand from relatives and family friends but, all the worse for the enrichment of history, none will be repeated here. It is enough to say that even after allowing for the sort of editorial improvements so usual in all family accounts of great moments, the dowager Mrs. McCormick undoubtedly put aside any restraints picked up among her diplomatic friends and did well for herself as a free-style Chicagoan and true daughter of Joseph Medill, the terror of the city room in his time.

No matter. Once again Bertie had demonstrated that nobody ever gained by underestimating him. He was tough and he had the instinct for survival.

CHAPTER NINE ★★★ Before taking off for the Grand Duke's headquarters, McCormick went around to the Russian embassy for a formal leave to go. His own, unelaborated account is that he was given a large box, high enough to sit upon, "which I was told contained the secret signals to the British fleet which they wished to get into Russia to be used when the fleets met in the Black Sea or the Bosporus."

On the *Kaisar-i-Hind* to Malta the box was kept in the ship's safe. After that McCormick and his bride were on their own. They made it to Athens on a "frate" boat, as McCormick had it in his 1952 broadcast text. Two porters carried the box around to his hotel. McCormick was warned by the manager this was not the Ritz, so "I cannot be responsible for Mrs. Robert Rockefeller McCormick's jewelry." That story, McCormick said, ran on ahead and served as a nice distraction from any suspicion that he was up to secret service.

In Athens, where he was impressed by the sight of narcotics openly for sale on the streets, McCormick demonstrated to his bride that no matter where they might be put down he could always find connections. The family of a law school classmate at Northwestern took over and did them well. And when the venturers got to Salonika he picked up fresh points on how to browbeat serfs. A hotel porter told him it was demeaning to show his passport. He should merely present his card to authorities. McCormick handed over a large tip and the news of his coming thereafter kept well ahead among state functionaries. Even so one of these behaved in a manner McCormick in 1952 still remembered with severity. There was a typhoid epidemic in Serbia and disinfectants made things most disagreeable. The Crown Prince of Serbia had a car all to himself and was selfish enough to leave distinguished foreigners to look out for themselves as he sat in splendor, lunching with the very best of company, himself. To which McCormick's footnote thirty-seven years later was the pure best of himself, too: "As it was, we took bread, sausages, cheese, and wine in a basket. I still have the basket." It was never McCormick's idea to get caught short and if he ever did the record does not disclose it. Well before the Government of the United States ever got around to organizing a civil defense program, McCormick organized the Tribune Tower against atomic war with pick axes, cases of pineapple juice, medical supplies and a comprehensive plan to keep the paper on the streets. In 1871 the *Tribune* had been knocked out for two whole days by the great fire that laid waste to the city, but with proper understanding of logistics that could be prevented a second time. Furthermore, save the basket.

All along the way, McCormick continued to have the time of his life. As usual, he had regular run-ins with the police and once was bailed out by a medical inspector at Sofia, who turned out to be another handy Northwestern alumnus. And there was the necessary, mysterious "little man with lemon-colored hair" who latched on at Salonika and stayed until they reached Russia. His duty, if any, was not discovered, but if he meant to be invisible he failed. He kept changing his clothes, which made him noticeable. The McCormicks stayed in their own quarters most of the time, for the sake of the box. Once they risked a trip to the dining car. There some men, whether just low Boeotians on a tear or German agents attending to business, invited a fight by imitating Mrs. McCormick's speech. McCormick remembered the box. Thereafter, he laid low in the room until the train was over the border. All passengers were then paraded for inspection, but it appeared the rascals must have slipped away somewhere in Rumania. So McCormick telegraphed for orders: should he take the box to the navy at Odcssa? Hc was told to bring it directly to the Foreign Office at Petrograd. There he turned it over to an assistant of the foreign minister, Serge Sazonoff.

Now it was Mrs. McCormick's turn to show her worldly connections. One of the Foreign Office ladies chanced to be a chum from San Francisco girlhood days. And what was in the box? If McCormick ever learned he kept the secret, faithful to the box unto death.

Mrs. McCormick was left in good hands. The usher of the box got onto his own purposes. Sazonoff knew American affairs well enough to surprise McCormick with a homey little chat on Republican politics in Chicago and filled up the rest of the meeting with just what his visitor was delighted to accept as realistic, a formula for expanding Russian-American trade. Then, Sazonoff really did something that made the whole trip worth while by any test.

At one o'clock in the afternoon, McCormick was off by train to Tsarskoye Selo, tricked out in white tie and tails, to see the last Romanoff. McCormick used to say that his own name would be remembered in history for only one reason: *With the Russian Army* was the book Nicholas II carried with him in captivity and it was found by his night table after he was shot. How McCormick learned this has proved beyond discovery by the researchers used in this present account. History will have to find its documentation on its own, for the above is positive only to the degree that McCormick claimed it. But as for the actual meeting with the Tsar in 1915, journalists would agree that McCormick, who confessed that he felt an obligation to live up to the standard of a justly famous editorial room, came off with full honors. If he missed a single thing it does not show. He counted the steps up to the palace door. Going in, the footman insisted on taking his coat ahead of his hat. He was handed around as "Mr. Cormick." A foxy old chamberlain sidled up and wondered in English just what year it had been "your father left us." McCormick was so rattled, he said, that he couldn't remember. But he wasn't so rattled he didn't notice the windows were doubled-paned. Outside, the thermometers registered 8° Centigrade; 12° between the panes; in the room, 15°. His eye caught everything down to the pictures in some books scattered on a table, all on subjects of lively interest to any man already established in the machinery line, such as hydraulic engineering and the makeup of military vehicles. Then, as the clock struck two, in marched a brace of sentinel-officers all in scarlet. These beings, so natural in their setting and the setting so exotic, caused McCormick to feel for a moment "as Marco Polo must have felt in the great and strange court of China." But it is not fair that a really great passage of reporting should be mutilated by picking over for bits that strike a single fancy. If anybody but McCormick had turned out the copy to be found on pages 36–45 of *With the Russian Army,* the makers of anthologies would have seized on it long ago as a model of reportage. From beginning to end, it is clear, simple and compelling, as freshly interesting today as a set of notes by the real Marco Polo, himself no mean hand at the mention of those particulars which make one man's experience vivid in the mind of another.

McCormick didn't say so outright, but a reader may gather that when the sentinel-officers let him into the presence, he found the Tsar of All the Russias rather a dim little man with "the largest eyes I have ever seen in living mortal." Anyone who has ever studied the portraiture of Queen Victoria and her many crossconnections among European royalty bred out of the great stables of Hesse and Hanover, will know this as a standard of the strain. The Tsar's English, McCormick noted, was better than that of his cousin, the Prince of Wales, out on that great occasion so long ago with another cousin, Wilhelm II of Hohenzollern. The Tsar remembered to ask after McCormick's father, and came up with the news that the war had been "very sudden and very unexpected." He thought the Grand Duke would let McCormick see it all. Conversation would now seem to have run down. "A pretty girl popped her head in the door behind the Emperor and said in all probability—the language being Russian—that luncheon was ready." So the Tsar said, "I am sorry I must go now," and stood there. It came to McCormick that the move was up to him. He backed out, squared up in the anteroom and this time, as he made it out among the living, was handed first the hat and then the coat. Now there were no beings in scarlet fluttering before him. There was only a line of outstretched palms, as the utensils of true power in the imperial household gathered their tips. McCormick finally bought his way to the railroad station and called for a menu. He marked up four dishes at random and got back two kinds of caviar, a cheese sandwich and a bottle of kvass, Russia's ancient, everyday excuse for beer and nothing to make a noise about in any language. But a man in a dress suit calling for lunch at three in the afternoon has to take life as it comes. McCormick choked it down and caught the 3:17 to Petrograd.

Right there he was a made man as a working journalist. It is true that McCormick was always unsteady and inclined to bombast at expository writing, but at narrative he had a true gift. He need never have been intimidated by any Grotonian red-ink sadist. All he ever wanted was an assignment sufficiently intriguing to hold his restless attention, then his eye for detail and his memory could dominate his uncertainty before the challenge of words. The proof that his interview with Nicholas II was no single-shot triumph is abundant to any reader of his memoirs. Those passages which left aside bombinations against hateful personages and told of his adventures with Indians and timber cruisers along the St. Lawrence and of his flights after 1945 among a myriad of men and nations new, are vivid evidence that McCormick not only had the Frank Merriwell heart himself, but also could convey his feeling to others.

After his call at Tsarkoye Selo, he was off to see the war in the East under the patronage of Nicholas Nicolaievitch. He arrived at headquarters in the last moment that establishment was to be seen by anybody on earth as a living organism with direction and purpose. The Grand Duke operated out of a train along the main line between Petrograd and Warsaw. When McCormick did his book he was still under the influences of censorship and so it is not certain where or when he got aboard. A fair guess, based on his dispatches, would put him onto the headquarters train at Vilna, 450 miles down from Petrograd, as of April 1, 1915. He had come to test himself in another facing up to death. In fact, he had another lively forty years to go, to the day, if that was the day, and much history to meddle into, both abroad and at home. But in Russia, just then, he did a turn for history that deserves special mention.

The *Tribune* was one of the most aggressive newspapers at all aspects of photography, both as news and as entertainment. While he was in the grip of his socialist yearnings, Patterson wrote a tract on "the nickelodeon" as art form to educate and uplift the working man. He saw to it that the *Tribune,* and later in New York, the *News,* paid careful attention to all movie developments and thought nothing, except a seat behind home plate when the Yankees were playing, could match an afternoon in any neighborhood theater. He had violent attachments, and equally violent antipathies, in his estimates of the performers, but unlike W. R. Hearst, never permitted himself any involvements.

In 1913, a *Tribune* photographer, E. F. Weigle, followed Patterson to Vera Cruz and photographed the shooting, in which a Marine from Chicago was one of those killed. The result was to make Weigle a *Tribune* hero, so that in 1914, Patterson took him to Europe where Weigle recorded the fall of Antwerp and other major events.

Now, in his own adventure, McCormick found a freelance Kansan, Donald F. Thompson, who was only too glad to risk his neck on the Eastern Front. On September 20, 1915, the combined Weigle-Thompson product was opened in New York under the title, *The German Side of the War*. There had never been anything like it. Lines waiting for the box office stretched four blocks and scalpers, unable to supply the demand with legitimate tickets, did well for themselves selling soda fountain tickets in substitution.

Historians wishing to study exotic aspects of the great war have found these films, especially the portions from the Grand Duke's operation, of unmatched importance.

The story has been told ten thousand times of the classic exercise at war begun on the Western Front in August, 1914. The Germans were to put everything into one monumental maneuver, swing wide around the opposition and squeeze them in another Cannae. On the Eastern Front there was to be nothing but a waiting-out. The Russian railways were on a different gauge from those in the rest of Europe, so the border was the end of the line for mass transport. And the fact was well known that Russia had no munitions industry. The general military appraisal, proved correct, was that imported stocks were just enough for one year of steady fighting. Russian communications were so primitive their wireless operated "in clear," without codes or ciphers. And the whole history of Russian militarism leaned away from a charge into the heart of Europe. But, as so often, nothing followed professional judgment. The Grand Duke attacked. The slaughter was so fantastic that even yet historians quarrel about the dimension of it. Just one immeasurable consequence was degeneration in the West to that timeless horror, the trench warfare of 1915–18.

The Eastern Front entered the winter of 1914–15 on a line curved from Libau, on the Baltic, through the edge of East Prussia on down to a crossing of the Bug river some fifty miles west of Warsaw. From there it sloped off through the Carpathian mountains to Czernowitz in Bukovina, at the headwaters of the River Prut, which meets the Danube just before its entrance into the Black Sea.

On January 31, 1915, just as McCormick's mother was settling his affairs behind his back with Russian Ambassador Bakhmeteff in Washington, the Germans fired off some 18,000 shells of poison gas at the Russians, to introduce into war a horror which shook the world. The Winter Campaign of 1914–15 bogged down toward the end of February as the mud suddenly thawed all through Masuria. For two months the line was stable, but far south in the Carpathians, just as McCormick was taking his leave of the Grand Duke after a tour of the whole front, the German mincing machine roared free. Rasputin offered to come down and exorcise it. The Grand Duke's response was, "Come here and I will hang you." Rasputin's medicine for such blasphemy was a prophecy that no Russian armies could prosper until the Tsar took them in his personal hand, and so, on August 21, 1915, Nicholas Nicolaievitch was relieved as commander in chief. He was shipped out to the Caucasus and the Revolution caught him still out there in what amounted to exile, at Tiflis. The Tsar's last official act was to hand him back the title of commander in chief of armies now little better than fleeing mobs. Twenty-four hours later he was fired again by Prince Lvov, head of the least of all the transitionary governments between the Romanoff dynasty and the Soviet power. He spent two years wandering in the Crimea, and at last, in March, 1919, was taken out by the British aboard the cruiser *Marlborough.* Thereafter, he was just another of the many ghosts floating between Paris and the Riviera until he died in 1929. One who did not forget him was McCormick. The old wanderer asked his friend to raise money for him with a couple of diamonds and McCormick, with his usual hard practicality in such things, made his own friends do the buying at top dollars. But first he got several crosschecked appraisals.

When he came to speak of all these things again in 1952, McCormick remembered to dispose of a slight at the hands of a supercilious lieutenant of guards, the Grand Duke Dmitri Pavlovich, who eyed McCormick indifferently in 1915 and neglected to salute him. So McCormick told how such things end. Dmitri Pavlovich botched his part in Rasputin's assassination and wound up in Paris being kept by one of Chanel's dressmakers. But that was the only flaw in an otherwise seamless cloak of hospitality. The headquarters mess was a moving show of Old Russia. McCormick was put in the hands of a young officer he first thought Japanese, who turned out to be a prince of the Kalmuks and one of the great champions of the Russian team which swept the riding contest at Vienna just before the war. He was also briefed on the whole Eastern Front situation by the chief of staff, General Nicholas Yanouskevitch, one of the worst among the many evil choices for friends the Tsar made among men. But in 1915 that could hardly have been something for McCormick to discover. Instead, he was impressed by all he heard. Then, he was taken to Nicholas Nicolaievitch and on the way in to dinner was introduced to the Grand Duke Peter, younger brother of the commander in chief. McCormick thought of "Aaron bearing up the arms of Moses," and was touched one day, as news of the terrible defeat at Tarnow came in, to see Peter fetch a cane and carry the stricken general's chair to a corner out of the sun. He dined in the midst of princes, generals, high foreign military observers. The Grand Duke was so careful a host as to spot McCormick about to mix claret with Narzan water and warn him the two would not go happily together. One of the staff that buzzed night and day was the Prince Cantacuzene, whose American wife, a granddaughter of Ulysses S. Grant, still lived fifty years later. Before McCormick was let off to see the front, the Grand Duke neatly wound him up to proper pitch with a fit of rage about a report that a seventeen-year-old nurse, having been raped by an entire enemy patrol, lay desperate with syphilis and peritonitis. He charged McCormick with a positive duty to see that "this horror be made known to the world." In time, McCormick came to wonder whether national policy ought to turn on such points and for his doubts earned, or anyhow had to endure, considerable reprobation.

From headquarters he went down to Warsaw where, as he later put it, he was "not unknown," because of his Patterson kinships. He was greatly moved at the spectacle of ladies who kept their gentlemen cheerful in the evenings with candlelight and wine, and then, at the hospitals, carried out sawed-off pieces of the wounded. Somewhere along the way McCormick's ruminations on courage led him to a solution. As he told it, he no longer traveled in constant fear of death and was certain he would never be captured, but he was left by his Russian tour with a powerful horror of lying alone on a battlefield, wounded, another Prince Andrey, to watch the pitiless clouds roll indifferently across the sky. So, in 1917, when it came his own turn to face the guns on the Western Front, he sewed some morphine pills into his coat and, as was his custom, stood ready against come-what-may.

After the terrible encounters in East Prussia during August and September of 1914, Hindenburg moved within twelve miles of Warsaw but had to withdraw after a loss of 40,000 men. McCormick went on a tour of the great battlefield and got up to the extreme front line along the Narew and Wkra rivers above Warsaw. Very sensibly, he improved "Wkra" to read "Rawka" in his text, but otherwise he did a manful job of sticking to less improved spelling of names and places which were not, after all, utterly alien to much of Chicago. He saw everything: French aviators; Russian experiments in antiaircraft artillery; infantry; cavalry; snipers' outposts, and was torn by a regimental band at one forest headquarters that played "My Country, 'tis of Thee." His dispatches on this wild and open front disclose that McCormick had his problems, struggling against the temptation to try out a few Richard Harding Davis touches contrary to the preferred matter-of-fact *Tribune* style, and so far fell from grace as to mention that he had tasted "the wine of death." But he lost any illusions of war as adventure. At one Warsaw hospital he found a soldier who spoke English. When the man said he had once worked in the South Chicago steel mills, McCormick told him that after the war they must meet again by Lake Michigan. But the soldier, after saying he could never go back to America, lifted the bedcovers, showing two stumps where his legs had been, "and over his face came an expression that I would not describe if I could."

It was approximately April 18 that McCormick finished his tour of the front before Warsaw. Then he trailed the Tsar down to Polish Galicia, where Eleanor Patterson, six years before, had come to the bitter end of her effort as the Countess Gizycka, and had got away only after the Tsar had granted leave with a passport inscribed on lambskin. Administrators of her estate in 1948 discovered that passport carelessly folded away in a hatbox, quite likely the last such Imperial writ anywhere to be seen, except perhaps in museums. McCormick got to the provincial capital, Lemberg, just behind the Tsar's party. He went all through the shattered fortress city of Przemysl and saw again that, as on the Western Front, civilians in the shadow of guns lived in misery but those behind the lines were flush. This was enemy country—the Russians had given the Austrian forces of Francis Joseph a terrible beating—yet McCormick found General Yanouskevitch strolling Lemberg unattended, like any tourist. The general public was all excited by the Tsar's passages through Lemberg, but if there was any hostility McCormick made no mention of it. His own tour took him to the extreme forward line along the Carpathians below Gorlice. There, Thompson, the fearless cameraman, took what McCormick thought to be the first 360° panoramic sweep of a battle front ever put on film. With that, he headed back to the Grand Duke's train.

He had seen Cossacks and Mongols, Germans and Austrians. He had discovered armies carry lice and lice carry typhus. He had eaten Russian bread and salt with high and low. For the rest of his life he refused to join in anybody's hymn of hate against Russians, no matter what their politics. He did come to claim that "as early as 1936" the *Tribune* had warned the United States against the perils in Marxism, or as he accepted it, of Communism. But he was ever fair in distinguishing between Russians and their masters' politics. In fact, for all his roaring against Communist agents in the United States, McCormick never did do a very precise or skillful job to show what he thought fundamentally wrong about Marxism itself. His literature on the vice of the British Foreign Office was detailed and copious. He was explicit and authoritative in delineating the material damages that he considered an inevitable consequence of Britain's aristocratic pecking order. By comparison, his Marxist strictures come off as thin stuff. His heart was not really in it.

A good sample of what got to McCormick about the Russian spirit—or one sort of Russian spirit—shows up in his account of his last night on the line in 1915. He and the Tsar got out of Galicia surely not more than a day or so ahead of the great assault at Gorlice, which announced the death of the Russian army-in-being. McCormick picked up the Grand Duke's train somewhere in the vicinity of Warsaw. He had dinner at a general's mess in a beautiful Polish villa, just at sunset. The general sat in the garden as if he were at his own home, in peace. The ejected Polish owners' collie puppies played about him. Word came that Italy was now in the war, a happy change from the dismal news out of Gorlice.

After dinner, McCormick went up to the trenches for the last time, machine-gun bullets cracking over his head. Once again, this was a long way from Chicago. Suddenly, a Russian spotlight snapped on and transfixed a German scout hardly a hundred yards away. McCormick watched through a loophole for a man to die before his eyes. But no. The firing held up as the German recovered his senses and ran for a shelter pit. McCormick wondered about this to an officer, who, in the fashion of his kind, asked what advantage there could be in slaughtering just one poor devil?

Of course, if logic were the real governor of men's ways, even the most jejune of philosophers could dispose of that, but it was the sort of thing that could get a man of McCormick's sentiments and if it helped save the Russians from his wrath in times to come, surely it did no great harm to affairs of state.

After his tour of the line, McCormick fell in with Besobrasov, that Ancient Pistol who had done so much to start the Russian Empire down the skids along the Yalu River back when McCormick's father was fumbling for a key to the riddle of the Tsar's court. Ever willing to show himself up on the latest thing, Besobrasov explained fixed warfare. McCormick was impressed, and went up into Lithuania to see for himself at Ossovets, a small, third-rank layout put together in 1888 and redone in 1910. McCormick had seen that the Russians could grind down the modern, beautifully done Austrian fortress of Przemysl. Here was something very much less, yet neither sixteen-inch siege guns nor infantry had yet been able to crack it open. It was just the sort of problem to engage the best thought of a man who had proved himself digging canals and building paper mills. Out of his study McCormick came up with his first, but not his happiest essay on the doctrine of war. He called it *Upon Modern Fortifications* and he charged every reader to study it with the closest care as a gift from the Russians—sent through him alone—out of friendship for the American people. McCormick thought it especially necessary to get this message out, "because our government has forbidden American army officers to educate the American people in military affairs," his sideswipe at President Wilson for not springing into action as the *Tribune* had suggested, to build a proper army and navy to protect Fortress America from Europe's war.

There is no hope of conveying in any condensation a just impression of McCormick's revelations about fortress warfare. He began with explanation of how to stock a strong point; how to fight from it; and what must be expected of it in the long run, to wit: any fortress must yield, eventually, to somebody strong enough to take it—a proposition against which none may argue safely—but every soldier in a garrison cut off should fight to the last man, last round. For the safety of the United States he prescribed bastions kept up to scratch at Albany, Buffalo, Pittsburgh, Atlanta, Vicksburg, Houston and "the passes of the Sierra Nevadas and the Rocky Mountains." From these it should be possible to maneuver our less mobile and less effective troops against an invading enemy.

Now he was ready to quit the field. Someone insisted he should not miss Moscow, rather a backwater in the Russia of that day. So he went down and heard the Princess Yousoupoff tell how she, her husband, son and daughter had been caught at Carlsbad, taking the cure with old General Brusiloff, as the guns broke out in 1914. The general, a firm believer in the rule that he travels the fastest who travels alone, made a neat jump over the border. The Yousoupoffs were slower, and got arrested in Berlin. In a great rage, the Princess telephoned her cousin, the Crown Princess of Prussia, who promised to come around at once and apologize in person. The Kaiser surely would never permit mere fighting between soldiers to discommode cousins of the blood. But Wilhelm II flew into one of his fits and declared the Yousoupoffs his prisoners. Even so, they slipped away, with his guards in hot pursuit. This was further proof that the Hun was beyond the pale of civilized society. And as the Princess told her story to McCormick a captain of Cossacks wept for the shame of it all, that he must wet-nurse an ammunition factory while the war was running out before he could get in it.

Then McCormick went again to headquarters for a formal leave-taking from the Grand Duke. It happened that the Tsar was in the camp that day and McCormick was permitted to approach while the Emperor and the general were in discussion. McCormick told, in later years, that he was bothered either by a gnat or a fly and before he knew what he was about, had made a violent swipe before his own face. Whereupon, the Tsar of All the Russias cowered and shrank behind the Grand Duke, in fright for his life.

The Grand Duke managed to put down any clash of arms, however, and told McCormick he would be welcome in the camp again any time he liked. McCormick tested out the significance of this by asking Yanouskevitch if the same time in 1916 would do, to which the answer came: "Certainly, or if you prefer it, the year after." This, McCormick said in his 1915 account, should be pondered by some who had scoffed at his own estimate that 1914 was the bare beginning of a long and terrible war.

He collected his wife, his movie studies, his notes and his baggage and went out by train up around the Gulf of Bothnia, crossing into Sweden at Haparanda and so on down the coast to Stockholm. It was the time of the midnight sun and he stayed up to see Lapps, reindeer, outlandish architecture and some of the world's most strangely moving countryside. He also discovered smorgasbord. At Stockholm he stayed with the American minister, Ira Nelson Morris, from Chicago. He saw Swedes swim naked in the Stockholm harbor and met two lovely ash-blonde young women, the Countess Bundy and the Countess Hamilton. The Hamiltons were a Scottish family that had fought with Gustavus Adolphus and taken up land as reward. The ladies, he once took care to explain, were not among the swimmers.

McCormick went on down to Oslo, then called Christiana, and found a Mr. George Gade, whose brother was a Chicago friend of long standing. He called on both Fridtjof Nansen and Roald Amundsen and made a great friend of Amundsen. McCormick once brought off a great news hit by tying up Amundsen for exclusive accounts of a South Pole exploration.

From Norway, McCormick came on down to London for another round with Asquith and Sir Edward Grey. He was taken to see Lord Kitchener whose mind, McCormick later said, was so far gone by 1915 the government in desperation started the old man on a trip to Russia. And that was how Kitchener happened to drown in the Baltic. McCormick had a letter of introduction from the Grand Duke to Marshal Joffre. The savior of France invited him up to the Compiègne, no small honor. In Paris, he remembered to do some business with Senator George Menier, whose family owned the Anticosti Island in the Gulf of St. Lawrence from which McCormick had been buying pulpwood since 1912.

Back in London again, for the third time, McCormick—who never hesitated to arrange such fixes when it suited him—managed so the Admiralty would let go one of the *Tribune*'s paper ships it had commandeered for Canadian patrol duty. He saw again a childhood friend from Chicago, once Hazel Martyn and by then Lady John Lavery, one of the great beauties of the Irish rebellion. Lady John had her try at settling the Irish Question by bringing Michael Collins and Winston Churchill into conversation. The most she got out of it all was her own portrait on Irish money eventually, done by her husband, and a gallant declaration by Sir Winston that she started him out as an artist.

Now there was no escaping business at home. He came back down the St. Lawrence and met Patterson at Montreal. They killed time waiting for the train by taking in McCormick's first sight of a minor league baseball game. His only criticism was that the pitchers seemed a little short on control. And once at his desk where his duty told him to study the balance sheets, McCormick read through the text of *With the Russian Army,* which he had dictated on his way across the Atlantic, and stuck on something he called "Envoi." Here, again, he fell from grace with more about that wine of death having fixed its flavor in his throat. He predicted that the United States would be drawn into "the great debauch," and would lose a million men "while we are striving to learn, in the stress of war, the lesson that could so easily have been taught in peace."

If such a passage lays him open to complaint of literary excess, at least he was not altogether blind to the road ahead. And just to remind himself of where he had been and what he had seen, there was on his desk a fragment from the cathedral at Arras where he first saw guns firing in anger. In that, we have the true McCormick.

For all his sophistication, his lifelong explorations of strange territory and his vast, odd acquaintance among kings, emperors, field marshals, hotel porters and lady revolutionists, McCormick liked to bring home souvenirs, to impress Chicago. By the time he died, the face of Tribune Tower was littered with such durable evidences: a piece of the Great Pyramid of Egypt [though how he got away with it would never do to guess]; a stone from the sibyl's cave at Cumae; one from the Antarctic, brought him by Amundsen; another from the Great Wall of China; another from a Kremlin tower; one from Bunker Hill; one from the White House; one more from Fort Sumter; altogether more than a hundred such pieces. Modestly set high in a wall about the Tower's Nathan Hale Courtyard there is a small red object and beneath it notice that this brick is from the doorway of 150 East Ontario St., "birthplace of Colonel Robert R. McCormick." It should still be there a hundred years from now, adding to the appreciation of a man who discovered for himself that he was a legend in his own time.

CHAPTER TEN ★★★ Until his return from Russia, McCormick had operated more among the foothills of public prominence than from the peaks, just as he had been up against it most of the time for unqualified praise and honor within his own family.

Now he could enjoy the change. The military invited him to lecture on what he had learned in the Grand Duke's camp. The public lined up and paid money to see in motion picture a little of what he had been through in person. Writers might hate to admit it, but they had to concede *With the Russian Army* a real and useful book. And very best of all, within the closed circle of newspaper proprietors it was now conceded that McCormick was one of themselves. The *Tribune* had turned a corner in the fight for dominance of Chicago. And in Canada, McCormick's personal test of himself as taker of business risk had proved out the foundation for a corporate power beyond anything imagined by his grandfather. McCormick had even outwitted his mother and, in the struggle of men to possess women, had managed a very chancy exercise without loss of public dignity. So far, so good.

The next problem was how to run the *Tribune* in a world unable to hear the voice of reason. The United States had so far managed to hold onto the notion of itself as a neutral power, willing to talk up peace while trading with belligerents on a basis of first-come-first-served, but neither McCormick nor his alternate in command of the *Tribune,* Patterson, had any illusion that such a policy was guaranteed to work. Nor was either blind to the dangers possible in the outcome of the war, even if the United States were not dragged into the fighting. There could come a new hegemony in Europe. The English and French systems, to which the United States was accustomed, could be swept away and there would be a strange, Germanic power to measure, probably to fight as the English and the French had been fought in past times and, after all, dealt with eventually. In a life of risk, this had to be remembered.

Such was the thought McCormick and Patterson both believed they projected in the opening phases of the 1914–18 war. For the rest of their lives they and all their family connections were outraged at the epithet "pro-German," which now must be weighed as close as may be to see what there is in it. For it was soon in coming, and once come, it stayed as long as McCormick lived. It outlived both his Patterson cousins, as it long outlived his brother. Any investigator of the charge will soon discover that, as in his examination of McCormick's unremitting conflict with President Franklin D. Roosevelt, understanding comes best through knowledge of what preceded the hard words exchanged day by day. In summary, McCormick saw the New Deal of 1933–37 in terms of what he had learned about the world up to, say, September, 1915. And to see how everything, everywhere, looked to him after 1937, it is essential to go deep into those events which impressed him between September, 1915, and the Presidential election of 1920. No single illustration can make it plainer than a comparison of the *Tribune* first page for November 11, 1918, with that for August 15, 1945. In typography, layout and whole treatment, the two are as nearly the same as possible. In 1945, as in 1918, the headline across the top of the page reads: "Great War Ends."

This was simply McCormick reminding the world he had warned it all along that Franklin D. Roosevelt would prove himself Woodrow Wilson returned to finish the ruin of the Republic.

The standard retort of both the McCormick and Patterson families to the "pro-German" charges of the First World War and to even worse accusations in the Second World War was that in 1917 Patterson and McCormick wasted no time getting to the front. They shot, and were shot at, with intent to kill. And the family view was that those who criticized them the loudest were the first to dive under desks and fight a safe war behind the line. It is a fact that some of these critics surely so did, but also a fact that some even beat McCormick and Patterson into uniform. And never came home. And in the Second World War it was much the same. If both men were far too old to be usable a second time in the military, at least they risked everything to stand for policies they believed best for the United States. And, rather simply, they liked nothing better than to take full-page advertisements in other newspapers, trade journals and magazines, to show that the *Tribune* in Chicago and the *News* in New York not only dominated readership and advertising, but also increased the dominance every time some effort was made to diminish them. This, they concluded, was the best evidence. Their papers were popular because they were "right."

Popular they surely were, if the test is that nobody could bear to pass the day without seeing what McCormick and Patterson were up to just then. But, of course, with newspapers, as with governments, "popular" is no test of "right." It is absurd to offer a short and simple verdict on the vast confusions that went into the relation between Woodrow Wilson, Franklin D. Roosevelt, Robert R. McCormick and Joseph M. Patterson. Leaving aside entirely the mysterious proposition of character, there are differences of authority, responsibility, knowledge, experience and of personality no outsider could possibly fathom. And there were, too, private stresses, experiences shared by Roosevelt, McCormick and Patterson from childhood to old age that none of them ever showed much sign of understanding, let alone of acknowledging. In this account, at least, a conclusion must wait on more compelling evidence than either circulation figures or polemical histories rushed out by Cabinet officers. But it is certainly possible to dismiss the "pro-German" charge as nonsense. The *Tribune* proprietors may have earned abuse for being wrongheaded, perverse, selfish, cowardly, stupid or hypocritical. They may have deserved to be called poltroons and scoundrels on general principles. One time or another, they were called all those things, too. But "pro-German," in the sense of adhering to a foreign power against the United States between 1914 and 1918, they were not. How to view their attitude in the period between 1937 and 1945 is another matter to be considered at its proper place in this chronicle.

But there again, it will be found necessary to emphasize that, leaving aside entirely the differences between Roosevelt on the one side and McCormick and Patterson on the other, there were differences, too, between McCormick and Patterson themselves, stemming from their very earliest days of work on the *Tribune* after 1910. If one would believe popular journalistic accounts now repeated so often as to have become articles of faith, Patterson and McCormick, until war got them out of the office, rotated direction so wildly neither staff nor readers could make head or tail of it. According to this doctrine, Patterson was out to make the *Tribune* a sort of socialist loonybin. McCormick, on the days he had a go at the editorial page, supposedly ran it as a deadly dull house organ of the Republican oligarchy.

This otherwise entertaining account of jealous confusions might do very well, except for some evidence to the contrary. The first fact is that no sooner did McCormick and Patterson begin their joint management than the paper began to recover its energy and run better than ever. The next is that in his earlier years, and we have his own word for it, McCormick lacked self-assurance at exactly the sort of thing Patterson did best, that is, to form editorial judgments and put them in writing for the world to kick against as it dared. Nothing demanded McCormick's respect more than that Patterson had already proved in the marketplace he did not have to depend on the *Tribune*. He could, if he had to, sell his writing for the high dollar on a national market. Patterson was a natural, well-proved master of language in general and an extraordinary specialist at thrusting ideas, naked raw, in the way of any made squeamish by the view. It is very unlikely that a piece of paper exists on which McCormick made conscious admission that he studied his cousin's method until he could make it his own. Nor has anything come out to show he ever confessed Patterson taught him what or how to think about the meaning in events. That would be asking too much. But there is in the public record real evidence to show Patterson's influence upon McCormick in the realm of ideas.

When the war began, Patterson was already well out front of McCormick at field observation. He had reported for the *Tribune* on the Russo-Japanese war, the Boxer rising in China, the insurrection against the United States in the Philippines and the sortie at Vera Cruz. And it may well be argued nothing more significant than the flip of a nickel led the *Tribune* into the "pro-German" morass. When the shooting started, Patterson couldn't decide whether he ought to head for Paris or for Berlin. The toss of the coin sent him just in time to hook on as the Germans began to sweep toward France according to plan laid out long before by Field Marshal Alfred von Schlieffen. As the marching line faltered in Belgium, Patterson slipped through to examine the great siege of Antwerp from the inside. There, his verbal impudence, as much as his reportorial intrusions, got him locked up. It took a serious effort by Lord Northcliffe in London to get him out, whereupon he went home to Chicago, much impressed by the social welfare services in Germany and the absence of such things in countries held to be more enlightened. In 1915, while McCormick was investigating the war in the East, Patterson resumed his examination of the Western Front.

The literary sensation of the day was *Germany and the Next War*, by General Friedrich von Bernhardi, a retired chief of the military history section in the German general staff, who would far better have been shot than allowed to get his hands on a printing press. All the barns in Iowa cannot hold the output of literary Teutons announcing a new line of thought that guarantees Utopia in human endeavors. Bertrand Russell, overcome by the spectacle, once put it that in England rain comes from Ireland and idealism comes from Germany. And it is part of their fatal talent, too, that these tireless system-builders manage to get out their news precisely at the moment and in precisely the form to make enemies of maximum number and quality.

Bernhardi's system, in its fundamentals, could hardly be thought anything unmentioned previously, nor was it at all a flying in the face of evidence commonly used in all manner of philosophical inquiries. But, like William Graham Sumner, who had also influenced Patterson, at Yale, Bernhardi offered his own brand of Social Darwinism. There is war and there is peace. War is a historical and biological necessity, nature's research system for moral, social and physical progress. Peace is only the interval of exhaustion and recovery for the next round of this wonderful method by which humanity is made better. Having now demonstrated war a good thing, Bernhardi explained that if one side wins the other side must lose. Winning is better. It followed that in the next war Germany must do anything necessary to win. The very worst to be said about Bernhardi's book is that it contained much nobody could deny. It had the ring of honest searching for truth and the courage to state that, as found. And it showed a strong interest in domestic social welfare work, a subject close to Patterson's heart. The fact that all Bernhardi's thought, including how to build strong bodies, had the simple aim of insuring that Germans could be more effective killers than anybody else, did not seem to offend Patterson. After all, people could refuse the aim and take the gain. Bernhardi got his book out, as one would expect, in 1912. Even Wilhelm II was impressed by the detonations abroad. When Louvain went up in smoke two years later it was not just another case of soldiers doing what they had done countless times before and have since. Bernhardi had fixed it so the Hun was at the gate of Rome.

On May 7, 1915, the British liner *Lusitania* was sunk by torpedoes off the Irish coast and of the 1,198 people drowned, 128 were Americans. The German submarine war seized the imagination of the world as nothing was to do again until the United States dropped the atomic bomb at Hiroshima. President Wilson was surely accurate in saying that a single order by some German naval lieutenant could now force the unimaginable. By September, Patterson had seen enough of the action and he had completed his analysis of Bernhardi, too. He was ready with a policy on war and peace he would give the country through the *Tribune,* based on both philosophical inquiry and experience in the field of war. He also had the courage to demonstrate his proposition in terms nobody could doubt. He bought passage home on a particularly slow British ship, the *Cymric*. He arranged for a message to reach the *Tribune* in event the *Cymric* were torpedoed. There was to be no scandal. He well knew the grain of wheat that thrusts itself between the millstones can expect to be crushed. No American boarding a British vessel in 1915 was innocent and his death ought not to be used as an excuse to send innocents to death in his name.

On the way across the Atlantic, Patterson put together the whole of his investigation. It was published in the *Tribune* in September, 1915, under the heading, "Notebook of a Neutral." In 1942, it was republished, with a historical introduction, in the *Tribune,* the New York *News* and the Washington *Times-Herald*.

It is plain to any analyst of *Tribune* editorial swings that the "Notebook of a Neutral" settled the question of how the paper should view the world and instruct the United States on the problems of the twentieth century. And it is equally plain that once it was all spelled out to him by somebody whose intelligence and character impressed him as Patterson's did, all McCormick had to do thereafter was hold fast. And so he did. For the rest of his life he knew what he was supposed to think and to do about peace, war and the interests of the United States.

And for the rest of his life, Patterson, too, was puzzled at the charge that he was "pro-German," because of the "Notebook." He found Germany in 1915 the only country that had acted to see its workers "shouldn't stand on their feet too long," that invested tax money to see its children saved from bad adenoids, bad teeth, illiteracy and utter poverty. Bismarck had shown the way. If England, France and the United States were so consumed with virtue, why had they nothing to compare? And Patterson put it in the *Tribune* for all the world to see that he thought "the amiable General Bernhardi," by and large, had the facts. War does erase the weak and point up the strong. Time would tell whether Germany would remain a military imperium or recover its Bismarckian solid sense and continue toward true socialist democracy. In any case, the cue for the United States was to stay neutral.

Patterson's definition of neutrality was different from anything else heard in the land. It embarrassed him not at all to concede that British control of the Atlantic was important to the United States. In fact, he advocated sending food and supplies to keep up England's strength, in the American interest. That interest he spelled out in language any Chicagoan, at least, would understand. It was to sit tight, "in the name of the holy Monroe Doctrine," and make money. If the timid and the hypocritical and the delicate-minded had not yet got Patterson's drift, he distilled all into one sentence:

"Any American in a position of power or influence who allows any consideration but the selfish interests of America to guide him is a traitor."

As far as the *Tribune* was concerned, that nailed the flag to the mast. Both cousins now applied themselves to discovering just which selfish interests of the United States required immediate consideration. Also, they made personal military commitments as members of the Illinois National Guard.

As election year rolled around with 1916, political professionals, without respect to party, were free of any early illusion that the professor in the White House lacked iron or technical skill at what was supposed to be their own, highly specialized trade of human management. He might sit up nights with his typewriter, tapping out language meant to glitter in the history books, but by day he showed himself the wiliest and most autocratic sort of partisan Commander in Chief. The United States was still then said to guarantee the Republican Party a "normal" majority, but there was good reason to doubt that anything in 1916 was going to be normal, whatever that was supposed to mean, anyhow.

Yet it wasn't so simple for Mr. Wilson, either, as he probed and picked for a path through the field of mines everywhere about. There was no doubt the country wanted really to do just what Patterson had said in his most offensive tone, sit tight and make money. Inevitably, purchasers of war goods let their debts pile up and inevitably, creditors worried about what would happen if one failed to appear for settlement, on account of being conquered and dead. And if that, and trouble in Mexico and collisions between partisans for one power or another were not enough, the German submarine campaign had put pressure on emotions to the point of explosion. Theodore Roosevelt was loose on the hustings. His language was worse than an artillery barrage.

Mexico boiled with German, Japanese and other agents. Carranza was not even master of his own house. The most popular man in Mexico was a cattle thief, Doroteo Arango, who had taken up the revolutionary trade and, in the fashion, adopted an alias, Pancho Villa. His idea appeared to be as much to bring down Carranza as to destroy the Yankee Colossus. One night in March of 1916 Villa's gang burned much of Columbus, New Mexico, and killed seventeen persons.

Mr. Wilson had given out that the policy of the United States toward Mexico would be one of "watchful waiting," but now events were shaping policy, rather than policy measuring out events. It was, after all, an election year. The United States was profoundly shaken to find the Atlantic Ocean a death trap and its own border not secure. Mr. Wilson called out the troops. The plan was that 150,000 members of the National Guard, seeded with Regulars, would hold the border so a 15,000-man striking force headed by Brigadier General John J. Pershing could bring in Villa. Pershing was the model of all "the Old Army" meant in American military

A great morning after headache for the *Tribune* that needs no explanation anywhere in the world of politics, as to its exquisite pleasure-giving. But there was more than blind bullheaded optimism behind the decision to risk that first edition headline. When it appeared in Chicago polls were still open in California, and television was sure to show it. So, who knows . . . ? Except that it didn't work.

Red Oak Farm at Wheaton, as Joseph Medill left it and from which McCormick's mother fled early and often as she could. She never saw it after her son made it over and renamed it Cantigny.

Colonel, sometime MFH of the DuPage Hunt, with Buster Boo and Red Oak as Cantigny, in full fig.

Copyright, 1952 by Time, Inc., reproduced by special permission

Cantigny exotica. Bride from Taiwan on the way to al fresco altar and McCormick standing in for her father, far away.

Joseph Medill, after 1894, and his four grandchildren; left to right, Robert R. McCormick, Eleanor M. Patterson, Joseph M. McCormick and Joseph M. Patterson.

Robert Sanderson McCormick, United States Ambassador to France, Mrs. McCormick, and aides who had served with them on post in Russia, Robert Wood Bliss and Spencer Eddy. Time, 1905–06. Taken at U.S. Embassy in Paris, supposedly.

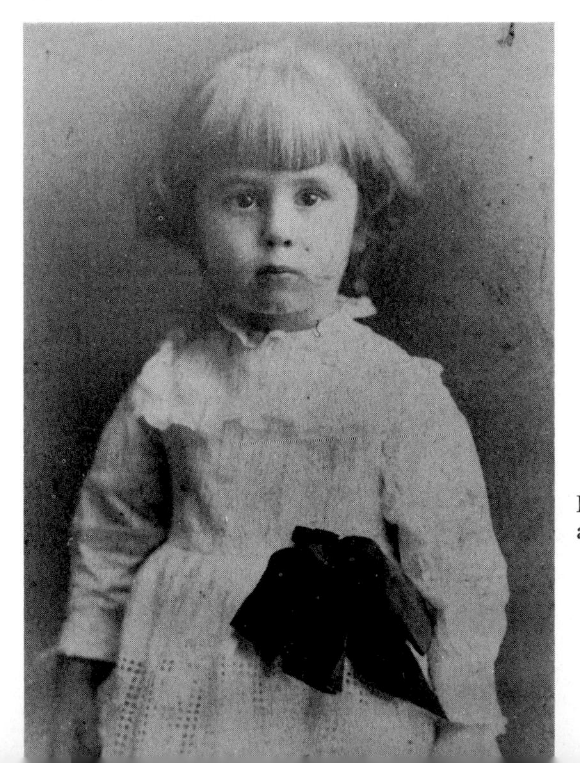

Robert Rutherford McCormick, aged three years.

Mrs. Robert S. McCormick and her sons, [Joseph Medill McCormick without hat, Robert R., with hat] just before sailing for London and her husband's first post as secretary to U.S. Minister Robert Todd Lincoln.

The McCormick sons in Ludgrove days [Robert R. on left] of their father's first diplomatic adventure.

Photo by Dana Hull

McCormick, post-Yale, the beginning lawyer-politician-journalist in the years of Chicago's conversion from overblown village to metropolis. About 1910.

Before the battle. It takes a magnifying glass to discover that McCormick here wore a colonel's eagles on his shoulders, which assures this was at the time he was about to join Pershing abroad. Also, that he is really carrying not a "heavy stick" as he liked to tell it, as an aid to his wounded knee, but a fashionable light crop. But he was alert enough not to be photographed with his monocle.

Somewhere in France, 1917–18. McCormick clam happy, if somewhat out of uniform. That is a French helmet, as near as can be made out, unless it was one he invented for himself. The glass also lets it be discovered that the first outlines are now forming of his moustache that ever afterward became a delight to caricaturists and a great support to McCormick's idea of himself as an austere aristocrat.

Photo by George Kalec

McCormick frequently advised public men in whom he took an interest to beware of smiling for the camera on great occasions for fear of seeming light-minded, also to avoid chance of being caught in ridiculous poses, but he could risk each without loss when he chose. Here he hurls horseshoes in company with Mrs. W. R. Hearst, Jr., and the late Speaker of the House, Sam Rayburn.

Photo by George Kalec

First copy off new presses at Fort Necessity, as McCormick called the *Times-Herald,* his unfortunate bastion in Washington.

Here is the sum of McCormick's judgment on notions of political action that would subject the United States to any form of authority outside itself. All Americans who would put any sort of limitation on sovereignty looked alike to him—natural descendants of the First Traitor.

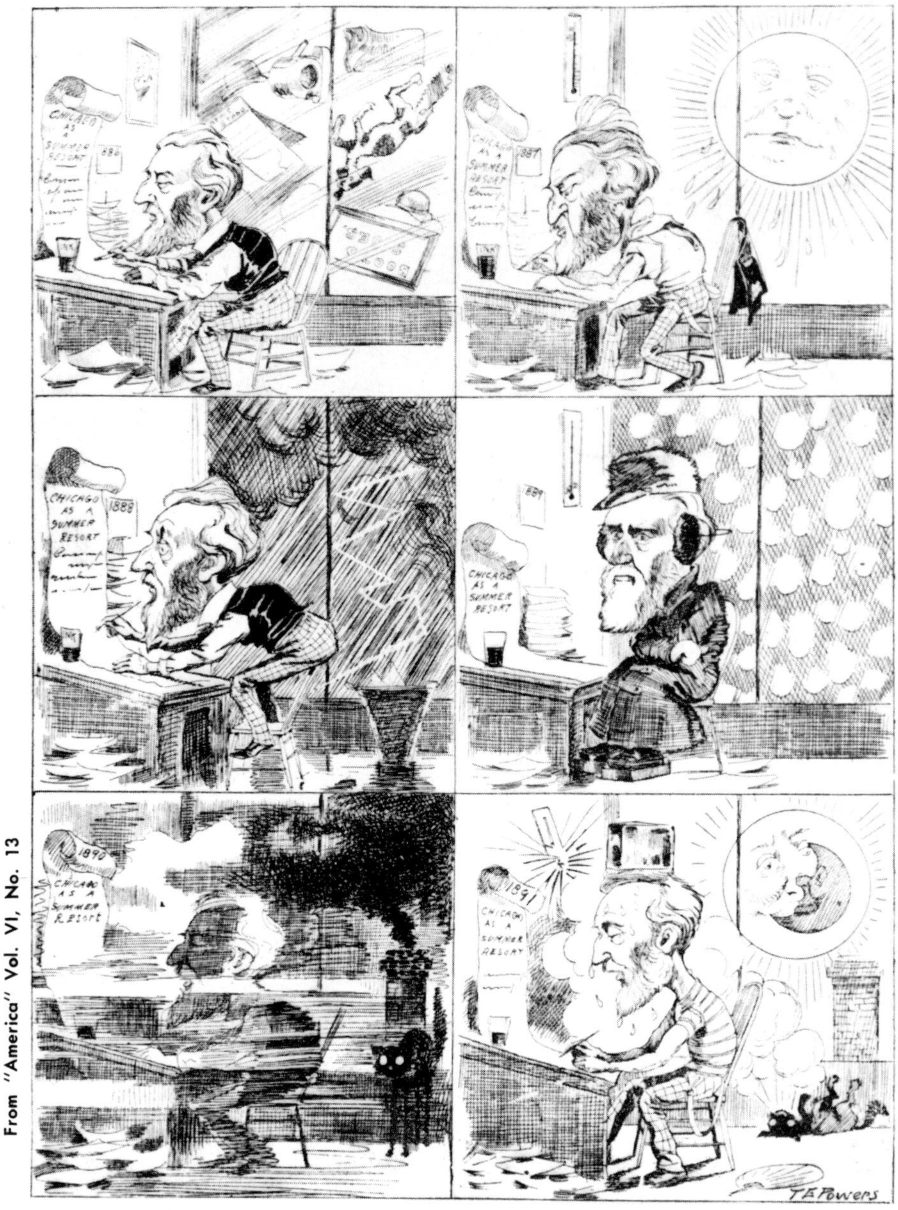

From "America" Vol. VI, No. 13

When McCormick pronounced the B'hai Temple in suburban Chicago superior to the Taj Mahal he was only following a family tradition of holding grandeur in thought superior to passing reality. Joseph Medill was famous in his day for contending Chicago an ideal place to enjoy the summer and is here portrayed in contemporary journalism "writing his annual rhapsody under varying conditions," between 1886 and 1891.

THE NEW LEARNING

In his effort to keep the English from capturing Chicago, Mayor William H. Thompson led a crusade to clear the city of books that might corrupt the public mind. Here is how the *Tribune* saw it.

Even as late as June 6, 1933, the *Tribune* was still trying to find something agreeable to say about Franklin D. Roosevelt, and in representing him as "vamp-proof" against European seductions, clearly attached itself to early New Deal tendencies toward autarchy.

IT LOOKS AS THOUGH AT LAST WE MIGHT HAVE A VAMP-PROOF PRESIDENT, June 6, 1933, John T. McCutcheon, Chicago *Tribune*

BOMBPROOF SHELTER, Oct. 9, 1940, Carey Orr and D.L.B., Chicago *Tribune*

As the foreign policy debate after 1937 grew more intense, the *Tribune* and Mr. Roosevelt made it personal, but the President had only silence as a weapon against such as this one of Oct. 9, 1940.

Rhodes Scholars and others who tangled with McCormick on America First found, as with this from the May 6, 1941, edition, that at polemic he had resources few could hope to match and no hesitation at using them.

AMONG OUR SOUVENIRS

Springfield, June 15. 1859

Press & Tribune Co.
Gentlemen

Herewith is a little draft to pay for your Daily another year from today. I suppose I shall take the Press & Tribune so long as it, and I both live, unless I become unable to pay for it. In its devotion to our cause always, and to me personally last year, I owe it a debt of gratitude, which I fear I shall never be able to pay.

Yours very truly
A. Lincoln.

PARRISH

How to use a President for a circulation builder. The letter from Lincoln is authentic, and was here part of the June 8, 1947 edition preliminary to the 100th Anniversary celebration two days later.

Fight for THOMPSON—He Fights for You

"You Know, You Are Famous, Like Babe Ruth... I Will See That the Tribune Gives You a Square Deal." — *Says Col. R. R. McCormick to Al Capone*

Chicago, February 14, 1931.

A LITTLE OVER TWO YEARS AGO, MAX ANNENBERG, DIRECTOR OF CIRCULATION OF THE CHICAGO TRIBUNE, CALLED ME ON THE TELEPHONE AND SAID HE WANTED TO MEET ME AT THE DRAKE HOTEL AND HAVE A TALK WITH ME. I ASKED HIM WHAT HE WANTED TO TALK ABOUT AND HE TOLD ME THE TRIBUNE WAS HAVING SOME TROUBLE WITH THEIR CHAUFFEURS AND DRIVERS. I WENT OVER TO THE DRAKE HOTEL, MET MAX ANNENBERG AND HE TOLD ME THAT HE WAS IN BAD WITH THE FLANNAGAN BROTHERS AND THEY WERE GOING TO CALL A STRIKE OF THE TRIBUNE'S CHAUFFEURS AND DRIVERS FOR THE FOLLOWING SATURDAY, AND HE WANTED TO GET SOMEONE TO TALK TO THE EXECUTIVE COMMITTEE OF THE CHAUFFEURS AND DRIVERS UNION TO SEE IF THE STRIKE COULD NOT BE CALLED OFF. HE SAID THAT DULLO, BUSINESS AGENT OF THE UNION AND MEMBER OF THE EXECUTIVE COMMITTEE, MET LOUIS ROLSE, CIRCULATION MANAGER OF THE CHICAGO TRIBUNE, AND THAT DULLO DEMANDED $25,000. TO STRAIGHTEN OUT THE STRIKE. ANNENBERG SAID HE WANTED TO TREAT THE BOYS RIGHT AND THAT HE WANTED TO REACH SOMEONE WHO COULD GET THE EXECUTIVE COMMITTEE TO FIX THE STRIKE UP.

I TOLD HIM THAT AS PRESIDENT OF THE NEWSBOYS' UNION THERE WAS NOTHING I COULD DO. THEN MAX ANNENBERG SAID HE WOULD CALL UP CAPONE AND SEE IF HE COULD DO ANYTHING IN THE MATTER, WHICH HE DID AND MADE AN APPOINTMENT WITH CAPONE TO MEET HIM IN THE TRIBUNE'S OFFICE. I ATTENDED THIS MEETING, AT WHICH CAPONE AGREED TO USE HIS INFLUENCE TO STOP THE STRIKE, WHICH PREVENTED THE SAME. MAX ANNENBERG THEN BROUGHT IN ROBERT McCORMICK, EDITOR AND PUBLISHER OF THE CHICAGO TRIBUNE, AND INTRODUCED McCORMICK TO CAPONE. McCORMICK THANKED CAPONE FOR CALLING OFF THE STRIKE FOR THE TRIBUNE AND SAID, "YOU KNOW, YOU ARE FAMOUS, LIKE BABE RUTH. WE CAN'T HELP PRINTING THINGS ABOUT YOU, BUT I WILL SEE THAT THE TRIBUNE GIVES YOU A SQUARE DEAL."

(SIGNED) DANIEL A. SERRITELLA.
PRESIDENT OF THE NEWSBOYS' UNION.

On this page is shown a sworn statement by Daniel Serritella about a conversation held in Colonel McCormick's office at the Chicago Tribune between Colonel R. R. McCormick and Al Capone.

After reading this statement you can judge for yourself where Capone is sitting. He is in the Tribune's lap.

Just one page from the campaign flyer put out by William Hale Thompson for 1932. Another page defined the Democratic candidate for mayor, Anthony Cermak, as a *Tribune* tool.

From the N.Y. Public Library's collection of American political ephemera.

thought. He was a cavalryman supreme. He graduated from West Point in 1886 and went at once against the Apache and the Sioux. He knew the region, and he knew how to handle troops. For eight months Pershing's horsemen raised the dust back and forth across the border. Carranza raised dust of his own. Villa, of course, enjoyed a world success in the field and in the newspapers. Not until 1920 did he allow himself to be caught by anybody, and then with a bribe from the establishment in Mexico City. High life ruined him. He switched over from horses to expensive automobiles, and one day while he was riding around, hired guns got him.

The farce of the Pershing expedition was no worse than that put on by the National Guard. The citizen-soldiers gathered for a mighty spring to arms. They then collapsed among their mismatched straps and buttons. Even so convinced a society of civilians as the United States could see that was not the way to run a country, and it was a formidable thought for Mr. Wilson that Chicago held a monster "Preparedness Parade" as the Republicans met there to select a candidate for President.

McCormick's memoir on the Mexican campaign is a reliable sampling of the general experience. His regiment was called The First Illinois National Guard, a cavalry unit. The colonel in chief was a Chicago alderman, described by McCormick as "irascible, suspicious, obese, lame, deaf and with defective eyesight," but still able to sit a horse within the requirements the regular army had laid down for its own. Guard cavalry organizations liked, then, to consider themselves "raised" through local patronage, as if they were English county regiments. Polo players, gentleman amateurs of the horse, young men hoping to meet such as these, and even some genuinely bent on military preparation, bought their own mounts, uniforms, weapons and texts. They elected their officers. McCormick came up as a major. Patterson, as might have been expected, enlisted as a private in an artillery formation. Of this, McCormick said: "Joe may like to wash harness, but not me." The First Illinois operated a commercial riding service to help raise money for horse feed but couldn't develop any great prowess at arms, allowed only one night a week for drill, plus two weeks in summer camp. The young bloods ran short, so it was necessary to fill the ranks from the floating supply of steel-puddlers, dock wallopers and any others looking for a change of pace, with a little cash to make it tolerable.

McCormick professed to be shocked at discovering that few knew how to ride. Of course, he was just indulging a fancy of himself as an aristocrat ignorant of proletarian limitations. He knew perfectly well that Chicago south of the Archer Road offered small use for anything comparable to the Onwentsia Club's pony class for six-year-olds. More to his credit, he was determined that the First Illinois should not want for the best of gear. Out of his Russian notes he came up with the designs for a rolling field kitchen. It was the first of its kind in an American operation. Another of his projects, entirely sensible and at least as important, laid the foundation for that literary shocker of 1942, known far and wide as "Col. McCosmic's letter to Sawyer." This was a letter to a former *Tribune* employee in which McCormick listed a few of his credits and debits as a patriot. The killing paragraph read:

> You do not know it, but the fact is that I introduced the ROTC into the schools; that I introduced machine guns into the army; that I introduced mechanization; I introduced automatic rifles; I was the first ground officer to go up in the air and observe artillery fire. Now I have succeeded in making that the regular practice in the army. I was the first to advocate an alliance with Canada. I forced the acquiring of the bases in the Atlantic Ocean.

A howler of such magnificent dimensions would hardly keep for long as private correspondence between men who differed about the state of public affairs as of the February following Pearl Harbor. President Roosevelt was not so busy that he let the war deter him. He sent his copy to General H. H. Arnold, chief of army air forces, with a set of questions to which he wanted official answers. Only a true adept at the inner politics of the period would know at once just why Roosevelt picked on Arnold. For the sake of unity in this narrative, explanation is withheld to the proper place. Among other things, Roosevelt wished to know whether McCormick or "Gatling Gun" Parker introduced the machine gun. Arnold reported that neither had, but that on March 11, 1863, General H. G. Wright recommended a manual type of machine gun. Credit for the automatic machine gun he assigned to John Browning and said the date of invention was approximately 1895. He misinformed the President badly on several counts, but the file was let out for public enjoyment and taken by those who already felt so inclined, anyhow, as proof McCormick at last had gone crazy.

General Arnold may be forgiven. He had other problems. But he certainly didn't come up with a reasonable statement of the facts about the great gun controversy, as anybody may discover who looks into Volume I of *The Machine Gun,* by Lieutenant Colonel G. M. Chinn, U.S. Marines, published in 1951 as an official survey by the Navy's Bureau of Ordnance. Of course, McCormick was incomparably absurd to say he introduced machine guns into the army, implying he discovered a weapon in principle before unknown. Multiple-firing guns date back to the fourteenth century. Long before that, the basic idea was applied with magazine-fed crossbows, slings filled with small stones and sets of spears fired from spring-loaded frames. But it is also true that for far too long after 1911 the Army's Ordnance Bureau refused to choose among many improved weapons. It stuck by the Benet-Mercier machine rifle, model 1909. Of this no more need be known than the excuse given by troops for failing to use it on Villa when he raided Columbus. He came by night and they could work the loading device only in daylight. Newspapers begged Villa to play fair, to be a sport, fight between dawn and dark. McCormick, who had seen what real machine guns could do, was not the man to be caught in any such trap. So, as his regiment struggled to mobilize, he put Charles Gates Dawes to raising money for a weapon he knew to be good. The First Illinois went off to Mexico armed with six of the best to be had in the world, a sort of machine gun Lieutenant Colonel Isaac N. Lewis, retired, had been trying to present to the United States without success.

For the rest of his life, McCormick used the case of the Lewis machine gun as his point of departure for savage and all too well-informed attacks on what he called the "professional military burocracy."

This much about the Lewis case is essential to any understanding of his attitude. Colonel Lewis graduated from West Point in 1884 and went into the Coast Artillery, which was, until airplanes put it out of business, the army's center of firepower. Lewis became recorder for the Board of Ordnance and Fortification and was sent to Europe to study changing weaponry. Then, he scandalized some of his fellow officers. In 1910, he quit the army and went to work for a gun company. In 1911 he made his first showing of a machine gun. By 1912, he had advanced it to the point that at College Park, Maryland, it was taken up in a biplane and fired successfully into a target on the ground. That made world news among the military, as Bernhardi's dissertation on the benefits in war made news elsewhere. By January, 1913, orders from England, France and Belgium were so huge Lewis's company let out manufacture on royalties. The only customer Lewis could not get was the United States army. McCormick said, in trying to extricate himself from the absurdities of the letter to Sawyer, that he first heard about the Lewis gun while in London. In fact, if he were in private and not put on the defensive, he tended to treat the Sawyer letter as if it were as funny to him as it was to people who hawked it around Chicago at one dollar per copy. He hadn't made any more of a fool of himself, at that, than anybody else in the whole encounter. After all, the Lewis gun did become an approved weapon for the United States army, but too late. Millions were under contract elsewhere. And as for Lewis, as fast as the War Department mailed royalty checks to him he sent them all back, to a final sum in excess of $1,000,000. It was, all around, just the sort of experience to set McCormick up in his own mind as obliged to keep an eye on the Ordnance Bureau and the weapons business, for life. Anybody who read the *Tribune*'s Sunday supplements over the years or kept up with McCormick's Saturday night radio performances, got the full benefit of his researches. If he missed anything on the history of killing machinery for land, sea or air, it was not for lack of industry. Even David Lilienthal, whom he had not before especially supported in public office, became a friend of sorts upon taking over the Atomic Energy Commission. McCormick wanted to investigate the latest thing in blowing up.

It is a pity the memoir on the Mexican campaign, so rich in delights, must be neglected for greater occasions. The First Illinois marched to San Antonio by train. Word was flashed that the Mexicans would attack shortly. Naturally, there was the customary ammunition shortage, so McCormick prepared for another Alamo. Sharpshooters were given all there was and the main body told to draw sabers for a last-man stand. The sun was terrible on the pale Illinois faces. For relief, men tried chalk, dirt, ladies' talcum. The

Mexicans must have been terrified by this war paint. Anyhow, they didn't show. As soon as it was clear there would be no war, McCormick took a house at Brownsville. Mrs. McCormick, even more at home on post than her husband, came down and ran things in high style. McCormick got in plenty of polo and sealed friendships that kept him briefed for life on the army's private politics. He became an intimate of Major General Frederick Funston, chief of the expedition, and thought it very democratic that Funston was cordial to Patterson. "After all," he would remind listeners as he recalled those campaign days, "Joe was only an enlisted man, you know."

There were other enlisted men who had worried about their civilian jobs. In December, 1915, Henry Ford set out for Europe on the charter ship *Oscar II,* in pursuit of his commitment that for the sake of peace he would sacrifice his fortune and his person. In his last interview before leaving, Ford's line was: "Tell the people to cry peace and fight preparedness." The *Tribune* had nothing against peace, but it was another thing for Ford to knock preparedness. In June, 1916, as the First Illinois was leaving Chicago, the *Tribune* published an interview with a Ford Company executive to the effect that any employe who answered the call to arms on the American border would lose his good job in Detroit. In the exchanges of abuse that followed, both Ford and the *Tribune* spent many thousands of dollars in legal fees. The word war lasted from 1916 through 1919. Ford's position was that he had suffered malice and unjust abuse, based on false witness. The *Tribune* took the high ground that it had acted from a patriotic concern and that the very foundations of the free press in a free republic were at stake.

So many thousands of words have been written about *Ford* vs. *Tribune* that little excuse remains for yet another doing it all over in detail just to display its period charms. The original interview appeared on June 22, 1916, under the heading, "Flivver Patriotism." This, of course, is a standard illustration of how to twist a supposedly straight news account for desired political effect. Quite sensibly, the *Tribune* was all for "preparedness," meaning a start toward mobilization. And it was not only popular, but utterly correct, in calling for a strong hand with Mexico, which was allowing itself to be used as the staging area for serious attacks on United States interests. Ford, with his cry for peace and one-way disarmament, was just the sort of butt the *Tribune* could use. To be sure, he was one of the most important of all advertisers and had great influence with others. He was loved and respected by *Tribune* readers as the farm boy who had gone to the city and made better than just good. His cry for peace was nowhere more than in the Middle West a cry of the public's heart. All of which, for the *Tribune,* made him that much more satisfactory as a target.

On the day after the "Flivver Patriotism" headline, the *Tribune* had an editorial: "Ford is an Anarchist." Years later, McCormick tried to make it appear that editorial was done by a staff writer without knowledge of higher authority. That would never wash. In the first place, no project of such importance as the prolonged assault on Ford would have been undertaken, let alone pursued, by underlings except on explicit orders. Second, "anarchist" was McCormick's own, personal hereditary hate-word. After all, had he not ridden with his cousin in their bicycle charge of 1887 against the pug dog, because its mistress had married the anarchist August Spies? Ford cured McCormick of being too loose with such language in print, but nobody ever cured him of using "anarchist" in verbal encounters. At the annual meeting of the Associated Press in 1942, when McCormick found himself back to the wall against government, fellow publishers, even against his associates on the AP board of governors, he was cornered by reporters for questioning about the suits being brought by the Department of Justice. He was polite enough until pressed by agents of one special publication, *PM,* financed by his Chicago competitor, Marshall Field. McCormick rose from his window seat, his face scarlet with rage. And as he stalked away, he shouted: "Communist." Then he turned and gave them the worst he could think of: "Anarchists! Anarchists!" There spoke the heart of old Chicago, frightened, confused and outraged by the Haymarket Riot of 1886.

The *Tribune* attack on Ford was as total as anything it had done to Cyrus McCormick in the Civil War or that it was yet to say against Franklin D. Roosevelt after 1941. It thought Ford should move his factory to Mexico. The crucial line in the editorial read: "If Ford allows this rule of his shop to stand, he will reveal himself not merely as an ignorant idealist but as an anarchistic enemy of the nation which protects him in his wealth." Ford sued, charging libel. The case finally was heard in Mt. Clemens, Michigan, in May of 1919. Who won? The jury found the *Tribune* guilty, but it awarded Ford six cents in damages. McCormick chose, in his memoirs, to claim the bill was twelve cents, but no other authority has ever said so. On the witness stand, Ford suffered humiliations that left him emotionally crippled for the rest of his life. Under oath, he had guessed that Benedict Arnold was a writer. He had defined a mobilized army as a large army, mobilized. He had been ruined. He had done it to himself. And was it really true the Ford Company bullied employes who answered the President's call to the colors? Nobody ever denied a company officer told the *Tribune* that men who quit would not be rehired. In the trial, the company introduced records to show that of seventy-eight men who left, most got better jobs on their return. Would they have, except for the *Tribune?* Allan Nevins and Frank Ernest Hill, in their three-volume authorized biography of Ford, skirt this point, but they do offer something else unique in any record of McCormick's performance as a public man. It is a letter, dated July 30, 1941, on which day McCormick was sixty-one years old and Ford seventy-eight:

> Dear Mr. Ford:
>
> It occurs to me on this, our birthday, to write and say I regret the editorial we published about you so many years ago. I only wonder why the idea never occurred to me before.
>
> It was the product of the war psychology which is bringing out so many similar expressions today.
>
> I am not planning to publish this myself, but you are perfectly welcome to use it in any way you wish.
>
> Yours sincerely,
> *Robert R. McCormick*

What Ford made of it Nevins and Hill do not say. There is nothing to indicate he even read it. Until the biographers made it public in 1957 there was no public evidence anywhere that McCormick had ever apologized to anybody for anything. But it is plain that in 1941, when he and Ford alike were again objects of even worse accusations than the *Tribune* had made so long ago, McCormick's mind was measuring everything in terms of 1916.

Things had come to pass between 1916 and 1941 that neither Ford nor McCormick, in their wildest flights of fancy, could have imagined. Government had become master of all. It had taught Ford to bargain with his employes not at his own pleasure and in a spirit of munificence, but with all the care he used for encounters with bankers and competing manufacturers. And government had taught McCormick that no matter how many times his telephone operators warned all callers that so and so many days remained to save the Republic, the *Tribune* could not win any struggle for power all that simply.

Ford and McCormick, in 1941, were being dragged in the wake of something they had no idea how to define. Some thought it a glory. Some thought it a disaster. All spoke of it, one way or another, as a revolution. So it was, a revolution by common men.

But nobody had seen anything yet, not Ford, not McCormick, nor the common men, either. In 1916, if not in 1941, there was a valor of ignorance abroad in the land that is the ignorant valor of the bull on its first charge through the gates.

In 1941, it was a dreadful thing to recall, to be sure.

CHAPTER ELEVEN ★★★ Understanding of a human creature does not always yield readily to its direct pursuit through time under the literary canon of the Railway Users' Guide. McCormick's performance in the great war of 1914–18 is incomprehensible as a linear account. He was journalist, soldier and political operative, sometimes in just one of these roles, most of the time in two, and for a while, in three at once. For the rest of his life he studied his own experience and the evidence that floated to the surface, generally, on men and nations. He formed some very hard judgments and he developed great skill at using his knowledge of facts, which was formidable.

His reflections and conclusions led him to one posture—a determination to frustrate the great change of direction in American life that followed the Presidential election of 1932. The common estimate is that the New Deal rolled McCormick under. Certainly, if one looks at the laws on the books and the state of society as it was when McCormick died in 1955 little enough can be found that he would claim for his own. But that is a simplistic test. What was he worth as a nay-sayer?

How effective he was at inhibiting the drive in Franklin D. Roosevelt's governing style is less a matter of concrete demonstrations and more an inference. But Mr. Roosevelt and his associates used up a vast amount of energy defending themselves against McCormick's concentrations that might otherwise have gone into carrying the country faster and in more ways toward their formal aims. Somehow, for all their scoffing and ridicule of his personal idiosyncrasies, McCormick still managed to ruffle the principal men in Mr. Roosevelt's organization with accusations that whatever they were up to at any moment was "repeating the mistakes of the past." The American role in the great war of 1914–18 became one of his very sharpest weapons at this and any who thought him short in power at its use soon suffered. Many a critic, before the event, liked to suppose McCormick an unfeeling monolith of reaction; that only the accident of birth had loaded him with money and journalistic machinery which ran in spite of his meddling with it; that his confusions about the age in which he lived were filtered through "the finest mind of the thirteenth century," and that he was an all-around abomination.

Entirely aside from its tactical deficiencies, this estimate made about as much sense as McCormick's own view, and he went to his grave still arguing with himself, and with the world, that his life had been a paragon of reason, logic and revealed wisdom.

McCormick had an intellectual heritage from Joseph Medill and from the totality of Middle Western life, amended by his cosmopolitan education and his tireless personal investigations abroad, so that it can hardly be argued he was ignorant of the news that the United States exists in a world and is not free of it. But, like everybody else, McCormick had elements in his being not of the intellect. If he ever made any serious, disciplined effort to liberate himself from these, available evidence does not so show. It is fair to suppose that, like almost anybody else, he would have been paralyzed with shock at first confrontation with those nameless powers that so often drove him to frenzies of the spirit.

McCormick's performance in the great war, and his reaction to it, were certainly no less affected than any other man's by feeling as well as thought. To demonstrate this, it is necessary to abandon the Railway Users' Guide that would just march him through the days, and instead pin him on a sort of mental shuttle that roves where it must to relate men, time and occasions to McCormick as he was caught up in one of the great human dramas of all time.

The path of the shuttle is eccentric. It is manipulated to one purpose only, discovery of moments and aspects that bore on McCormick. In some episodes he was personally present. Others, he studied until he had become as much involved as the true principals. All are described either to show how they actually appeared to McCormick or to indicate how he denied their appearance. Either way, they were powerful governors on him in his confrontation with the new day in the United States after 1932.

McCormick's true entanglement in the great war did not really begin with the Russian adventure, or even with the Mexican border campaign. The real entanglement came in Washington, where in 1916 a complicated politico-diplomatic struggle was under way, here reduced to the relation among Woodrow Wilson, Theodore Roosevelt, Cecil Spring-Rice and the German ambassador, Count Johann von Bernstorff. None was an amateur at his trade. Each had a most difficult part to play. Spring-Rice, as usual, arrived in Washington at the critical hour, 1913. He was by no means intimate with Wilson's set, but he had incomparable resources of another sort. Theodore Roosevelt counted him near to a brother. Henry Adams dealt with him almost as if he were a son. Henry Cabot Lodge loathed British public policy but he loved Cecil Spring-Rice as a man. With such an intelligence organization at his command, Spring-Rice had little need to fear William Jennings Bryan's goings-on at the State Department. Nor did he. These were no worse against his purposes than the performance of the United States ambassador in London, Walter Hines Page, so wildly committed to the notion of saving Canterbury Cathedral from the Hun that Woodrow Wilson called him "almost an Englishman" and dismissed his dispatches as worthless. Spring-Rice thought the old saying true, that one can defend himself against enemies, but heaven help us all against friends. He had been studying the United States since the days of that monstrous blunder by Baron Sackville of Knole, and he had no intention of being trapped into another such thing anytime at all, let alone in this most dangerous of moments.

There is no finer concise analysis of the American period, 1913 to 1918, than the letters and dispatches of Cecil Spring-Rice. He had extraordinary sources of technical information about all the main personalities, and he made superb use of his material. But all that would have been useless, except that he had the wisdom, the patience and the iron will to make no sudden, public motions. He knew what he was after and he knew how to get it and he knew, too, how easily it could all be lost. It should be confessed at once that he won, totally, finally and everything. He swept the board. But the pressure was deathly. In January, 1918, as he was just opening a delicate negotiation with Mr. Justice Brandeis of the Supreme Court to appease Zionist animosities toward British policy, Spring-Rice was summarily let out. His successor was the Marquis of Reading, a close crony of David Lloyd George, who was by then dominant in London and making plans toward a world settlement. Within weeks, Spring-Rice was dead. Henry Cabot Lodge thought that dismissal had destroyed his will to live. Lodge is usually presented in popular history as incapable of any human feeling common as grief, but of Spring-Rice he said:

"To me, he is an unspeakable loss. He was an intimate friend for more than thirty years. . . . Very few days passed that he was not at my house late in the afternoon to talk things over and I think he found it a comfort to be with someone to whom he could open his heart without reserve. I miss him more than words can say."

Lord Robert Cecil made a memorial speech in the House of Commons saying Spring-Rice had done a good job. A plate with his name was stuck up in the chapel at Eton, and Balliol College raised a $75,000 fund, putting the income over first to his widow and children, and later to educate diplomats. But never did one politician in London acknowledge any responsibility for the anguish Spring-Rice suffered in his years of struggle to prevent a disastrous error in coping with Woodrow Wilson. In 1916, the London cry was that Spring-Rice had "lost his grip," that he was "too American," that he made excuses for Wilson the American ambassador in London would not. He was thought blind to the urgent need for action. But London could not see, either, how Mr. Wilson searched every day for some excuse to duck further away from the war as Theodore Roosevelt, by 1916, was defining it. Roosevelt's beginning attitude might well have alarmed Spring-Rice, if he had not been both acutely sensitive to the nature of the man and free to talk in terms of closest intimacy. It was on the public record that T. R. professed great personal esteem for Wilhelm II. And when the Germans crashed the Belgian border, Roosevelt analyzed the action as a necessity of the German national purpose. His language all but echoed the very words of Chancellor Theobald von Bethmann-Hollweg. But a Spring-Rice could read this as having no special Germanic commitment. T. R. was the man who acted in 1903 in the interest of total human progress and left Congress "not to debate the canal but to debate me."

Getting him settled down and aimed in the right direction must have been another of those games of "grandmother's steps," two forward and one back, at which Spring-Rice was a born master, but any conclusions again must rest less on documentation and more on inference. T. R. had no illusions about Germany's general view of war as an instrument of national policy. As early as 1911, he put an estimate to Sir George Otto Trevelyan, that "Germany has the arrogance of a very strong power" without "that feeble aspiration toward international equity which one or two other strong powers, notably England and America, do at least begin to feel."

There have been some very handsome quarrels among analysts trying to prove a trend underlying Roosevelt's instant Vesuvius of speeches, letters to newspapers and yet more letters to eminent personages in the years just before and at the opening of the war. It is all a waste of time. The significant fact is that Cecil Spring-Rice was as welcome in Roosevelt's house as any member of the family and made the fullest use of his privileged status. Bernstorff had no such advantage. At Harvard, there was Hugo Münsterberg, a world-renowned authority on psychology and another of Roosevelt's "old friends." Münsterberg sought to defend German policy among academicians and intellectuals. And Roosevelt had some sort of peculiar literary relation with George Sylvester Viereck, whose performance as a German propagandist in both great wars seemed to infuriate more Americans than that of any other. But the professor, though he did not lose T. R.'s personal affection, found the going soon turned hard. Viereck wound up in an exchange of published recriminations which are as much a handbook for propagandists on how-not-to-do-it as they are a spectacle of T. R. Roosevelt losing his dignity.

The net effect of all the pulling and hauling comes down to the Presidential campaign of 1916. Wilson's line was that he had heard the country's prayer and had no apologies to make for keeping out of war. The Republicans were, officially, in a sort of confused straddle, much as they would be again after 1939. Mr. Justice Charles Evans Hughes had come off the Supreme Court and was offered as the candidate. His campaign line was timorous. The best he had to offer was that Wilson had flunked on "preparedness." In so totally mercantile and civilian a society as the United States of 1916, that lacked the necessary bite. But nobody could say of Theodore Roosevelt in 1916 that he suffered any such lack. All Spring-Rice had to do was remember the case of Sackville-West and keep his own head down from the line of fire. Wilson went up to New Jersey for a little rest at his summer White House, Shadow Lawn. Roosevelt rattled the windows with:

> There should be shadows now at Shadow Lawn; the shadows of the men, women and children who have risen from the ooze of the ocean bottom and from graves in foreign lands; the shadows of the helpless whom Mr. Wilson did not dare protect lest he might have to face the danger; the shadows of babies gasping pitifully as they sank beneath the waves; the shadows of women outraged and slain by bandits. . . .

Not even a man of utmost phlegm can be expected to ignore that as mere campaign oratory. And no President was ever more sensitive to slights upon his manhood than Woodrow Wilson. He had no gratitude that in the end Theodore Roosevelt, by roundabout, carried the election for him again in 1916 as he had before in 1912. Mr. Hughes was equivocal on more than one count, and Roosevelt's impassioned followers trusted him not at all. In California he neglected proper obeisances to Governor Hiram Johnson, who let no man forget that in 1912 he had been Theodore Roosevelt's running mate. Hughes went to bed on election night thinking himself the next President of the United States. He awoke to find Johnson's handful in California had done him down.

In such a melee, von Bernstorff, for all his many charms, was hopelessly outclassed. Like Spring-Rice, he was a gentleman of high cultivation and he, too, was accused at home as "pro-American." It has never yet been settled just how duplicitous Bernstorff was in his official role. Was he a dupe of his own government or was he a knowing party to the many undeniable offenses of its secret agents against the United States? In any case, Washington was split from the start between fashionables who thought him suitable at a neutral's dinner table, and fashionables who denounced anybody so much as polite to him. Bernstorff had been in Washington since 1908. He was on friendly terms with McCormick's mother and aunt, especially so with the footloose Patterson daughter. In consequence, whenever the *Tribune* had a word to say for the German side in the propaganda war, as it did following the sinking of the *Lusitania,* credit was given to Bernstorff as expert gallant. Whatever chance he might ever have had to be effective with Wilson, and it never was much, his own government ruined him. Once the election of 1916 was over, the Germans published that now they would sink any enemy ship on sight, no matter who or what was on board. Merchantmen were all armed, anyhow. The argument ran that nobody ever expected soldiers at Waterloo or Gettysburg to back off in the crisis if some witless milkmaid blundered between them with the cows. Women and children had no business on a sea embattled, and no man could justify letting them on it. All of which, of course, was the purest Bernhardi brand of logic, and made beautiful sense—to those who already had taken it in. The United States was told that it might send one ship a week of its own to England, under strict watch.

To say the least, the Germans had not estimated what it meant for the mightiest ex-President alive to have used toward the sitting President, one of the thinnest-skinned men alive, such words as "logothete," "sophist," "hypocrite," and to have said that Wilson stood for "the peace of cowardice and dishonor and indifference to the welfare of others." Now, after the election, he went further. On February 28, 1917, Roosevelt wrote Lodge this estimate of Wilson:

> He is so purely a demagogue that if the people were really roused and resolute as they were in '98, he would give them leadership in the direction they demanded tho [Roosevelt, too, was an "improved" speller] to do so stirred with fear his cold and timid heart. But his extreme adroitness in appealing to all that is basest in the hearts of our people has made him able for the time being to drug the soul of the nation into a coma. He is responsible for Germany's brutal wrong-doing to us; he is responsible for the very peace party which he brings forward as an excuse when told that he ought to act boldly.

That is rougher on Wilson than the *Tribune* was and may even match McCormick all-out on the subject of Franklin D. Roosevelt. The reader of Ickes' *Secret Diary* or brochures put out by the Union For Democratic Action after 1939 would also find sentiments on McCormick in near to identical words. Historical knowledge is rich in evidence that T. R. regularly left Wilson in a true hysteria of rage. The same happened with McCormick in the second great debate on foreign policy, as far as his personal emotions were concerned. But nothing changed him in action. Every attack only bound McCormick tighter to the wheel, holding a course he had set many years before. For whatever reason, that is not so of Wilson. On April 6, 1917, there was war. Wilson asked it.

McCormick got into the action immediately with a letter directly to General Pershing and was as directly accepted, which is an interesting little signal that Pershing, the iron soldier beyond guile, still hid somewhere within a faculty for maneuvering among civilians of influence. And it is worth recalling exactly here that George Catlett Marshall, Pershing's favorite among the younger performers in the first great war, did not neglect McCormick either, in the years of his own campaign to achieve final eminence.

McCormick went into service on June 13, 1917, a major in the First Cavalry, Illinois National Guard. He came out on December 31, 1918, a colonel of field artillery in the war army. In 1920, he published a view of the whole under the title, *The Army of 1918*. But for the rest of his life he was busy shaping and reshaping versions of both the general public experience and his own personal role. His last, frantic stab came in his memoir broadcasts of 1952–55.

A great deal about McCormick is uncovered by comparing his early version with the final revision.

He opened up in 1920 with one of those grandiloquent pronouncements that are the occupational hazard of the journalist attempting history. An editor does not use white space as a site for investigations, but as a platform from which to announce discoveries. He does not exhibit his evidence. He describes its effect on him. The public, which has paid money for the honor of watching him lucubrate, is supposed to go away impressed. McCormick, as historian, ran more toward essays than exhumations, though his two technical studies on the Civil War show how he could organize evidence if he had a mind to. And so does *The Army of 1918,* in part.

His first paragraph was a finding that in January of 1917 Germany risked war on the theory the United States was more dangerous as a neutral than as a belligerent, because our neutrality hindered full use of the submarines. If these could be unleashed with success, Germany had nothing else to fear from us. This bit of advanced mindreading might not satisfy every historical investigator, but few would resist McCormick's next, that the American performance on the Mexican border in 1916 was so awful any German could be excused for holding after 1918 that it had been a deliberate maneuver to deceive him. McCormick might also have added that if the Germans laughed at Wilson's claim that the United States was out to make the world safe for democracy, they were listening to the wrong part of his war message. There were also several points about force to the uttermost, force without stint. But it was no part of McCormick's purpose then or later to draw any attention to Wilson as a dangerous man in action. Instead, he turned immediately to a concise review of American historical military policy, his view of what it should be and a summation of all the belligerent powers' policies, achievements and failures.

Aspects out of date are surprisingly few and of no real importance to the main thoughts. And these, allowing for his partisan urge to get in licks against Wilson, are remarkably broad-gauged efforts to distinguish between patriotic pride in the United States' pursuit of force to the uttermost and the true means by which the war had been won. McCormick gave the palm to the French. They had not only provided the major intellectual resources for the fighting system, but their civil government had shown qualities the United States would do well to seek within itself. This was hardly the authorized view of the Compleat Chauvinist, but it ought not to be dismissed summarily as just another of his swipes at Wilson. McCormick certainly had a determined weakness for mixing up political arguments in any sort of analysis, to a degree that almost anybody could miss any other point in what he was trying to say. But a crosscheck between his 1920 exposition on the issue of universal military service and how he saw the same subject a quarter-century later sets out plain evidence that the McCormick who wrote *The Army of 1918* and the McCormick who, in December of 1954, with death just around the corner, thought it necessary to broadcast a series of polemics entitled "How The Roosevelts Cashed In" had some problems with each other.

The early reaction of the American people to discovery of themselves in the great war was hardly anything to terrify the battle-hardened Germans. The sinking of the *Lusitania* in 1915 is taken by most military historians as the provocation which led Congress to pass the National Defense Act of 1916, Wilson's weapon against the Republican charge of "unpreparedness." It was a sort of general outline for increasing the standing force of both Regulars and National Guard, forming a reserve officer corps and establishing officer training systems in colleges. It also sketched out some general principles for building a military supply system. There it stopped. Men were supposed to rush to the colors by invitation only. But they hadn't, and the declaration of war really changed nothing at all in this civilian hesitation to take the plunge.

Immediately after the war declaration an Allied high commission, with Marshal Joffre as its most impressive member, arrived in Washington. In secret meetings with members of Congress, Joffre gave a shocking account of conditions in France. He also criticized American weapons, training and attitude, and made an emphatic appeal for immediate compulsory service. In his 1920 book, McCormick praised Joffre as "the inspired ambassador," whose simple manners, venerable appearance and straightforward handling of facts touched the soul of the nation and made him, of all strangers who ever came here, the one of greatest influence on our destiny. Joffre spoke no English. His American aide edited out his opinion on the American military in the official translation of his first public speech but "hearers who understood French" supplied the missing parts to the press. It was only then the country came alert to its peril. The draft law was enacted on May 18, and by June 5, 1917, a million men were enrolled. Pershing got to Paris on June 13, exactly the day McCormick was sworn into the war army, and it was on Pershing's staff in Paris that McCormick went deep into the secret politics of the war. In his 1920 book he only hints at roles which, in his memoirs, he described in another of those narrative flights at which he had, for all his mumbling style of speech and his deviations into political savagery, almost a bazaar taleteller's pleasant smoothness.

But the main burden of the 1920 book is its analysis of how military power should be worked into the structure of American life. It is McCormick's revision of this from the very moment it became probable the United States would fight in Europe again that demonstrates his war with himself.

In 1920, he described the Draft Act as the outstanding legislative achievement of the war period. Prior to it, he held, the American outlook was dominated by weak national feeling and centrifugal propaganda, but the Draft Act had asserted the supremacy of the nation over all its citizens "to an extent that even our federalist and unionist ancestors had not attempted." He defined the Draft Act as one of the great milestones in our national evolution, and expected historians of the future to class it with the drawing up of the Constitution and the preservation of the Union in 1861–65. Every young American was now liable to fight for his country. Therefore, every parent would pay attention to the Government's behavior and nurture cultivation of the nation in arms. But he was already sensitive to the thought of power in the hands of men beyond ordinary reach.

McCormick thought the general staff a constant, profound menace to civil liberties. He saw it offering a hiding place for men afraid to fight; a bureaucracy gorged on authority and dictating to superior men which ones could enter the army; where they should serve; what industries should be commanded into military production; who should travel; who should be imprisoned. Worst of all, "as proposed by President Wilson," it would surely get around to gagging the press.

The main disposition of the general staff, which he said the Germans developed and the staffs of every Allied country showed tendencies to emulate, was nothing less than the assumption in wartime of an irresponsible government holding powers of tyranny "it has taken generations to drive out of our civil system."

McCormick's solution was the nation in arms. Men required to do military service when they are young lose their awe and fear in the presence of the career professionals. Once the nation had an engrained understanding of military necessities, assumptions of undue power would be put down. Citizen-soldiers would never again turn power over, blindly, to men as little known to the nation as the nation was known to them and knowledge of war too little known to either. That was McCormick on military posture for the Republic as he saw it in 1920.

A quarter of a century later, he approached the identical problem, and if one chose to read it so, he could be said to hold the same concept of society, that the citizens, to master the government, must array themselves so as to block off the cabals of careerists who try to keep secret a special key to power.

On February 8, 1947, McCormick broadcast his interpretation of how the manpower of the United States was brought under military authority for the two great wars, or the great war of 1914–18 resumed in 1939. This time he was not so magnanimous toward Joffre. Nor did he talk about "universal military training" or "drafts," but reached back to joggle the nation's sensibilities with an old fear-word of politics descended from Colonial days:

> . . . Congress and the courts parted from the word and spirit of the Constitution in permitting national conscription. Conscription came about in World War I from the almost total lack of volunteering and from the advice of Marshal Joffre of France, who, at that time, enjoyed enormous influence in the United States.
>
> Conscription for World War II was invoked in time of peace [1940] under the leadership of the Harvard Club of New York, many of whose members have prospered greatly from it. . . .
>
> I am very strongly of the opinion that our military policy should be returned to the form provided in the Constitution and that, in order to prevent any coup d'etat by some overambitious President, admiral, or general, such as General Hooker, the troops belonging to the states must far outnumber those under command of the central authority.

The whole case of General Hooker offered McCormick an excellent excuse to elaborate on the risks inherent in the citizen's relation to government. It also suggests the need to keep a cool head in considering these, not to say, also, in acting on them. Hooker was one of the great blabbermouths of the Civil War. He was a moderately good field soldier in his grade, as brigadier general, but success led him to give out a great deal of loud talk against his immediate commander, Burnside, and to describe the country's need of a dictator. Burnside challenged Lincoln to relieve a whole list of insubordinate officers, with Hooker's name at the top of the list, or to relieve himself. Lincoln let out Burnside and gave Hooker his job, with a letter it would have been interesting to hear McCormick read in 1947:

". . . I have heard, in such a way as to believe it, of your recently saying both the Army and the Government needed a Dictator. Of course it was not *for* this but in spite of it, that I have given you the command. Only those generals who gain successes, can set up dictators. What I now ask of you is military success, and I will risk the dictatorship. . . . A. Lincoln."

Unfortunately for his ambitions, General Hooker neglected the first requirement of dictatorship: he didn't win. And even McCormick would have been hard put, if he had ever risked a debate on the subject, to refute the evidence that the real dictator in American Presidential history—unmatched, yet—is A. Lincoln of Illinois. No amount of legendary festooning conceals this reality. Nor, it may be added, has any significant grievance lingered, either in public sentiment or in historical scholarship. By and large, the American position is that the republic was shot with luck to have Lincoln available.

No great amount of political insight is required to see that McCormick was using the case of General Hooker exactly 180 degrees opposite to its evident character. If his 1947 attitude on the power of the central government, also 180 degrees opposite to his attitude on the same subject in 1920, had been in effect in Lincoln's day, McCormick would have been living, if at all, in a very different role. So would everybody else.

But was he deliberately faking? Many a critic was always very sure of it, when McCormick entangled himself in such ruinous self-contradictions. It made the case easy and evident to say that he knew the truth but was so arrogant and self-centered he thought the general public would swallow anything at all, thrust at it with confidence. Against this, some evidence of McCormick's difficulty in understanding himself is worth considering.

When he came to Washington, in his later years, he stayed with his cousin, Mrs. Patterson, as long as she was alive. He was a welcome guest, to be sure, and she took pains to see that he got every attention to his customary routine. But she also learned to remove from his bedroom anything of importance to her that might break or be spoiled with stains or general abuse. In the dark hours, the terror could overtake him so that McCormick's shouts and battles with his demon would echo through the whole house. The next morning servants would find there was nothing to do but strip down and re-assemble the room. As for McCormick, his morning policy was to ignore the whole thing, never apologize and certainly never explain. His tips to the staff, on departure, were more than generous, so it was all taken as a matter of course by everybody. Mrs. Patterson, herself, was both discreet and sympathetic in saying it was "Bertie's affliction," something he could not help and, therefore, something for which he must never be embarrassed. Nor was he.

In his conscious behavior, McCormick fought the terrible battle another way. He could, and many a time did, set the *Tribune* to personal abuse of men with whom he differed on public policies. Wilson, Thompson, Ickes and F. D. Roosevelt were savaged without mercy. It is only fair to the record to say that with the possible exception of Wilson, who could make anybody furious by the devices of the professor handling a roomful of ignorant sophomores, this abuse of person was a reciprocal action. Nor is it as easy as it ought to be, to say McCormick threw the first stone—or that he didn't. But as to McCormick's behavior in such savaging, the record is as plain as it is full. He could let himself go only if he could stay out of human encounter. He dared not risk much of his will against any man with whom he continued to break bread, or even exchange conversation. Examples of this will be given, in due course, both ways; his violent resistances to the temptation to meet, and his loss of control on meeting. His need to hate and loathe, in conflict with his shame for such conduct, if it may be summed up so, made a curious and understandably confusing spectacle to those who had little opportunity to observe his torments.

And so, for all the violent language that burst through against individuals, once he had steeled his resolve, the main force of his invective, like much else in his life, was de-personalized and abstracted so that he could really let himself go best against supernatural malignancies by denouncing "burocracy." He was against it, whatever it was, but he was confused, and confusing, on details, so that the consistency of his internal feeling could lead him into disastrous contradictions in public performance. Few Americans of his time knew the details of national and political history of the Civil War period better than McCormick. His 1920 dissertation illustrates his ability, in a proper state of feeling, to appraise realistic national needs. But his goings-on in 1947 illustrate equally well how life experiences could also drive him into a corner.

In 1947, the *Tribune* celebrated its "first hundred years of existence," with a performance treated by McCormick as a sort of combined July 4 and Bastille Day. There were pageants, speeches, and great exhumations of evidence to show that Abraham Lincoln and Joseph Medill had saved the Union; that the *Tribune* had recorded the life of Chicago with total fidelity; that its virtue had been rewarded with prosperity and triumphs all the more demonstrated by the failures of lesser journals; and some thirty-two columns of reading matter were devoted to the efforts of mayors, governors, Presidents and endless combinations of "burocrats" who had tried mightily, and failed, to dent Chicago's trust and confidence in its protector. As far as it went, it was a remarkably accurate, as it was lively, exercise in journalistic history. But Joseph Medill was something of a problem.

Toward the end of his life, Medill was sought out regularly for interviews on the forming of the Republican party and his encounters with the great figures of American history among whom he had moved. In its hundred-year memorial edition, the *Tribune,* of course, had to do something about all this, and so it met the problem with all its usual skill and aplomb. For two columns it laid on heavily concerning Medill's meetings with Horace Greeley, the breakup of the Whigs, the Free Soilers, and arguments between the new men as to what their movement should be called. It quoted various authorities to show Medill's right to honors as one of the handful, if not in fact the very first among equals, who put the party of Lincoln into effective political action. Buried well down in the text was a concession to external, established record. Salmon P. Chase, who became Lincoln's Secretary of the Treasury and later Chief Justice of the United States, never managed to stabilize his partisan identity. In 1854, Chase attended a meeting at the office of the Cleveland, Ohio, *Leader,* of which Medill was then editor. The new men were hammering out their doctrine with its capstone, "slavery is sectional; liberty is national." Medill stood for the party title "National Republican." Chase wanted "Free Democracy."

Medill said Chase never really accepted the idea any more than he did the name, grumbled for years and finally went back to the Democratic Party, to which in spirit he belonged all the time. Medill said Chase "admired the form of the loose Greek federation rather than that of the firm and compact Roman republic. And that, I think, has been the real basis of every defection from the Republican Party—not the tariff or any such issue, but the question of the relative rights and powers of the states. It was the name [National Republican] which drew the party together, and when that name is gone there won't be much to hold the party together."

In 1947, McCormick was using the *Tribune* as Julius Caesar had once used the *bucina,* the great brass Roman horn of war, both to rally the troops and scare the barbarians. But what he had to tell those who would listen was hardly what his grandfather had thought in 1854. It did not square with McCormick himself as of 1920. The McCormick of 1947 held that liberty is sectional and slavery is national. On being asked how he thought Medill's comment fitted with what the Republican Party should be doing in 1947, he was abrupt. "Medill was a man of his time." Not then or ever did he attempt any formal explanation of the particulars he expected from his own philosophy. Nor did he attempt to reconcile Medill's axiom with his own.

The main body of the 1920 book is less useful at illuminating McCormick in action than the memoirs, through which he described details of his career in France that are nowhere else available. But it at least shows he felt for the French, as he did for the Russians, strong ties of personal affection and sentiment. He was unsparing in his tributes to the toughness and competency of the individual French soldier, as he was in his assay of the fashion in which the civil government had survived military invasion and grave ruptures within its policy-making agencies. Yet, in 1947, when he spoke of the United States Government in Washington as a "german silver court," toadying to a President mad for monarchic absolute power, McCormick thought the total collapse of French civilization, too, was very near. He laid the ruin of France, as he predicted the ruin of the United States, to the working of what he called "a narrow, grafting burocracy." The uses of this in peace he thought worse than anything he had seen in war. And he had, indeed, enjoyed an exceptionally good look at the inside workings of the French system during the First World War, as a member of Pershing's staff. He set out in high style, having already seen more of the war than Pershing, and sure of a warm welcome within the center of power in a country he had known from childhood. Like a monarch of old, he took his wife along. Pershing's own war diary lists Major and Mrs. Robert R. McCormick among dinner guests on an evening of negotiation between the commander of the American Expeditionary

Force and high dignitaries of Mr. Wilson's civil authority. Very few majors, indeed, have ever been let in on such transactions. And, too, a knowledgeable reader of Pershing's two-volume memoir, *My Experiences in the World War,* can spot more than one aspect of great affairs brought to his attention by McCormick, whose business it was to find out what was really happening among the French.

At that sort of thing, McCormick moved in his natural element. He and Mrs. McCormick traveled as honored guests of the French Line. It was the general manager of the line himself who rustled up the morphine pills for McCormick to sew in his coat against the chance of being left to die on some abandoned field. McCormick also tricked himself out with a monocle and stick, but evidently this was a little more than he could endure with entire comfort.

In his memoirs, he tried to handle the stories. His eye trouble dated from childhood. Spectacles were a nuisance. British and German officers wore monocles. Many Frenchmen even carried *lorgnons.* And of course it was true that English officers did sometimes walk the parapets, glass in eye and stick under arm, to demonstrate that a gentleman-at-arms dares to die first. Brigadier General Douglas MacArthur of the 42nd Rainbow Division was a spectacular performer at this art, for the education of Americans fresh on the line. McCormick once had a chance to make off with a gas mask borrowed from MacArthur and regretted ever after that he didn't. In any case, as he told it later, he carried a stick himself only because he had a bad football knee, something not previously noted in his annals.

Among the many other assets McCormick already had going when he reached Paris was an overseas edition of the *Tribune.* The staff was a wild and roaring outfit, headed by Floyd Gibbons, whose eyepatch and breathless writing style were the delight of *Tribune* readers for years. During the war McCormick had the paper concentrate, of course, on discovering warrior sons of the Middle West to one another. After the war, he directed the staff to leave the affairs of "lobster palace Americans" to the Paris edition of the New York *Herald-Tribune* and stick to the same formula, as adapted to the tourist trade. Unfortunately, civilians from Kankakee, Lima and Burlington did not much care for reading about one another in the shadow of the Louvre so the staff, since it was forbid to elevate New Yorkers, tried for sophisticates by reporting on the literary adventurists who made Paris in the 1920's their world headquarters. In 1934, McCormick surrendered the field. Modern cultural historians of the period, however, read the microfilms of back files on the Paris edition—when they can find any—with unrestrained fascination. McCormick never spelled out the details of how he used the Paris *Tribune* during the war as part of his work force for keeping Pershing briefed, and more's the pity. In fact, the Paris edition was in more ways than one a very important weapon and before it was done, had a part in the *Tribune*'s most significant journalistic feat in all its years.

The intrigues began at once. No sooner had Major and Mrs. McCormick set up their house than they were captured for dinner. An English officer, no doubt well briefed on McCormick's family and personal career, warned that he should be careful of the French and proposed that McCormick advise Pershing to put American forces under British command. McCormick told it in 1953 that he did not accept the suggestion as quietly as he might have, but was apprehensive about what he should do. Majors do not ordinarily tell commanding generals they come as chosen instruments for conveying highest policy suggestions from foreign powers, no matter how important such a major might be if he were still a civilian. Still, there was duty. He got up his nerve and reported. Pershing turned fiery red, but said: "You acted exactly right, McCormick, as I would have expected you to do." After that it was all downhill.

Among the French, McCormick's lines were deep, not only on account of connections with elders from his father's time but also among his own contemporaries. There were, for example, the brothers De Chambrun, whose descent from the Marquis de La Fayette qualified them to claim dual status as citizens of the United States and the Republic of France alike. One brother, Pierre, had been counselor to the French embassy in Washington and while on that duty, married a daughter of Bellamy Storer, an amateur diplomat from Cincinnati, into whose unfortunate wrangles with T. R. Roosevelt McCormick's mother had meddled, to her sorrow. In 1917, Pierre de Chambrun was a Deputy of France with more than an ordinary sophistication about the politics of two continents. His brother, Aldebert, had married Miss Clara Longworth of Cincinnati, who was not only a cousin of Miss Storer, but sister to Nicholas Longworth, Theodore Roosevelt's son-in-law. Aldebert de

Chambrun was a major on the French general staff, assigned to help the Americans find their way around Paris. And all of them together, wives, husbands, sisters, brothers, cousins and in-laws alike, were McCormick's friends of long standing.

Pershing had hard enough going. On the one hand, the British and French tugged at him separately to come under their own commands, and jointly bucked his efforts to set up as an equal, independent war lord. The French would not even let him have a copy of their battle dispositions. McCormick found out where the map was kept and organized a fight in the hall outside. The guardian ran out to see what was happening and McCormick ran in, a maneuver that suggests he had not been blind to the devices of city-room journalism. He brought home the goods, too, and once the war was over, hung the original sketches and notes on his office wall.

In that crisis spring of 1917, as the French army came near to total collapse, there broke out a complicated plot among high authorities in the civil government to reach the Germans by way of the Vatican and make a separate peace. McCormick learned of this, he said, not only through his French connections but also from the head of the British Secret Service in France, Lord Esher. He filed a full report to headquarters, as he had also done on his knowledge of prewar trading between the powers for shares in the Turkish Empire, following up in Paris leads from his 1915 trip.

He professed, in his memoirs, to be surprised that Wilson, when he got to Paris in 1919 to settle up the world's affairs, said he had never heard of such things. McCormick did not specify whether he thought the President an ignoramus, a liar, both or even a statesman trying to stay out of traps. In any case, general histories have amplified both matters considerably, though none has thrown much light on the workings of agents at McCormick's level in the inter-Allied combinations.

Another case that fascinated him was that of Mata Hari, which he also reported to Pershing. She is generally presented as a German agent who drove French dignitaries to shower her with secrets for the excitements of her company. Her true name was Gertrud Zelle and she was half Dutch, half Indonesian. In Paris, she set up as a dancer and took the stage name Mata Hari, Malay for "sun." Her spying, according to McCormick, was nothing but simple-minded obedience to her patron at the arts, one of the Cabinet officials in on the illegal peace negotiations, who sent her as a courier between France, Germany and Spain. When the peace plot blew up, her high-ranking lover told her to go along with a charade in which she would be shot at with blanks to keep the opposition happy. In the best operatic fashion, she was to fall and then she could be carried off to Spain, safe enough. But, of course, the bullets were real.

Another such victim of the high life was a Spaniard, Miguel Almareyda, editor of the socialist paper *Le Bonnet Rouge*. Almareyda was taken at the same time as Mata Hari. Charges of treason, traffic with the enemy and defeatism, brought down one Cabinet and set up another. McCormick several times reviewed the whole period in close detail and never failed to wonder how historians have since repeated the official report that Almareyda committed suicide by hanging himself with his suspenders. Investigation showed there wasn't anything in his cell to hang from; he was found on the floor; the suspenders weren't strong enough, and besides, the police had already given out that he had been carried off with typhoid fever. If one is to judge by the zest with which he explored the Mata Hari-Almareyda case, what he learned in the shadow world of French Cabinet politics went a long way to convince McCormick that such is the real nature of government, anyhow. Certainly he was fascinated by the sort of intrigue found in executive institutions and dwelt on it to the exclusion of legislative or judicial machines and the men who inhabit these.

For all his love of detail in describing things in which he really had an important part, McCormick was vague and unclear in facing up to a charge he very well knew, that in the actual shooting war of 1917–18, he had been a laggard. It was not that he avoided the subject entirely, for in fact as he grew older his language became very expansive. A careless listener might gain the impression that McCormick had several times charged across No Man's Land, and particularly that he had been one of the men who saw the First Division through in its victory at Cantigny, the first American offensive of the war. But if one listened closely, it was otherwise. As a matter of fact, McCormick did not fight the battle of Cantigny at all. His very indirect and unclear account was that on the morning of the great offensive he was ordered out of the line by his medical officer because he was down with influenza. High dignitaries in the Franklin D. Roosevelt period told it that they had looked up his file and that none of this was so. They flatly accused McCormick of rigging an excuse to duck out, and they promoted the idea that he was a coward under fire. McCormick's detailed file is not available until the year 2005, but in 1964, an official summation was made. It is only fair that this be spread on the record exactly as furnished.

Statement of Military Service of Robert R. McCormick 0 119 986
Born 30 July 1880, Chicago, Illinois
Major, 1st Calvary, Illinois National Guard

Mustered into federal service	21 June 1916
Mustered out of federal service	17 Nov. 1916
Reported for World War I service	13 June 1917
Lieutenant Colonel Illinois National Guard	17 June 1918
Colonel, Field Artillery, United States Army	5 Sept. 1918
Honorably discharged, Colonel Field Artillery United States Army	31 Dec. 1918
Colonel, Field Artillery, Officers' Reserve Corps	8 Oct. 1919
Commission in Officers' Reserve Corps terminated (honorably)	30 Sept. 1929

SERVICE SCHOOLS

Army General Staff College, Langers, France	1917

SERVICE

	FROM	TO
Regimental duties on Mexican Border	June 1916	Nov. 1916
General Staff Duties, American Expeditionary Force	" 1917	Sept. 1917
Regimental duties, 5th Field Artillery, 1st Division	Sept. 1917	Dec. 1917
Commanding 1st Battalion, 5th Field Artillery	Dec. 1917	May 1918
Regimental duties, 122 Field Artillery, 58th Field Artillery Brigade, American Expeditionary Forces	June 1918	Aug. 1918
Regimental duties, 61st Field Artillery, Fort Sheridan, Illinois and Camp Jackson, South Carolina	Aug. 1918	Dec. 1918

BATTLES

Defensive sectors: Ansauville (18 January to 4 April 1918) and Cantigny (20 April to 28 May 1918)

DECORATIONS AND AWARDS

Colonel McCormick was awarded the Distinguished Service Medal by the President through General Pershing with the following citation:

"Colonel Robert R. McCormick:

For exceptionally meritorious and distinguished services. As commander of the 1st Battalion, 5th Field Artillery, in the Ansauville Sector and in the Cantigny Sector, France, between January 18 and May 28, 1918; and as lieutenant colonel, 122nd Field Artillery, May 13 to July 29, 1918; and as colonel, 61st Field Artillery, July 30 to December 31, 1918; he displayed rare leadership and organizing ability, unusual executive ability, and sound technical judgment. By his ceaseless energy and his close supervision of training, discipline and command in action against the enemy he contributed materially to the successful operations of the artillery of the American Expenditionary Forces."

He was authorized the World War I Victory Medal with clasp for Defensive Sector, and the Mexican Border Service Medal.

ACTIVE SERVICE

Colonel McCormick is credited with active service as a commissioned officer of the United States Army from 21 June to 17 November 1916 and from 13 June to 31 December 1918.

By Authority of the Secretary of the Army:

J. C. Lambert
Major General, USA
The Adjutant General

McCormick was certainly a regimental field soldier under fire. And just as certainly, he did not take part in the Cantigny offensive. But if there was anything shady about his behavior, what accounts for his promotion, his citation and the undeniable fact that at the war's end he was in charge of a regiment in training for Europe? McCormick liked to say he discovered, from that final assignment, the "terrors of military ambition." It was in his mind that if he could get back to France with his own regiment he might wind up a major general. Taken all around, the official record argues that he was a real enough campaigner. And anyone who ever collided with him in his role as president of the Tribune Company would have to agree that he was certainly due some kind of medal there for "rare leadership and organizing ability, unusual executive ability and sound technical judgment," not to mention "ceaseless energy." And any *Tribune* employee could testify McCormick was given to "close supervision of training, discipline and command in action against the enemy."

It was a good thing. Enemies began to multiply faster than the dragon's teeth in 1919, and they were to last many a year.

During the Second World War, a favorite *Tribune* target was the poet, playwright and sometimes Librarian of Congress, Archibald MacLeish, who had assignments from Mr. Roosevelt officially described as producing governmental facts and figures. But the *Tribune* thought MacLeish only a sort of Roosevelt press agent. In July of 1942, after one of its special attentions, Mr. MacLeish got a note of consolation from the President:

"I welcome you to the society of immortals. Bertie McCormick started it many years ago even before we entered the First World War and he incorporated it in 1918 when he broke Woodrow Wilson's heart and made him the first of the immortals." To some, this might have seemed a rather feeble effort and lacking point. Not so, to any of Mr. Roosevelt's vintage in political encounter.

The Battle of Europe suspended at eleven A.M., November 11, 1918, and it was announced that the powers would gather in Paris to decide what should happen next. The most stunning news after the Armistice itself was that Woodrow Wilson would be there to see that peace would reign without victory. Why and how did it not? The great historical conundrum of Versailles eludes all efforts to riddle it. Whatever the one great truth about the peace conference may be, supposing there really ever was any, it is long since lost. Here the single effort is to delineate just how Franklin D. Roosevelt was charging up Woodrow Wilson's broken heart to McCormick and the *Tribune*. It is an accusation far from original with Mr. Roosevelt, and it has been extended by many an earnest believer to argue that the *Tribune,* with a single news article in June of 1919, destroyed the Peace of Versailles, defeated the League of Nations, generated Adolf Hitler, the Second World War and all that has come in its train. And if there are those who suggest that is giving the *Tribune* more credit than really it deserves, still enough fact is of record to require that here the case be organized for a judgment.

Mr. Wilson sailed for Europe aboard the S.S. *George Washington* on December 4, 1918. There was an almost unearthly touch to his journey. Millions prayed for him and millions believed—none more than he—that once in the Hall of Mirrors, Mr. Wilson would magic up an age of peace. But confusions were already at work. On May 27, 1918, Wilson went before Congress to discuss the war, which then looked to be as long as it was grim. And Mr. Wilson said: "Politics is adjourned. The election will go to those who think least of it; to those who go to the constituencies without explanations or excuses, with a plain record of duty faithfully and disinterestedly performed." In days that followed the German army came near to a breakthrough, then abruptly lost its will to do any more dying and headed for home. All the world knew the end was now near. On October 24, 1918, Mr. Wilson called on the country to give him a Congress on which he could rely. In fact, he asked the nation to give him Democrats. On November 5, 1918, what Mr. Wilson got was a warning against himself. The House of Representatives turned Republican by fifty votes and the Senate by two.

But still Mr. Wilson sailed, to pass through one capital after another before crowds weeping, cheering, kneeling, waving. At Versailles the politicians, and such statesmen as there were, stood waiting as Mr. Wilson delayed his arrival until all the world could see that in him rested hope and power. During all of which high drama abroad, Theodore Roosevelt, at home, was dying. But he did not go until he had put in motion his own plan to break the President's heart. Hiram Johnson had come on to the Senate from California in 1917, and he was one of Mr. Roosevelt's very own. Medill McCormick switched from House to Senate with the election of 1918. To these, Mr. Roosevelt let it be known that Woodrow Wilson must never be allowed to run himself for "President of the world." In as near the apostolic manner as it is possible to achieve among politicians, he laid on hands and assigned Henry Cabot Lodge the duty to see "that our Allies and our enemies and Mr. Wilson himself should understand that Mr. Wilson has no authority to speak for the American people at this time . . ."

And, then, on January 6, 1919, Theodore Roosevelt died, having both written and made history in copious amount since Graduation Day, 1880.

Nor was the work all a matter of high-flown rhetoric. Mr. Wilson's travel plan intrigued the nation, but it was also frightening. Never before had an American President ventured his body beyond the jurisdiction of his writ. Who knew what nameless dangers might rise up, once the army and the people no longer stood between the Chief Executive and the world? In Congress there was a clamor, by no means limited along party lines, to know just how this strange departure squared with the Constitution. To such as this the President turned back an icy stare. And in the women's quarters, Mrs. Wilson counseled with the authorities on fashion for an equipage which would not shame the nation before the world. Then a bomb was let off in New York. Of all legalists in his day, George W. Wickersham was held the supreme advisor on international law. He was also a Republican and had served William Howard Taft as Attorney General. Mr. Wickersham said there was no telling what ruptures might occur within the engine of the law once the President had passed onto the high seas. He recommended that instantly the *George Washington* got beyond United States sovereignty, the Vice President of the United States be sworn to guard duty in higher office. And with that the man of the hour was one of history's least assuming heroes, Thomas Riley Marshall, Presbyterian, Mason, teacher of Sunday School classes, trustee of Wabash College and sometime Governor of Indiana, who in all his life had never, except possibly once, done a single thing that others should stop and stare. In a thousand American political histories it is told that one day, wearied beyond measure at some Senator's ear-splitting oratory on America's need of this or that, Vice President Marshall wantonly murmured that what America needs is a good five-cent cigar. There are those who deny it, and for more than thirty years there were Senate clerks who swore they heard him say it. In any case, Mr. Marshall is best remembered as author of that classic in folk-truth and less for an experience which was to him, if not to others, dangerously electrified.

When the Wickersham opinion was handed down at a dinner of the Foreign Policy Association in New York City, Mr. Marshall was, in the strict corporeal sense, in Boston on affairs of his own.

The New York Times hunted him down, and suddenly the Vice President wasn't anywhere but up to his neck in the hottest, also the chilliest, of Washington water. Nor was there anyone to guide him, for at the White House all shutters were drawn and there radiated only a silence, deafening, polar and as of wolves in the night. The *Times* pressed for an answer. So, Mr. Marshall bleakly accepted the Wickersham ruling, with one proviso. He would take the oath, but first he would have to be so ordered by a court of competent jurisdiction.

Here the Supreme Court snapped awake.

And though nobody ever pressed Mr. Marshall into being sworn, still Mr. Wilson left behind him a federal government seriously agitated in all its constituent parts. By the time he got to the council on January 18, 1919, his edifice of power was already seriously damaged. Nor could he ever say it was entirely without his knowledge, either, for at one point he made a trip back to Washington specifically to calm, or try to calm, the general apprehensions that permeated the life of the capital as the President pursued "a great charter for a new order of affairs in the world."

But it was no less true that, in America as all across Europe, common men, their women and their children, still prayed for him. So, Wilson never doubted that in the end the peace would be his. The strategy was to enunciate broad principles and disclose nothing on the bill of particulars being haggled together in staff meetings. Then he would bring the treaty home as a total contract, including the League of Nations. He would combine logic, surprise and moral horsepower with such force the Senate could not deny ratification. But it was slow work, and it was the first of June, 1919, before the teams of experts felt they had a draft treaty fit for the principals to examine.

On Monday, June 9, 1919, the Chicago *Tribune* carried a headline, "Tribune Has Treaty." Below it was a Washington dispatch by Frazier Hunt, who wrote that on his way home from Soviet Russia he had stopped off in Paris. There, by means he did not describe, Hunt said he got hold of a compendium entitled "Conditions of Peace," making up 416 pages and about 75,000 words of text, with four maps attached. It was the draft treaty, without any doubt at all, as shortly was proved. Hunt landed in New York on Friday, June 6, and brought the draft straight to Washington. The initial article carried in the *Tribune* on the morning of the 9th was more a generalized commentary than any spelling out of treaty language, but it was obvious that more would be heard. As the Senate convened at noon, Mr. Borah handed the whole text in to the *Congressional Record.* On June 10, *The New York Times* made up a special eight-page section carrying every word of it, the only newspaper to do so. With that, the fox was among the chickens.

Mr. Wilson was trapped on the opposite shore, ill, enraged but helpless to stop the ruin of his strategy. The treaty was signed on June 28, 1919, in that very same Hall of Mirrors from which Bismarck had proclaimed Germany an empire in 1871. But the debate in Washington and all across the United States had already escaped logic. Never was Mr. Wilson's vision pursued, then or thereafter, as more than a row between politicians for domestic advantage.

The forces opposing the treaty, epitomized by the *Tribune,* Senators Lodge, Borah, Johnson and Medill McCormick, of course were political, but they could quite properly say Mr. Wilson had been political, too, in his 1918 appeals for the election of Democrats and in his short supply of Republicans at Versailles. Just the same, the Senate did not ratify the treaty and in 1942 Mr. Roosevelt spoke for a whole school of historical writing which has held ever since that the *Tribune* faction turned the course of world events away from light. It was a charge to which McCormick and his family connections always showed a peculiar sensitivity. Their public rebuttal was that if the Wilson peace plan really had all the merit claimed for it, no newspaper's publication of its tenor a few days before Wilson chose to make disclosure on his own terms could possibly have made much difference. But there always was something lacking in McCormick's discussion of how the treaty came to the paper. In the hundred-year memorial issue of June 10, 1947, the credit for getting the Versailles text was laid to Spearman Lewis, who in 1919 was editor of the *Tribune*'s Paris edition. Elsewhere it has been said that Lewis got the document from someone in the Chinese delegation. The public record does not clarify in any way, and McCormick, himself, died strangely vague on this most debated news article to appear in his lifetime in any publication anywhere. But about the phase in his affairs immediately following his return to Chicago as the shooting suspended, he never tired of telling anybody who would listen. Nor was it in any part dull, either.

CHAPTER TWELVE ★★★ McCormick's life from 1919 to his death had a singular consistency of purpose, carried out in three distinct phases. His aim was simple: to put down "the burocracy." The phases of execution divide plainly. From 1919 to 1937 his concern was with domestic affairs. From 1937 to 1945, it was to stop the "burocrats" on war and peace. His last ten years were spent exploring a world it would be entirely false to say he found incomprehensible. He was just absolutely against it in every part. Nothing better sums his final stage than the spectacle, analyzed in detail at its proper point in this account, of McCormick reading the Republican Party itself out of his further service, as a rotted failure. And if there were those who laughed at the moment, they found later that even in death McCormick had his own way of delivering blows. He was not a man to leave the house of his fathers in a fit of simple spite. He was never joking when he said, as he so often came to do, that the *Tribune* kept the Republican Party alive between 1933 and 1937. All who saw the party's day-to-day gasping for oxygen grant him at least a very genuine part. Magnates and their hangers-on might hold white-tie dinners of the Liberty League in New York to tell one another horror stories about the Revolution. McCormick threw his effort into the ward politics of Chicago and an even more Byzantine culture familiar to Illinois under the trade name "Downstate." He spared nothing and risked everything to save even the most obscure representatives in Congress, just so they were Republican. What he managed cannot be better signified than with the case of Representative Everett McKinley Dirksen of Pekin, in Tazewell County, close enough to the Sangamon River to call itself "Lincoln country," which is potent medicine in "Downstate." Mr. Dirksen began in 1933 as a freshman member of the 73rd Congress. In 1949, he dared mightily and, against established doctrine, won a seat in the Senate. He would have been first to agree that none had been greater in the cause than McCormick. Except, of course, Mrs. Dirksen. In 1952, Mr. Dirksen made a famous oration on the floor of the Republican convention at Chicago against the faction that sought General Eisenhower's nomination. He was at that moment McCormick's last, best hope and when he failed to carry the day, that was McCormick's moment of departure from Republican discipline. Yet, in 1964, there was a revulsion and the party, after long years of other-directedness, suddenly accepted McCormick's interpretation of the world. No man could say Mr. Dirksen failed, then, to keep the faith. He was orthodox and accepted the new order—or sudden rediscovery of a very old order—with his notable aplomb. But, unfortunately, if he had not failed in the spirit, the flesh failed him in the crisis. Mr. Dirksen, in the campaign of 1964, was frequently sick a-bed. His orations were little noted nor long remembered. To which may be added a clinical note. Mr. Dirksen, unlike others, survived. But who, in 1964, remembered McCormick's part in the elevation of Dirksen and the great upheaval of 1964 itself? By then he was best recalled, if recalled at all, for the malediction and anathema of his final year in Presidential politics, his curse upon a world he had come to hate. It was all a long way in more measures than by time alone from 1918, when the first order of business had been only to decide how he and his cousin should divide up the management of Tribune Company.

Patterson's war had been as different from McCormick's as harness washing in Texas was from polo. When McCormick was ready to sail for France, he thought it would be nice to do something for his cousin, too. He intervened with the governor and shortly Patterson found himself a first lieutenant in the First Illinois Field Artillery. This organization went to France as part of the 42nd Division. Patterson tended to make himself out to be so terrified in action he could not think. He would never discuss his experiences much, except to tell how he celebrated the Armistice by throwing furniture out his hotel window in Paris. But just the same, he must have done something useful, for he was promoted to captain in the field.

At the war's end, Patterson was in a serious fit of emotional and mental disturbance on several counts, not least the fact that his marriage was no longer harmonious. He was ready enough to let McCormick take increasing command in Chicago while he looked for a new departure.

It always amused the cousins to play on the credulity of the simple by telling it that they sat on a manure pile somewhere in France to plan out an assault on New York. In fact, they had been trying to get into New York even before the war, and that meeting in France was just a matter of personal goodbyes before taking off for home.

They had already consulted with Lord Northcliffe in London, who had once again shown himself a friend in need. Nobody ever understood better than Northcliffe how to stop a Londoner in his tracks and make him turn loose a penny. In the early years of this century it was magic near to television for newspapers to have pictures jump from between masses of type. Northcliffe showed his mastery of London's public mind with one gesture. He ran a street scene showing a girl's face encircled and a single word: "Who?" Nor did he ever answer, though the city almost rioted for a name to go with the face in the crowd.

Patterson and McCormick took Northcliffe's illustrated *Daily Mirror* as their model, rented a loft and printing service from the New York *Daily Mail,* now long vanished. Patterson was not yet ready to abandon Chicago, but he was a tireless commuter. A handful of *Tribune* adventurers tested the greatest of all cities for experimental journals. The name taken for the new departure was *The Illustrated Daily News,* which Patterson was no time at all cutting down to *The Daily News*. He couldn't think of a title saying more in less or he would have used it. In time, one came against him trying to compress all into the cryptic logotype, *PM*, but found Patterson had long since achieved an irreducible name, style and performance. It did not seem likely, at first, that the *News* would make a go of itself. Patterson took up his troubles with the *Tribune*'s Sunday editor, Mary King, who had come to the paper as a secretary and proved herself as a journalist. The problem was that the *News* did not know which of New York's many audiences to seek, except that Patterson's natural passion for hanging out with working people kept him sure that it lay somewhere among these.

In a few years, the *News* was the awe of all other newspaper proprietors. Patterson seldom let himself be trapped among them, but when pressed to reveal his secret, his answer never varied. He would point at Mary King and say: "I never had a good idea in my life that she wasn't at least the first half of it." In 1938, he separated from his wife, married Miss King and they adopted a son. It was Miss King, he said, who told him where to look for an audience in New York. She was a working girl herself. The war had put the working girl into the life of all great cities. She needed someone to notice her. The *News* began to run dress patterns, to build the working girl's fashion sense. Horoscopes kept her alert to threats and promises. Serial romances, at which Miss King was a specialist, kept up her hopes that all would turn right with the next day's instalment. Then Patterson hit on the power in a literature of human stress: men and women shooting one another, eloping, doing anything to shatter the humdrum present. Melville Stone's nineteenth-century quiddities on the farmer come to town were adjusted to fit what was suddenly known everywhere as The Jazz Age. And Patterson had, at last, his own audience in the great metropolis of the twentieth century. He was made.

McCormick's problem was very different. William Field was exhausted and must retire. Keeley was out of journalism; McCormick beat him in just one morning by a long-distance telephone call in 1916 that cornered the last 20,000 tons of newsprint on the open market. All the money his backers had to throw around could not find Keeley enough to carry on the fight. The Chicago battle was now really down to *Hearst* vs. *Tribune,* though the *News* sought to save itself through those who felt it time to "bring the Middle West into the modern age." These had everything except sufficient number to provide for the *News* in Chicago what the working girl was doing for the *News* in New York.

High on McCormick's list of urgent business was also the Ford libel suit. Neither party had felt it quite safe to push this high-octane uncertainty in wartime, though each made a great show of demanding to be heard. McCormick had never left his law firm, for all that he had put into the reorganization of the *Tribune* and the conduct of the war. He invited one of his partners, Samuel Emory Thomason, to try the job left open after Field. And to a less grandified member of the firm, who had joined as trial counsel after terrifying traction companies, railroads and utilities with his wolfish pursuit of damage claims, McCormick gave a simple, blanket order: "Beat Ford." If it can be said any single event took from Ford all that had made his life agreeable, McCormick did it with his choice of Weymouth Kirkland to manage the *Tribune*'s law side.

In 1950, McCormick gave himself a seventieth birthday party. At his right hand was his second wife, Mrs. Maryland Mathison Hooper McCormick, whom he liked to describe as "my beautiful ambassadress." On his left was his niece, Mrs. Peter Miller. He had some years earlier announced Mrs. Miller would be his successor in command. It was an evening of great sentimental feeling, with many elaborations on grand occasions past. But nobody ever came close to matching Kirkland's opening line:

"People ask me how in the world I have gotten along with McCormick all these years. It is really very simple. I find out what he wants and I give it to him."

It was a maxim that other member of the law firm, Thomason, allowed to get away from him as he rose in title to be called not only business manager, but also a vice president of Tribune Company. As the paper prospered, so did Thomason. He came to draw a salary so large that, so he later said, "it frightened me." It disturbed him, also, that nothing definite about work, pay or authority was anywhere on paper. McCormick, who never forgot his experience with Keeley and the narrow squeak home from the North Woods to stifle that *Tribune* panic, would not explain to Thomason exactly where the line of authority lay. Thomason told the outcome: "I said that I couldn't keep on drawing that much money just on a day-by-day basis, and I wanted him to spell it out. What were my duties, anyhow?" What he got back was just the sort of thing Weymouth Kirkland would have told him to expect: "For the kind of money I'm paying, you'll do what I tell you." And so the friends parted.

McCormick himself never discussed the blowup, nor did cither man ever hint there was more to it than met the eye. But it is not the wildest guess to suppose there was some difference of view also touching on the by then grievous problem of the mayor of Chicago.

In 1915, William Hale Thompson came to power with a four-year term at precisely the worst possible moment for the city's interest. In another time his instincts and behavior might very well have made short work of him in a position of such high exposure, but in 1915 there was a war to distract thought and by the time he was up for re-election, he had been loose on Chicago almost with a free hand while many of the city's able younger men, such as Patterson and McCormick, were out of the country. It was many a long day before he was finally knocked loose from the powerhouse.

The *Tribune* actually helped Thompson in 1915, though it never was shown by anybody, or confessed by McCormick, that the service was intentional. During the campaign, the *Tribune* published a series of attacks on British propaganda and soothing descriptions of Germany, done by R. J. Thompson, a former United States consul in Germany. Naturally, Candidate Thompson reprinted these and scattered them through the Teutonic wards, a critically important segment of his public. Among the more sober-sided elements of the city, which included all the newspapers, he was being snubbed, but among the simpler-minded and the excitables, his bull-roaring was a vote-getting device of power.

During the war, Thompson played so heavily to Chicago's German and Irish wards he was considered by many persons a downright adherent of the Kaiser. He was really an adherent only of Thompson. In 1918 he ran against Representative Medill McCormick for the Republican senatorial nomination, but lost. McCormick went on to Washington and had one term in the select company of the Republican oligarchs, but when he came up for renomination in 1924, Thompson used his by then real power in Illinois to defeat him.

Senator McCormick had never really recovered his poise from that time in 1910 when he was removed from the *Tribune* editorship. He fell into a deep melancholy. Suddenly, he was found in his Washington apartment in February, 1925, dead. It appeared that in the night he had been seized with hemorrhages. And so, Medill McCormick bled to a finish as lonely as much of his life. That ending, too, was part of the matter between Mayor Thompson and the *Tribune*.

Thompson never discussed issues if he could find a man to illustrate his view. Of all his performances, leaving aside some against the *Tribune* and McCormick, which really would have warranted anybody's horsewhip, as good an illustration as any was his exercise with the rats and the cage. In this he delighted to go about the city holding up his exhibit and addressing the rats as "Doc" and "Fred," after two associates on whom he had turned. "Doc" had not endured a bath for twenty years until the day before, and against all efforts to improve him still smelled like a billygoat. As for "Fred," who could believe that even a rat could be so ungrateful after the mayor had saved him from the penitentiary? These diversions took notice away from the reality, that Chicago was in serious trouble. McCormick set out to break the mayor. It was fatal to mistake Thompson's method for his purpose. He was a thorough student of Chicago's human organization. Thompson was early to exploit Negroes from the South who were flooding the slums around the stockyards. And there were his other friends, the Italian Primitives. Immediately after the 18th Amendment to the Constitution took hold, these natural humanists put their large common sense to extracting its benefits. They might not have heard it said civilization is a byproduct of life around the Mediterranean and so is wine; but they needed nobody to tell them civilized society does not permit itself to be cut off from getting drunk. That is just ancient wisdom. And so these servants of culture found in Mayor Thompson a special friend. In McCormick they had only a customer and a difficult one to serve, at that. But like everybody of his generation, McCormick could buy through such fences as chauffeurs and those semipolice found around any large enterprise, whose official tradenames, however dignified, are ignored for the more accurate "bodyguard."

In Mayor Thompson's era of public safety, bodyguards were held in large respect. No citizen was so lacking in self-esteem that he would say he had no market value. Every man felt that for him, too, the dark limousine could come. He might very well be returned in less than good service condition, if returned at all, even though his sureties were prompt with redemption money. The day of the kidnaper brought on interesting variants of Thorstein Veblen's law on conspicuous consumption. The more bodyguards, the higher a citizen stood in the scale. McCormick had a whole private police system. Nor would any Chicagoan, then or now, say he was only trying to make himself feel wanted. He was, and more than once.

It is a very special pity no impartial scrivener was present to keep a record of McCormick's personal negotiations with Al Capone, *bella figuera* from that best known of all Chicago suburbs, Cicero. There was a threat that the *Tribune*'s chauffeurs and drivers would be called out on strike, and there was reason to imagine the Mayor had hopes it would do more than just impede *Tribune* sales of race news from Arlington Park, where Capone could be gaped at in season, but not approached. Capone kept near him at all times a troupe of what Chicago liked to call "musicians," performing artists of the hand-carried machine gun.

It has never been shown that Mayor Thompson had personal identification with the renowned device that bore his name and fit so well in a violin case, but a standard Chicago joke held it His Honor's branding iron, and not entirely because any newspaper made so much noise about him. Some few researchers, repelled at the thought McCormick could ever have been right on any question, have tried to redeem Thompson as a sort of first robin in South Side Chicago, a sign to the poor that their day would come against monsters of privilege. So far, it has turned out unprofitable work. No matter who studies the evidence in *Tribune* vs. *Thompson* it seems to end the same way. A residue of gold notes, odd lots of currency and negotiables, was found in the Mayor's lockbox after he died in 1944, in sum near to two million dollars. Such a monument has impeded his municipal, if not his supernatural redemption.

It is not correct to portray Thompson's Chicago as a pond of tadpoles afflicted first with King Log and then with King Stork. Nobody will ever know what the Arch-Respectables might have done following Mayor Busse's cue, because what they did do, one way and another, was to put Chicago aside at the crucial moment for part in a great war. When they came home their city was degraded in the eyes of the world, and in its own. The problem of its relief from Thompson was such that many, who otherwise might have returned to public affairs, abandoned hope and surrendered to him. More can be understood from a brief look at *The Tribune Shadow, Chicago's Greatest Curse* than from plowing through a hundred filing cabinets filled with the product of sociologists' research. This was Thompson's official campaign flyer for 1931. It shows the *Tribune* driven to open support of Democrats, amazing as that might seem. The flyer laid the charge that Anthony Cermak,

Thompson's opponent, was nothing but a tool of the "organ of organized wealth." The first page showed in the balance a choice between more soup houses with "Tony and the *Tribune*" or more jobs with "Thompson and the people." However all that might be, Cermak won and went on to catch the bullet fired at President-elect Roosevelt in early 1933. Cermak's statue in Chicago bears a phrase attributed as his dying gasp to Roosevelt: "I'm glad it was me instead of you." Whether he really said exactly that or it was made up, as some say, by a journalist hoping to enhance his legend, is no matter. It is the language of the one city in which a Roosevelt and a McCormick each could be hated and supported, alike, in every segment of society.

The inner pages of the flyer make out a case that is persuasive of a crimson-faced McCormick scuffing with a low hoodlum. The witness was one Daniel A. Serritella, at the time holding Thompson's commission as City Sealer for Chicago. Just what a city sealer does is not too clear in any municipal code book, but roughly it is within his duties to see that thumbs do not fall too heavily on scales that weigh up the housewife's purchase. It is the sort of post men of ambition in public affairs do not scorn. Before his elevation to municipal responsibilities, Serritella had been president of a newsboys' union only. One of his experiences in that role cannot be described better than in his own account as it appeared in *The Tribune Shadow:*

> Chicago, February 14, 1931
>
> A little over two years ago, Max Annenberg, director of circulation of the *Chicago Tribune,* called me on the telephone and said he wanted to meet me at the Drake Hotel and have a talk with me. I asked him what he wanted to talk about and he told me the *Tribune* was having some trouble with their chauffeurs and drivers. I went over to the Drake Hotel, met Max Annenberg and he told me he was in bad with the Flannagan brothers and they were going to call a strike of the *Tribune*'s chauffeurs and drivers for the following Saturday, and he wanted to get someone to talk to the executive committee of the chauffeurs and drivers union to see if the strike could not be called off. He said that Dullo, business agent of the union and member of the executive committee, met Louis Rolse [sic], circulation manager of the *Chicago Tribune,* and that Dullo demanded $25,000 to straighten out the strike. Annenberg said he

wanted to treat the boys right and that he wanted to reach someone who could get the executive committee to fix the strike up.

I told him that as president of the newsboys' union there was nothing I could do. Then Max Annenberg said he would call up Capone and see if he could do anything in the matter, which he did and made an appointment with Capone to meet him in the *Tribune*'s office. I attended this meeting, at which Capone agreed to use his influence to stop the strike, which prevented the same. Max Annenberg then brought in Robert McCormick, editor and publisher of the *Chicago Tribune,* and introduced McCormick to Capone. McCormick thanked Capone for calling off the strike for the *Tribune* and said, "You know, you are famous, like Babe Ruth. We can't help printing things about you, but I will see that the *Tribune* gives you a square deal."

[Signed] Daniel A. Serritella
President of the Newsboys' Union

Nothing in Thompson's flyer intimated that Mr. Serritella was also, at that moment, the municipal guardian of chicken weights, not to mention liege man to the mayor.

Then there was a demonstration to support the theory of the *Tribune* as false witness on criminalities. A page from the Congressional Record was reproduced in which Representative Oscar de Priest, both a Democrat and a South Side early spokesman for the newest ethnic wave to hit Chicago, the Negroes, offered refutation.

Of eighty-one cities measured for crime in the nine months preceding September 30, 1930, Mr. de Priest wished it known that Number One was Toledo, Ohio. Chicago was Number Sixty-eight. This was all worked out by the Department of Justice, with its Uniform Crime Reports tabulated to weigh comparative virtue in proportion to population. Mr. de Priest did not mention, for perhaps he did not know, that the Department of Justice repeated with every issue of Uniform Crime Reports a notice that it took no responsibility for anything except that it put out the figures as received. Each city had its own method of arriving at its volume of criminality. If Toledo were stupid enough to run up big numbers by putting down every little jot and tittle, nobody could say that against the intelligence of His Honor in Chicago.

And on the same page, to show that he kept much more elegant company than Capone did, Thompson produced this:

San Simeon, California
February 9, 1931

Hon. William Hale Thompson
Mayor, Chicago, Ill.
Thanks for your message to City Council. I am arranging to have *Chicago American* statement which you approve printed in all our papers throughout the nation so that it will get the widest possible publicity.
W. R. Hearst.

The mayor's footnote to this news was irrefutable evidence that when a great editor and a great public servant get together on a great city, let all beware:

An Interesting Telegram

To the right [on that page of the flyer] is pictured a telegram from William Randolph Hearst assuring the mayor that a story on the above table [on crime] would appear in every Hearst paper throughout the country. That is the kind of co-operation that he is giving our city. The *Tribune,* because of the lies they had told, did not dare print the story.

Well, so there it all is, the story of Chicago's life with Thompson, all in one exhibit. Nor is it difficult to translate. Hearst and Thompson were leaning on the *Tribune,* each for his own purpose. McCormick felt the weight enough to humble himself before Capone. It paid to do so, in the end. Thompson died in disgrace. Hearst was run out of Chicago and almost out of New York. And one day not long after the treaty with Capone, McCormick had a stiff little meeting with Herbert Hoover, who wished the *Tribune* were more co-operative with his effort to enforce the 18th Amendment to the Constitution. McCormick gave the ordinary man's rebuttal. The President should quit sending his agents to chase the corner bootlegger and go after somebody worth catching, for example, Al Capone. For aesthetic if no other reasons, one has to believe McCormick's account, that Mr. Hoover asked: "Who is Al Capone?" Then, it was not long until the day of the *bella figuera* from Brooklyn, Cicero and Arlington Park, was done. But that is no excuse to fall for McCormick's wan little passage in his broadcast of July 14, 1954. This is his impression of himself as he liked it in what proved to be his final year of life:

> There was talk of a strike and the publishers called a meeting to hear the demands. I arrived late. As I entered an outer office I saw several swarthy, evil-looking men, who eyed me coldly. Inside, I saw to my amazement that Al Capone brazenly had invaded the meeting with the aim of terrorizing those present. I ordered Capone to leave and to take his pluguglies with him. I knew his reputation but I also knew he had never killed anyone himself and I didn't think he'd start then. Capone got out. He didn't muscle in on the newspapers. We continued to expose him.

McCormick, by 1954, had seen many more interesting demons than Al Capone fly off to the graveyard, to the penitentiary or into the silence of plain retirement. He had outfaced them all. He had, then, an opportunity to describe his collision with Capone for what it really was, the best possible evidence of how terrible the citizen's distress could be in Thompson's Chicago. It was solid evidence that McCormick was right, as Thompson was wrong, on how the city ought to live. But by 1954, McCormick was too far gone, had suffered too much within and was too much lost to his senile vision of himself triumphant, to see any such point. Instead, he went on in the same broadcast to tell another of those little gems that ought to be false but is true, precisely the sort of turn with which any researcher into McCormick's affairs must be prepared to live.

In the Capone treaty-making period, he bought an armored car. It was good sense. Among people who had business with Capone the test was not whether they needed an armored car but whether they could afford to pay for it. McCormick, all things considered, could not afford anything less. Even so, he found that when he went out for walks, pluguglies followed. Max Annenberg assigned some *Tribune* circulation department associates to hunt the hunters. There was an encounter, an exchange of views and when the hoodlums got out of the hospital it would appear they reasoned McCormick must prefer solitude. Anyhow, thereafter he continued his life-long habit, walking alone.

Thompson's Chicago was a dangerous place, just in general. For McCormick, it had many very special dangers. It is no part a myth that people disaffected toward the *Tribune* have tried more than once to blow up pressrooms or kill somebody around the place just to express their attitude. McCormick's defense methods inspired elaborate accounts of an eagle's nest at the top of the Gothic

Tower. He had an axe and telephone in his toilet so he could break out if overcome with panic, so it was faithfully told. But those who liked the story best would have found it difficult to claim first-hand knowledge of its truth. Then, there was the matter of The Door. The panels of his office wall were said to be so done that none could tell which was on hinges. The visitor leaving would vainly scrabble for a clue to the exit until McCormick's cruel pleasure was sated. He would press a secret button. Guard dogs would leap from dark corners and stand at attention. A panel would give way, as in a horror movie, to let out the by now emotionally empulped prisoner. As to all this, it need only be said that in Serritella's account of the Capone meeting nothing is more convincing than his description of McCormick fumbling to preserve his dignity with a thug who had him in the corner, and yet maintain his obligation to himself as a gentleman. McCormick would never be discourteous enough to harass someone present in his office by invitation, even Capone. The mumbling about Capone and Babe Ruth is pure McCormick, caught without his self-possession.

McCormick's office, in fact, was also very much McCormick. It was large. So was he. It tended to cast a feeling of gloom on the caller at first glance. So, heaven knows, did he. But if one paid attention, both man and office, without losing one whit of solemn appearance, could produce some lively particulars. McCormick worked at a large, polished slab of stone for a table. In window recesses or on walls, or anywhere around the place, he kept his amusements: a bronze cast of Lincoln's hand holding the Emancipation Proclamation pen; a death mask some said was also Lincoln's, though others held out for Joseph Medill and others thought nobody had ever heard him say; souvenirs of his doings as warrior, secret agent and man-about-the-world; swamps of *Tribune* clippings inscribed with his cryptograms to be puzzled out, and, dozing in some corner, either a German shepherd dog that had the politest manners or an English pit bulldog, frightful to see but in fact an endless nuisance, begging to be reassured for the thousandth time that it was really beautiful and loved.

McCormick did have a secret signal device, all right, and he needed it, as do all men in such position. Aside from the prospect that someone enclosed with him in all that hushed cathedral really might be overcome with an urge to have a pop, there was the need to get rid of bores. And so, on his indication, secretaries would bring in mail, cartoonists in shirtsleeves would present him sketches for approval and editorialists would flutter proofs. McCormick would regret that for all the fascination of the present moment, duty called. And it was true there was no knob to pull in making a getaway. But it was still possible to escape independently, given a minimum of sense. McCormick moved around the office with his hands full of papers and often read as he walked. So he had the doorknob taken off and a brass plate put across the bottom of the door, obvious to anybody who had come into the place, anyhow. And as he approached, McCormick would kick without pause or glance, never doubting the result. The brass plate was experienced, if not especially intelligent, and had long since learned to keep out of harm's way. It got so it would do as much for anybody and take the door with it.

The rest of McCormick's floor was taken up with his immediate convoy of secretaries, researchers, cartoonists, editorial writers and uniformed house police, part of such a force all through the building. The street floor was used much as in any such building having traffic with the general community, except that it was, and still is, better kept than most. Promotion essays were on display to keep up spirits against invidious reference to The Second City. Uniformed guards were polite except to holdup men. In one such affray, a *Tribune* policeman was killed and another wounded. The bandits thought they had got away, but in the end the *Tribune* said it downed them, as it always claimed to do. One such claim has for years been a matter of some contention. A *Tribune* criminal specialist of the Thompson period, by name, Jake Lingle, was shot on the way to a horse race. A professional killer, hired by parties not to this day specified, was brought to trial and sentenced to fourteen years in prison. If he had anything to say about it, nothing has ever come out. But McCormick had plenty. Lingle was killed at 1:30 P.M. on June 9, 1930, in a pedestrian tunnel beneath Michigan Avenue, at the very peak of the long, really roweling fight with Thompson in which the *Tribune* had used every bomb it could, of paper and ink. Chicago was filled with direct-action types of less narrow view about bombs of another kind. McCormick can be pardoned, surely, for at first supposing poor Lingle had been struck down in line of duty. Within minutes after the word of his death reached the Tower, a reward of $25,000 was offered for the killer.

In a few days McCormick was devastated to learn that if Lingle had died in some cause, it was not the *Tribune*'s. He was shown to have assets unreasonable on his salary and unaccountable otherwise. Men began to hint that he was certainly not less than a friend of friends of Capone. Other Chicago newspapers, then papers from other cities, began to use Lingle's affairs in such humiliation of McCormick that he put the whole *Tribune* executive force through a rigorous system of clearances. Then he began to get back some of his own, for at knowledge of Chicago's inner life the *Tribune* had then, and has now, no match except possibly the Federal Bureau of Investigation. McCormick's private housecleaning was all in his honor and he was merciless, as far as he had any housecleaning to do. In none of it was any major personage found wanting. This was not so in some cases elsewhere, to this day tiptoed past by Chicago's press historians. The whole Lingle case, noisome as its details are, again is more to McCormick's credit than he ever had the perspective to see. Chicago was never mistaken by anybody for the Holy City, but with a mayor such as Thompson to set the pace, those who wished to go in for its total dissolution had their finest hour. His Honor's campaign flyer for 1931 and the Lingle case are alike, as evidence that McCormick had his back to the wall. For all his antic style, he was a man desperate on a better side of the battle for Chicago than not, and the city gained by it. But there is still the fact that his performance was sometimes so far off balance that men having transactions with him made it appear the top of Tribune Tower was a sort of lunatic's attic. This following is perhaps the ultimate specimen of its class.

Shortly after the excitements of the 1952 Republican convention, a Senator under heavy obligation paid him a call of courtesy. On return to Washington the Senator told it to more than one person of high reliability that conversation was entirely amiable, but he felt an uneasy sense the two of them were not alone. He happened to glance up toward the ceiling behind McCormick. A flap had been let down. An unblinking eye was fixed on him and a machine gun was aimed squarely at the great, curl-decked senatorial head. Nothing more is going to be attempted here to make out the sense of the story beyond the record that there can be no doubt the Senator went to the Tower and he lived to tell his story. The Senator's reputation was that of a man with great gift. None of his gifts included a claim that, either as a private or public man, he tended to lie about his friends. And McCormick was his friend.

Just what it was about McCormick that inspired so much repetition of such matters as literal truth remains an open and unsolved question. There was nothing jocose, really, about any part of the Battle for Chicago, reduced to the form of a collision between the mayor and the editor. The end of it left Thompson defeated, discredited and if any still could not say he was degraded, then the opening of his bank boxes after his death invited them to speak up. Who did? The end of it left McCormick inflated with a sense of invulnerable power and with no capacity for restraint, once his suspicions were aroused. He tended to find every hostile holder of public power thereafter another Thompson. At bottom that was exactly how he came to see Franklin D. Roosevelt. There is no better way to sum up McCormick's experience with Thompson, and furthermore to draw the distinction plain between the *opera bouffe* surface appearance and the desperate underlying issues, than to offer brief synopses of three lawsuits which typify the whole. The first was a personal libel suit by the mayor against the *Tribune*. The second was a libel suit against the *Tribune* by the city government itself. The third was a suit by the *Tribune* to recover from Thompson and others, in the name of the taxpayers. The first and third are in the ordinary nature of such things and need little elaboration. The mayor spent just one day on the witness stand in his own libel complaint. After Weymouth Kirkland had finished with him in that very opening round, he pulled up lame and dropped his case. In the suit to recover on behalf of the taxpayers, the *Tribune* won in the trial court but lost the appeal on a finding that though the defendants had not acted on information and reports of waste, extravagance and mishandling, the evidence fell short of showing them guilty of "intentional, deliberate and wrongful conduct."

It was the suit brought against the paper by Chicago's corporation counsel that put everything in an entirely different class. The charge was that the *Tribune* had falsely and maliciously described conditions in Chicago with such effect the municipality's credit with lenders had been gravely impaired. Damages, in the name of the city of Chicago, were asked to the total of $10 million. Here was a case brought by the city government, to be tried by the city's legal staff before a judge in the city's system of law. The verdict, if it fell for the city government, would mean the knackers for not only the newspaper, but for McCormick personally. He would be the blunderer who had misused his office and betrayed all the stockholders. If he lost, he would be bankrupt, like his father, and there was no rich wife or father-in-law with influence to get him a government job abroad for the sake of his feelings. He could not hope to practice law in the town where he had been born, even if Thompson would allow him to try. It was unimaginable that Robert R. McCormick would ever again show his face in Chicago after wrecking the *Tribune* and losing his last nickel, as well.

The case, which is recorded officially as *City of Chicago* vs. *Tribune Co. April 1923 307 Ill. 595,* rested on the issue of libel on government, a proposition which reappeared following the Supreme Court decision of 1954 that it is not lawful to administer tax-supported education in such a way that pupils are segregated by race. More than one newspaper then found itself accused of willful damages because of commentaries on various cities' official activities in the aftermath of that finding. Few, if any, remembered the first such case in the United States was fought out between McCormick and Thompson. McCormick won it, not least because of his own memory for facts and his knowledge of law. But he was prompt, always, in his many writings and speeches centered on it, to say that the master of the case from start to finish was Kirkland. There cannot be any doubt Kirkland saved him then as he had in the Ford case and as he was to do many a time more.

When McCormick, in 1942, fell into another lawsuit of at least equal dimensions with that one which had tested the doctrine of libel on government, Kirkland violated his own house rule. Instead of finding out what McCormick wanted and giving to him, Kirkland offered his lifelong friend, unasked, advice on how to stay out of a senseless personal fight with another man who had been McCormick's friend from childhood.

McCormick rejected the suggestion and he lost, all around. So did many others tied to his judgment. The man to whom he lost was Marshall Field III, whose grandfather once had loaned McCormick's grandfather the money to buy control of the *Tribune.*

CHAPTER THIRTEEN ★★★ Until his collision with Franklin D. Roosevelt, McCormick was moderately peaceable on the national scene after 1919. He opposed the Democratic ticket for 1920, as a matter of course, but had little enough to do about selecting the Republican. To some degree, anyhow, that honor went more to another sometime Chicago journalist, who exemplifies the kind of party operative McCormick came to define as the "Eastern, Pocketbook Republican." By this, he meant people who interfered with his rulings of how the Grand Old Party should proceed.

McCormick was still a very small boy when George Brinton McClellan Harvey had a look at Chicago, on Melville Stone's *News*, and was a schoolboy in England when Harvey returned East to edit the New Jersey supplement of Joseph Pulitzer's New York *World*, then the great power among Democrats. From that start Harvey moved up to be managing editor of the *World*'s main edition in Manhattan. He came as a colonel in the New Jersey household guard to His Excellency, the Governor.

Colonel Harvey was never windy about doctrinaire politics, and soon quit journalism to grow rich procuring utility franchises for William C. Whitney, himself an urbane exemplar of the school that holds it not impossible for an intelligent man to be a Democrat and still make a moderately good living on Wall Street. Colonel Harvey never lost his love for the uses of print. His first acquisition was the *North American Review*. Then he heard J. P. Morgan had grown weary of holding notes on Harper & Brothers. So, Colonel Harvey next had in his kit bag a really important publication, *Harper's Weekly*. As of 1901 he was ready to apply his wisdom at the art of making Presidents. It was a time when the Republicans flourished Henry Cabot Lodge as their "scholar in politics" and the Democrats felt their own champion, William Jennings Bryan, lacked something as answer. In 1906, at the Lotos Club in New York City, Colonel Harvey elevated the tone of politics by proposing the President of Princeton University for President of the United States. Such was Mr. Wilson's entrance into public affairs. Most politicians thought he would be of little success, but certainly tractable as a stalking horse. They seemed not to hear him murmur that any who could survive the machinations of faculty life could meet the simple-minded gropings of "practical" men blindfolded. In 1911, the shock of recognition sobered Colonel Harvey into taking his patronage elsewhere. He became so total a critic of Wilson that in the debate on the Versailles Treaty none surpassed and few matched Harvey in assault.

Just the same, he was out in the cold until 1920, when the deadlock between Governor Frank O. Lowden of Illinois and General Leonard Wood gave him opportunity to be, at last, the man in possession. That legendary "smoke-filled room" at the Blackstone Hotel in Chicago was Colonel Harvey's and his was the argument, started well before he left New York City, that the convention should avoid stress. The consequence was that mellow-toned Senator from Ohio, Warren Gamaliel Harding. Later, Mr. Harding's Attorney General and special agent, Harry A. Daugherty, tried to downgrade the colonel's claim to honors for the settlement. So have others. But if ever an Eastern Pocketbook Republican had his way, Colonel Harvey had it in Chicago, 1920, and much good did it do him. To McCormick, who had been trying to settle between Lowden and Wood, the Pocketbook Gang were his party's curse, and curse them he did as he called the roll in 1952 of "Middle Western boys" he considered captives of Colonel Harvey's successors. His list of casualties was, at least, distinctive. It included every Republican candidate for President after 1936.

If anybody had ever asked McCormick whether his own attempts to shift Republican control to his jurisdiction had pocketbook purpose, he had a patent answer. The *Tribune* stood for the Declaration of Independence, the Northwest Ordinances, the U.S. Constitution and the Middle West as the Seedbed of the Free American Spirit. It seemed to escape his notice that great as those expressions of the human spirit have proved to be, and powerful as their impact in the Middle West most certainly has been, not one had its origin within the shadow of the Tribune Tower. Whatever wind blew them to Chicago, it was a wind from the East. Just the same, as far as McCormick was concerned, the Republican Party was a Middle-Western invention. He might even have dared to say it was an invention of the Chicago *Tribune* itself, if shoved roughly enough. Attempts to use it contrary to his views, therefore, were inevitably corrupt. And since he knew a great deal more about the inner workings of the Republican Party than most of its members, not to say a *very* great deal more than any Democrat, his commentaries tended to make members of the Pocketbook Gang jump. They seemed slow to grasp the point that it was an error to suppose McCormick, just because he was obviously no slouch at looking after his own pocketbook, must be pretty much just like themselves.

At looking after his own pocketbook, McCormick, indeed, was no slouch. He used the years between Harding and Hoover about as well as anybody in the United States. James W. Gerard, who had been Woodrow Wilson's ambassador to Germany and then treasurer of the Democratic Party during its fallow years, drew up a list in 1930 of the ten most influential men in the country, as he measured them from his perspective. He put McCormick right there among the Rockefellers, Mellons and other such finance capitalists who, in Gerard's opinion, made up a sort of supergovernment apart from the public authority. If it was giving all of them credit they were soon to discover they did not really have, at least Mr. Gerard's estimate was pretty close to the magnates' own.

McCormick did not make the kind of money in the great decade that attracted such capital operators as the Mellons and Rockefellers. Magnates on that order put their money into the extraction, processing and marketing of substances and objects around which the very industrial system itself had been evolved.

McCormick could say, and be absolutely accurate about it, that he owed the great finance capitalists nothing, either literally or emotionally, for the development of the Tribune Company. It was a bootstrap operation, and all the more remarkable that by 1930 it was a fully formed project in the best tradition of the great industrial systems. By then, the Tribune Company started in Quebec with trees. It cut these down and ran them through mills; brought paper out of the millends onto boats and by water to its warehouses in Chicago and New York, and in those cities ran the paper through its machines and sold the product to all comers. But more than that, it had a sales force distributing news stories, comic strips, fashion and medical notes, all the special excitements at which Patterson was a master, and for which consuming newspapers clamored. The Tribune Company's syndicated features were of such high quality at drawing readers no publisher ever let one get away if he could help himself.

And that was not the end of it. The Tribune Company by 1930 was already well out beyond the limitations of paper and ink in vending its merchandise. It was on the air. The Chicago meatpackers used to boast that they had learned how to market everything about the pig except the squeal. McCormick, if he had liked, could say he had managed that sort of total extraction, too. At the integrated vending of news products, which came to be done in much more sophisticated style later by very different sorts of men in great combines of audio, visual and printing systems, McCormick was, in his day, really the true breaker of new ground.

To appreciate his achievement it is necessary to have a few fundamentals on the technical facts of life in the news industry. News is difficult to define, but easy to identify. News is whatever people think it is. One thing has been proved beyond argument. News is vendible merchandise. People will pay to get it. Once they have settled on a chosen source of supply, they will even pay in advance.

The first important supply of news in this country was, of course, the great politico-military encounter begun in the eighteenth century between the Colonists and the government of George III in London. It continued in the same basic tradition until, as of 1865, the United States made up its mind to be a national establishment, as against a loose confederation of regional interests. Then, the Gilded Age opened up the market for news on a broader scale, as people began to take interest in one another, as such. Affairs of government had to compete for attention inside the boundaries of the total human drama, ships burned at sea, breaks in the cotton market, girls ruined in the big city and quarrels of seminarians on Alpha and Omega.

Rising literacy and a sense of involvement sent the market for news going up at a geometric rate of progression. Finance capital had its chance, if it liked, to take over the works. It missed. Men who understand gold movement, extraction of ores from the earth and fabrication of objects to wear, use or eat, and how to organize rational enterprises in such traditional sources of profit, never have been comfortable taking the risks that go with really important investment in ideas, which, after all, is the final thing to call news. News is an idea.

The idea-mongers of the nineteenth century ran a poor sort of shop. Joseph Medill was in the tradition, a country boy with some vague notion of being a lawyer who learned to set type as a means of picking up cash, and with brains, gall, frugality, luck and a friend willing to lend him some money at last got control of a plant. In the late nineteenth century things began to change. Before, type was set by hand. Paper was made from rags. It was beautiful and durable, but very hard to get and even harder to pay for. Printers struck off their sheets on flatbed presses that started out being run by hand and finally used steam power.

But then a constellation of inventions hit in sequence. The telegraph made news available in strings of cities at once, as it happened. Paper from woodpulp was not so beautiful or durable, but it was in ample supply and the price was easier. Machines set type, with men only guiding them. More machines cast curved metal plates to fit on cylinders. So now the old flatbed became a high speed rolling machine, at one end taking in a web of paper from a reel and at the other chopping the printed, folded total into segments ready for the customer.

It was a revolution.

Such was the business as McCormick stumbled into it before the First World War. He had used his opening years to lay a foundation for making the most of that revolution, but before he could get really into it, the war took him away.

By 1919 journalism was up against still another revolution.

Everything had changed, really, except the ordinary publisher's approach to the marketplace. He got into business any way he could, using enough down money to get the use of plant and equipment and some paydays ahead for his working force. Then and thereafter, the feat of his life consisted in collecting circulation and advertising fees faster than his creditors could get at him with their bills.

Such, in very truth, was still the general way in American journalism when McCormick settled down in 1920 to see what he could do on a long-range plan for the Tribune Company.

While the ordinary publisher was absorbed in watching the spectaculars of such as W. R. Hearst, McCormick was building an industrial machine. Hearst was a sight, all right. He started with his family's fortune in mining and land and bought up newspapers, magazines, book publishers and motion picture companies. He collected huge sums as a great expansion in reading hit the world of the common man, but spent it back on more newspapers, magazines, book publishing, motion pictures, castles, armor, hotels and at entertaining himself with an ever-shifting herd of admirals, generals, mayors and publicans of any sort or nationality he could catch. The ordinary publisher, instead of gaping at this latter-day Lorenzo the Magnificent, would have done well to notice the structure of trees, ships, machines and men McCormick was organizing. For instance, there was the early warning that radio transmission of information, "the wireless," would be important to the ordinary publisher, sooner or later.

In his memoirs, McCormick claimed he was alerted to radio in the First World War. If so, he was one of the very few who caught the drift, but he had evidence that he was telling the truth about it. Immediately on his return to Chicago he put the Tribune Company to work on the formation of the News Traffic Board, Ltd., which set up a receiving station at Halifax, Nova Scotia, to handle transoceanic traffic for not only the *Tribune,* but also other newspapers bright enough to subscribe. By the time commercial cable companies waked up, it was too late. In 1929, the old station at Halifax was no longer efficient. The subscribing papers organized Press Wireless which operated both sending and receiving stations on Long Island. During the Second World War, Press Wireless furnished a world-wide communications net from battlefronts to newspapers, press associations and radio stations. If anybody bothered to drop McCormick a note of appreciation for having germinated this traffic system, he never mentioned it, but the record is undeniable. He started it.

In the broadcasting business, too, he wasted no time finding a place. In December, 1921, the *Tribune* entered agreement with a primitive Chicago station to furnish sports and market news and summaries of general commentary on current events. In 1923, it leased a station started up the year before without any clear idea except to broadcast dance music from the Drake Hotel. Already, the *Tribune* had a license for one of its Great Lakes paper ships to operate point-to-point communication under the call letters WGN for "World's Greatest Newspaper." This was adopted for the new operation. After a while the Tribune Company bought the whole station for sixteen thousand dollars and got a transfer of the operating license, something very few publishers had yet bothered to do. It also picked up two more stations in the Chicago suburbs, so that by the time of the National Radio Conference in 1925, McCormick could come to the table with three licenses.

Broadcasting was a babble of confusion by 1925. Stations jumped power and shifted channels to get at audiences. If there was no street-fighting there was outcry in surfeit. McCormick was always quick enough to resent government interference with the commercial traffic of the *Tribune* in printed form. It embarrassed him not one whit now to invoke government help against commercial interference with the *Tribune* in its radio form. And, as usual, Weymouth Kirkland was ready with just the man for the job. A member of the law firm, Louis Caldwell, Phi Beta Kappa from Amherst, was told off to study the only statute on the books, the Radio Act of 1912, and come up with a plan. Then the *Tribune* sued to enjoin another station from interfering with WGN's sole enjoyment of its chosen frequency. The victory in *Tribune Company* vs. *Oak Leaves Broadcasting Station* is the landmark case on which broadcasting in the United States has been guided ever since. Caldwell was moved to Washington and advised the Congressional committees which drafted the Radio Act of 1927, the first real effort to get a foundation in law for total electronic communication methods. The central achievement of this act was creation of the quasi-judicial independent agency which still has that responsibility, the Federal Communications Commission.

Caldwell sat in for a while as general counsel of the commission and then returned to his real business. For the rest of his life he had his hands full at the law firm's Washington office, seeing after local details of a running war with taxing agencies, regulators of paper imports and all the other demonries of the central power. Caldwell's personal specialty was to see that WGN got the best in radio, and on McCormick's terms, which were to operate as an independent competitor against the network systems run from New York. WGN, in the great period of radio, had one of the very few super-power "clear channel" stations in the country. With this, it squashed the signals of competitors for hundreds of square miles around Chicago. In New York, Patterson could not do so well. The *News* was limited to contract operation with an independent station, but introduced a novel feature, five minutes of bulletin news on the hour and in between a great deal of dance music, with added newspaper promotion stunts, all of which became commonplace, later. When television came along, Tribune Company was in at once with stations of its own in Chicago and New York, both independent of network controls. If McCormick ever longed for the easy life of shelter within chain systems dominated by someone else, he never let on, and neither did he let independence punish his pocketbook. On the air as on the printing press, Tribune Company of Illinois pursued its own, lone, hardheaded way and made money doing it. Ten years after McCormick was dead and as even more portentous technological changes confronted the ingenuity of newspaper management, there was none in the country more willing to see the changes come than Tribune Company.

In the Harding to Hoover years, therefore, McCormick's best work was at discovering new forms of selling news, of printing it better, faster and in four colors, in short, at corporate enterprise. Except when it was in some frenzy or other about William Hale Thompson and the ruination of Chicago, the *Tribune* editorial page was a cool and supercilious analyst of low life among politicians, with little respect for party. When Harding's flop put the Republicans on the defensive, the *Tribune* laid the basic trouble to Prohibition and traced a straight line from the pomposities of the Anti-Saloon League to the prison cell waiting for Albert Fall, an old-fashioned, Western hard-rock prospector who had been Harding's Secretary of the Interior. That took care of the great Teapot Dome scandal. Down in Tennessee, a high school teacher was brought to book for teaching, contrary to state law, Darwinian ideas on the evolution of man. The *Tribune* considered this unwarranted religious meddling in affairs of state. Several times it explained to its readers that it had no wish to give up its Republican Party responsibilities but that crooks, no matter what their label, had better beware. But the *Tribune* presented no arguments for fundamental social change. It took the world as the world chose to come, saving a granite opposition to suggestion that government, of right, may regulate the judgment and tastes of newspaper proprietors.

Having been very sensibly frightened by that $10 million suit in the name of the city of Chicago, McCormick stayed alert to any chance that final rules of safety could be established without the *Tribune* as defendant in chief again. His chance came in Minnesota. An obscure publication in Minneapolis called *The Saturday Press* was driven to the wall, following accounts of life to the north. In 1925, the Minnesota legislature passed a statute that a judge in a court of equity could shut down any newspaper, and keep it shut down, on a showing to him, alone, of information that its product was "malicious, scandalous and defamatory." This was invoked against the *Saturday Press* in 1927, and the editors, J. M. Near and Howard Guilford, appealed to McCormick for help. He put the *Tribune* into their case as a friend at court and then, to establish himself as first among equals in the whole journalistic establishment, invited the American Newspaper Publishers' Association to show the color of its own money. It came in for five thousand dollars, and all across the country newspapers lectured their readers about the great cause at issue. Nor, for all their pomposities and self-righteous tone, were they faking the sense of it.

Near vs. *Minnesota* finally got to the Supreme Court in 1931, to test the clause in the Bill of Rights, "Congress shall make no law respecting an establishment of religion, or prohibiting the free exercise thereof; or abridging the freedom of speech, or of the press; or the right of the people peaceably to assemble, and to petition the Government for a redress of grievances."

The Minnesota authorities had an ingenious argument. If a man in the dairy business persists in selling bad milk a judge can enjoin him from selling any more milk at all. This is endured by the public on the theory the law is just in saying that in such cases the past is a reliable prediction about the future.

If it is lawful to restrain a man who persists in selling bad milk, why is it not lawful to do the same about bad ideas? The Minnesota doctrine was that its judges could perfectly well tell from past issues of the *Saturday Press* and all the ructions between its operators and claimants against them, that future issues would also contain material that would be "malicious, scandalous and defamatory," in the meaning of the statute and under verdict of court. How is the peddler of printed paper any different from the peddler of milk, cat food, stocks and bonds, or anything else, for that matter?

The Minnesota argument in essence came down to posing two Constitutional points in opposition: the right of people to defend themselves against certified predators in the marketplace, as against the right of people to risk their necks at self-expression. Here is how the Supreme Court chose to answer the cry for justice:

> The fact that the liberty of the press may be abused by miscreant purveyors of scandal does not make any the less necessary the immunity of the press from previous restraint in dealing with official misconduct. Subsequent punishment for such abuses as may exist is the appropriate remedy, consistent with constitutional privilege.

The language was that of Charles Evans Hughes, now once more well out of lines of fire in politics and back on the Supreme Court as Chief Justice. Voting with him were Associate Justices Oliver Wendell Holmes, Louis D. Brandeis, Harlan F. Stone and Owen J. Roberts. Against: George Sutherland, Pierce Butler, Willis Van Devanter and James Clark McReynolds. Students of Supreme Court political philosophical loyalties can make of that close call what they will. By five to four, that decision saved the essence McCormick, as the years galloped by, somehow treated as one with himself, and which he labeled The Freedom of the Press.

It has already been fairly well indicated that McCormick tended to develop strong feelings toward men in political power, and his feelings were almost always negative to them. There was one who suited him very well. President Coolidge saw government as administration. Taxation was a dangerous explosive. Innovation was near to sin. And careless handling of the people's money was theft, just as much as deliberate misappropriation. "Gingerly" was the watchword all around in Coolidge's day and McCormick made the most of it. In sum, he taught his production force to think a South Side quarrel on street names bigger news than the fall of a ministry in Graustark. He was in tune with the times. Like all the rest of the nation, Chicago was fascinated mostly with itself. The *Tribune*'s

Paris edition did its best to elevate tone with accounts of new departures in literature and the arts, but late-coming adventurers in the Tribune Press Service overseas, who mistook themselves for Richard Harding Davis, like those on the paper at home, were in for shocks. The experience of George Seldes, who told it more than once in a long, embittered memoir on the whole American press, was standard. He was sent from Paris to examine the German railway system and report what a mess it had fallen into under management by the socialists. He sent back an explanation that it was doing fine. There was considerable traffic between Paris and Chicago before he got the point that nobody had asked him *whether* the railroads were badly run, but only to shape up the details of evidence. The verdict was already established. Like Emory Thomason, Mr. Seldes learned the hardest way that McCormick made no exceptions to the rule, "for what I'm paying, you'll do what I tell you." But even Seldes conceded McCormick, as employer, was generous enough. If some errant had to be cast back into the country of the blind from which he had been taken through some underling's blunder, the severance check was larger than any other publisher was ever likely to surrender, except under court order.

By the time the Jazz Age had begun to go stale, McCormick had long since got the reputation among the working press as a curiosity beyond their reckoning. The Tribune Company in all its branches was well ahead of the times, in general, at social welfare services, insurance, medical aid, home financing and far beyond the rest of journalism, taken as a whole, for job security. Furthermore, it was all business, from top to bottom. It fought for news with organized platoons of photographers, reporters and specialists on whatever the case might need. And its men were sure of being backed to the hilt, no matter who tried to deflect them or complained about them after having lost the test of will. McCormick, as employer, was a model.

But no man could guess how he would behave about any of the ordinary sentimentalities so dear to working journalism. In Washington, where the *Tribune* had kept a bureau since Joseph Medill first came down to spy out the land for Abraham Lincoln in 1860, the chief of bureau would inevitably be elected to the Gridiron Club, the insiders' inside, or at least so its members like to think, of political journalism. McCormick would turn up occasionally for the Gridiron's semiannual dinners at the Willard Hotel, but he was not a very exciting guest. His tendency was to sit as if alone and to show little interest in the political skits and speeches, though he was known to react with mighty rumblings and even to smile if the songs hit him right. But after dinner he wasted little time roving colleagues' suites.

Most publishers treated this pastime as if the fate of the world were settled between jokes about the low quality of the bootleg whisky they split up in their suites with members of Congress and other high-flying guests. Those were the years of the affectation in Washington, "drink wet but vote dry." The theory was that the voters were mortally opposed to traffic in liquor and political survival depended on public obedience to the received view, no matter what was done in private. It was also taken as a demonstration of governmental probity for federal agents to hack their way through doors to get at evidence of evil-doing. But no agent was ever so delusional as to go near the Willard during a Gridiron weekend.

McCormick had his own way of handling the off-hours liquor problem on the *Tribune*. In Chicago, families were made to feel they were part of the paper and staff outings made it difficult for wastrels to conceal themselves. In Washington, he used an interesting variation. The National Press Club is to the political community of the capital what Rotary is to a city centering its life around another sort of merchandise. The Press Club put together a great plan during the Coolidge years for a central building to be filled with representatives of the whole community of journalists, lawyers, lobbyists and press agents interested in the news business. The top floor was set aside for the club itself. It was an idea most publishers found congenial and subscriptions to underwrite the project went smoothly enough, until the managers reached McCormick. He said he had no intention whatsoever of putting money into some place for journalists to hide in when they were through work. *Tribune* men already knew that when he was done with them each day, they belonged at home. As for the rest, what they did was none of his business.

The Washington bureau of the Chicago *Tribune* kept its old quarters several blocks away from the Press Building, and neither then nor after did any *Tribune* man with the will to rise ever make the mistake of getting his name on the list of Press Club worthies who rotated the various titles and perquisites of that amiable institution among their handful—until, at last, television and radio broke up the writing journalists' fun. Then everything had to be redefined. The meaning of "The Freedom of the Press" itself was confronted with challenges of technology far more shaking than anything attempted by any minion of law, from the mayor of Chicago to the President of the United States.

By that time McCormick was well out of it, and nowhere among journalists of any sort, verbal or addicted to printing, was there one visible who had his contrary determination to buck the tide.

Whether a television camera has the same Constitutional rights and immunities as a human being who has been rigged to form ideas about events and nonevents was the heart of the question. But nobody pressed very firmly for answer. For one reason among many, nobody quite knew how to frame the question itself, let alone argue for the answer.

CHAPTER FOURTEEN ★★★ As Election Day approached in 1932 all the world knew it could only confirm a judgment already passed.

In 1865 the country's reaction to suffering at the hand of power gone berserk was a rush into The Gilded Age of every man for himself. Fortunately, there were plains and mountains, Indians and rough weather still in ample supply to absorb those energies quite new, on which Henry Adams pondered.

In 1932, the country was in reaction to horror quite as terrible as any civil war, but not so easily called by name. Just exactly what share government had in bringing it on was part of a general doubt. There was doubt, too, about great captains of enterprise, hitherto generally thought wise as they thought themselves powerful. The field of battle was littered with reputations, dead as the dead from Sumter to Appomattox. The surrogate for every otherwise unidentified object of national animosity was a sad man in the White House waiting the end.

It was a frightful time. There had been no physical frontier to explore in the new version of The Gilded Age that came after 1918 and called itself The Jazz Age. And now the country found its energies had exploded against something silent, motionless, invisible, and all the more terrifying in its mystery. Just a few years before, learned doctors had spoken of achieving what the less artful had phrased as "a permanently rising plateau of prosperity." It had not worked out exactly that way.

In the years following Franklin D. Roosevelt, learned doctors again groped for a phrase. This next time it was called "people's capitalism." Government was not again so timid about its relation to the form and substance of enterprise; free, as some liked to define it; or as McCormick faithfully believed, enchained. His behavior, on contemplating this inner vision, was such that exploration of the evidence must begin with some attempt to define, or at least try to discover, whatever it was McCormick thought capitalism to be. If he ever bothered to make such an effort for himself, the record does not so show in this research. Therefore a substitute, with which he did not quarrel in the *Tribune,* is offered as a guess at McCormick's own view in the prime years of The Jazz Age.

On October 22, 1928, Herbert Hoover spoke in New York City. The Republican National Committee had spread advertisements throughout the country's press, reading:

"Republican prosperity has reduced hours and increased earning capacity, silenced discontent, put the proverbial 'chicken in every pot,' and a car in every backyard to boot."

Mr. Hoover had adapted this to read: "The slogan of progress is changing from the full dinnerpail to the full garage." Now in his climactic moment he spoke as an Iowa blacksmith's orphaned son who had yet battered his way upward, in exercise of an option held by every free-born citizen of the great Republic. In 1918, Woodrow Wilson had sailed on the S.S. *George Washington* saying the New World was now off to redress the grievance of a universal tragedy sprung on mankind from within the Old. How, now, in 1928, did the record seem to Herbert Hoover? He spoke for the generation:

> We were challenged with a peacetime choice between the American system of rugged individualism and a European philosophy of diametrically opposed doctrines—doctrines of paternalism and state socialism. The acceptance of these ideas would have meant the undermining of the individual initiative and enterprise through which our people have grown to unparalleled greatness.

And what, in retrospect, is the climax of The Jazz Age to be called, after all? Was it not a "people's capitalism"? Barbers jumped aboard stock tips, heedless as bankers of J. P. Morgan's thought that "the market will fluctuate." Some workingmen really did build two-car garages. And had it not all come about with every citizen feeling himself both rugged and very definitely individual?

In 1928 it was all so. In 1932, there were those who spoke of the world's end, the finish of civilized intercourse. Some buried gold bars, put rifles, canned goods and family mementoes underground, much as another generation would do on first hearing that governments now had weapons with which to blow whole continents apart. Except that the second time around any citizen found in possession of gold bars could expect to be frog-marched off to jail. And, as some were to do again that second time, there were those in 1932 who fled to islands in the south, pursuing sanctuary among fried fish and hurricanes. Once boredom had driven them from swapping spouses to bouts with alcohol and doleful talk about swimming for the horizon one night just to let the sharks settle everything, those who dared finally drifted back to a society caught up in a great swirl of change. Nobody, except a few irritated relatives, quite recalled they had been away.

Among the many shocks that had come to Herbert Hoover, after 1928, was discovery that one of the most rugged individualists on the American scene did not see eye-to-eye with him.

As far as McCormick was concerned, his conscience was clear. He had not wasted the years of opportunity in riotous abandon. He had no apologies for living according to his right, as he saw it. At the war's end his mother had faced up the presence of a daughter-in-law who took nobody's snubs calmly. The dowager Mrs. McCormick set out to make peace as best she could. She gave the couple their handsome house on Astor Street and her son a Rolls-Royce cut to fit him in his opera hat. He clambered in and out of it without the slightest notice of any who might have tendencies to giggle. His dignity was total. When it suited him he retired to Paris for diversion, free of any concern that Mayor Thompson's minions might cause him to regret. He and his wife kept a house down in South Carolina for the hunting and polo at Aiken. McCormick was also a founding member of an elegant establishment calling itself Grasslands, in the Tennessee fox country near Nashville. It had a course laid out on the lines of Aintree in England, and gentlemen rode for a gold cup donated by the King of Spain, with all the hazard of the Grand National. As long as the fun lasted.

But McCormick never let the sporting life confuse his memory of a father's ruin. In 1928 he wrote his mother a warning that the market in stocks had gone beyond the bounds of reason. Disaster was certain unless somebody could stop it, but who he could not say. When he died, McCormick had a copy of that letter on his dressing table. But his interest was no more negative than trivial. Even in so provincial a capital as Nashville, he found opportunity to acquire important assets as the shadows lengthened. He had already found one Nashville political cartoonist to his liking. That was Carey Orr. Now, he spotted another, Joseph Parrish. In the years of the New Deal and in the war years that followed, the Orr and Parrish executions of McCormick's humors grew to be objects of absorbing interest to political analysts all over the world. It was no idle rumor that men who knew their business took care to stay out of harm's way, if possible, on days that Mr. Roosevelt, Mr. Ickes and other dignitaries of quick-firing temperament, had been depicted.

Orr's style was hard and simple, direct as a mace, and as little used in fun. Cartoons by Parrish had a wit sly as Mickey Mousc, but the effect was ruinous. No man can feel too grand after having seen himself portrayed to millions with his pants fallen down. And the number to see such sights really ran to millions. Cartoons by Orr, Parrish and McCutcheon, too, were sold through the *Tribune*'s syndicate after they had been first used in Chicago. They reappeared in every part of the country, and in such a way McCormick not only had the pleasure of forming minds far beyond his own bailiwick but he had the even greater pleasure of making money at it, too.

In the Fall of 1929, the roof of the world came down again.

It seems beyond the powers of historians, logicians, orators or dramatists, to convince any generation that some great event within which it has lived can be conveyed to a next with full meaning. So with the veterans of that momentous decade, 1929–1939. The literature is already vast and yet there is no end to it. Nor does it appear that any single man, or even any likely combination of them, is ever going to get the whole of it together in one account, though John Kenneth Galbraith has come very near doing just that on the opening round, with *The Great Crash, 1929*. Nobody who lived through it can read his report without a clutching at the heart.

By now it should be plain enough to any reader that McCormick had problems with himself. Out of his childhood he brought the frights of the Haymarket Riot and his loneliness, not helped by listening to Joseph Medill recall his own hard life, the pair of them shunted away from the old man's wrangling daughters. The great crash and the strains that followed it were, of course, hard on everybody. On McCormick, in more ways than one, the total was unhinging, so that in final crises of judgment which later cornered him, it is clear that he was governed less by his splendid, hard, Scots-Irish sense of reality and driven frantic by private, slavering demons. If it had been his temper, McCormick, too, would have cut and run for an island in the Caribbean. In panic fits, so the psychological scholars put it, the animal choice is "flight or fight." McCormick was one of those who dared not ever flee. So all he really knew how to do, in a panic state, was to fight.

The panic did not come to him all at once. In his years of clear-headed sense he had put the Tribune Company in superb condition to meet its tests. In the publishing industry, as in so many others, that was a rarity. W. R. Hearst, to whom the ordinary publisher had looked in dazzlement, was caught short as any tyro. Three times, Hearst's frantic stewards put through flat 10 percent cuts in wages for the terrified hands, who skulked in hallways and hid behind pillars on hearing that "efficiency experts" were back. "Efficiency" consisted in reducing light bulbs from sixty to forty watts in already dismal washrooms, and ordering waste paper be used for hand towels. It was common belief and well-founded, too, that these "experts" had not the slightest regard for merit, service or family problems. They came to get rid of bodies. They selected as they saw. Even so, before it was finally brought to some semblance of order, Hearst's madhouse of interests reached the point that more bills were in than the stewards could hope to meet. They would have to declare their master bankrupt. Two ladies saved him by posting guaranties of their own, well-guarded funds. One was his friend, Marion Davies. The other was McCormick's cousin, Eleanor M. Patterson. Even so, a prolonged anaconda squeeze by the Tribune Company choked Hearst out of Chicago and in New York reduced him to the point that he was no longer a serious problem.

It was not all roses for anybody. McCormick and Patterson had their narrow squeaks, but McCormick was the cannier. Patterson had decided he would have a fling in the stock market. In one day his holdings in bank stocks lost five million dollars in face value. Nothing even close to that distracted McCormick.

When the smoke began to clear away and men could examine the details of the Great Depression with something less than total panic, a great new bitterness rose. Congressional inquiry disclosed that twenty partners in the great banking house of Morgan and Company had paid only trivial sums as income taxes in 1930, and none at all for 1931 or 1932. They had done nothing worse than avail themselves of the full sanctions allowed by law, but that hardly satisfied the public fury. McCormick also came in for a solid round of curses. He had, in the crisis, run one of his ferocious campaigns against large property owners who had been delinquent from 1929 forward and were in some cases actually charged with deliberate refusals to pay what they knew they owed. The post-mortem Congressional records turned up evidence that McCormick had claimed for himself, in 1931, to own personal property of such low value that he paid a tax on it of $1,515. To which his answer was that he paid it, anyhow, and on the dot. Furthermore, the Tribune Company not only kept salaries and employment stable all the way through, but even maintained bonuses at Christmas every year except in 1931. McCormick said of that suspension, rather feebly, that he thought it well to remind that such things are not automatic.

On the morning of January 2, 1932, he called a meeting of the *Tribune*'s advertising space salesmen at the Drake Hotel. There were some 700,000 people hunting work in Chicago, near to 40 percent of all in the city capable of gainful employment, supposing it could be had. The *Tribune* men were lucky, and they knew it, just as they knew they were the envy of competitors for the advertiser's dollar who still had any jobs at all. McCormick wasted no time in breaking the news in a fashion plainly calculated to jar every man free of illusion and yet send him out in a fighting mood:

> It is a hard year that is coming and your opportunity is correspondingly large. There has been a good deal about the last year that was not happy. There was something about the year before that gave no cause for comfort, but so far as the *Tribune* is concerned, 1932 will be better.

If anybody thought he was now about to loosen up and pass out bonus checks after all they were soon disillusioned. His good news was of a different order.

Tribune team research, he said, had proved the reason for the Great Depression, and he wished members to receive the appreciation they deserved. He listed them by name, and in the years following he demonstrated that his accolade was no more campaign oratory, either. Leon Stolz, who had begun on the Paris edition and worked his way home again to Chicago, rose to become chief editorial writer of the *Tribune*. Stolz infuriated friends of Mr. Roosevelt as much for the polish and scholarship of his demonstrations in *Tribune* logic as for their hair-lifting invective. John Howard Wood had been guilty of leaving Downer's Grove, Illinois, for Harvard University and a try at teaching English at Middlesex school, in Concord, Massachusetts, but made safe harbor in 1925 as a *Tribune* reporter. McCormick moved him into the auditor's department to shine among those fearsome experts at discovering the lost weekends buried inside expense accounts. In 1960, Wood became president of the parent Tribune Company and chief trustee of the welfare fund McCormick had endowed with his share in the enterprise.

McCormick never doubted his team had found the secret of the world's tragedy, for its verdict agreed with his own. He opened his chilling revelations to the space salesmen with a roll call of ruined societies. Germany and Austria had gone to the wall, he found, and in evidence mentioned that the great Anhalt family, after centuries of power, was now down to hawking Martin Luther's Bible around Chicago for one last haul of cash. In the British Empire, New Zealand and Australia were ready to be sold up for bankruptcy. England itself, even after repudiating debts, reducing interest payments, cutting wages and deflating every money cost, still could not meet its bills. The only part of the Empire still solvent was not even British, but French, he said. That was a neat obeisance to friends in the Province of Quebec. He did not mention it, but he was even then quietly organizing an extension up there with timber, water and subsoil rights that built the Tribune Company into one of the very great land proprietors within the jurisdiction that in 1932 still liked to believe itself an empire and British.

He surveyed the state of public finance in every quarter of the

United States and found it all ruinous. And as for the federal establishment:

> Our own national deficit runs between two and three billions of dollars and will certainly exhaust the credit of the nation before next New Year's Day. Yet nobody in public office in Washington has the combined knowledge and courage to tell the truth; no finance bills proposed either by the Treasury or by opposition Congressmen offer hope to equal the drain.

None of which was news. What, then, could he have meant by saying 1932 would be better? Here the *Tribune* researchers had fortified him and William Graham Sumner should have been there to hear. The source of disaster was the cost of government, clumsiest and least useful tool of society. The *Tribune* would explain this and so civilization would be saved. And with that, the space salesmen were off to beat the streets and keep the money coming in, even if there wasn't any. They did it, too.

As for McCormick, he set out to cry the news anywhere he could get himself asked. His favorite lecture, and he gave it in nearly every principal city, reviewed the horrible tragedy of Anticosti, the great island in the Gulf of St. Lawrence once noted for its caribou and its Indians. The caribou ate lichens. The Indians ate caribou. This policy had gone on equably, at least from the Indians' point of view, until a winter storm blew a cake of ice over from the north shore to Anticosti. The ice was loaded with wolves which appear to have been sorted out for age and sex by some poltergeist of the most cruel humor, to increase and multiply at others' expense. This they were prompt to do. The Indians took to their canoes, but the wolves had not arranged return passage and, in the end, they paid for their neglect. After they had eaten all the caribou they went after the fox, then the rabbits, the ptarmigan and finally even the field mice. But when it came down to eating lichens, they handed in their portfolios and nobody in all the world shed a tear for them. Anticosti was ruined, just the same.

McCormick saw civilization was now up against the same problem. The wolves were the "burocrats" of government everywhere, and he made it plain Herbert Hoover had done little to suppress them. But the speeches of Robert R. McCormick in 1932 which chilled the sad man in the White House, warmed another. The governor of New York had been at Groton in McCormick's time and was long established in the art of elevating above the crowd to exchange knowing looks with other adepts. All Mr. Roosevelt had to do was find the right words and he would have McCormick. He found them, and he had him. For a while and to a degree, anyhow.

Those who look among the papers of Franklin D. Roosevelt in the Memorial Library at Hyde Park, so sure before they start that they know what they will find, are in for a mild shock. On June 24, 1932, Mr. Roosevelt received a telegram reading, "Please wire collect four hundred words your attitude on governmental expeditures how much should federal expense be cut what would be your plan for economy = Chicago *Tribune*." Mr. Roosevelt was not ignorant of newspaper formulations. He knew perfectly well the operating staff was executing some general instruction. It is common practice for newspapers to fire off such queries to all candidates for any office. McCormick was not aiming at him, specifically, from behind some blind.

But his reply was not sent to any "Chicago *Tribune*." Mr. Roosevelt sent a personal telegram to McCormick. He used up 107 neatly ordered words to say that he could not give any exclusive newspaper statements for publication just yet, but: ". . . for your personal information and not for publication preliminary survey leads me believe federal expenditures can be cut twenty percent by eliminating many functions not absolutely essential and by complete reorganization of many departments stop I have been giving deep study to this during past month and have excellent basis of comparison of present day with the status of expenditures in nineteen fifteen stop Should much like to talk this over with you some day Franklin D. Roosevelt."

That got results. McCormick addressed the Governor of New York in as cordial a manner as he could muster for anybody, considering how he felt at the moment:

> Dear Frank:
>
> The telegram asking you for four hundred words on economy was identical to those sent to the other candidates for nomination. I was away at the time, trying to attend the recent mishap at New London, but was called back because of the bank crisis that precipitated Thursday.

I am glad you entertain these views on public expenditures, although I doubt that there will be enough money in the country to meet half the present budget by March fourth next.

Yours sincerely,
Robert R. McCormick

It would be false to say the *Tribune,* in the 1932 campaign, was enthusiastic about anybody or anything. All is told, really, through a single editorial on the 18th Amendment. The *Tribune* explained that it hadn't ever really believed the Constitution should attempt prohibition of people's right to get drunk, but since that was the general majority idea, it had limited itself to discussing pros and cons and hoped for the best. Now it thought repeal was the only way out. In other words, what it had taken at the time to be a great movement in public feeling had put the *Tribune* up a stump. Instead of taking its customary hard line of knowing all the answers it had wobbled. Now the feeling had gone down, it was willing to say so.

The whole condition of society in the 1932 Presidential campaign, however, had McCormick back up the stump again, more ways than one. Ancient loyalties pulled him one way. Brutal realities drove him another. Both in his editorials and in other ways, he showed himself, as the summer wore on, to be capable of doubting his past certainties. Mr. Roosevelt had done a masterly job of reaching McCormick's wobbling point with that business about the cost of government. But that was not all, by any means. A great wind was shaking the world and it would have been an obtuse citizen, indeed, who did not feel it.

McCormick was anything but obtuse. In fact, he had a lengthy discussion with one newspaper colleague he thought knowledgeable, Robert McLean, publisher of the Philadelphia *Bulletin* and fellow member with McCormick on the board of trustees of the Associated Press. As McLean recalled it long afterward, McCormick recognized that some power would be surrendered and that it would probably wind up in the hands of the "burocrats." He was preparing himself to live with it. Or so he liked to think that he thought.

His correspondence with Mr. Roosevelt shows that he really tried. When the Democrats held their convention at Chicago, he offered the Roosevelt family use of his grandfather's old Red Oak Farm, now done over as a great country seat and titled Cantigny, after McCormick's favorite field of war. But Mr. Roosevelt was onto that one. Next, McCormick wrote a very amiable letter on July 19, 1932, introducing the *Tribune*'s reporter assigned to travel on the Democratic campaign train. His name was John Boettiger. McCormick said Boettiger had been told to do a comprehensive account of Mr. Roosevelt's candidacy. One thing is sure. Mr. Roosevelt did a comprehensive job on Boettiger. After the election, Boettiger, in keeping with journalistic practice, followed his man to Washington and in no time was one of the favorites at the Roosevelt Sunday evenings of scrambled eggs and concertina. Then he fell to asking the President questions at press conferences of a sort Mr. Roosevelt could use, with all his grace and style, to make McCormick seem foolish. The one most often repeated, and erroneously attributed to an exchange between the President and Walter Trohan, touched on communists in government. Mr. Roosevelt was all set with an upward cock of his cigarette holder and a wonderfully biting drawl: "Oh, now, John, tell Bertie he is just seeing things under the bed." The press claque roared and shortly Boettiger left the *Tribune*. He and the Roosevelt daughter, Anna, rearranged their lives and married.

But in 1932, both McCormick and Mr. Roosevelt were playing a very different and, in their way, each a very skillful game, in which McCormick was up against the all-time, all-around champion at political grandmother's steps. Mr. Roosevelt was prompt to return McCormick's offer of hospitality during the convention, and had him come up to the dowager Mrs. Roosevelt's Hyde Park house for a quiet talk between old friends. On August 6, 1932, McCormick wrote:

> Dear Frank:
>
> A line to thank you for your hospitality to me. I enjoyed every minute of it. . . .
>
> As my eyes struck the enclosed clipping I recalled your remarks about the people who wish to tax corporation surpluses in order to force their distribution.
>
> Booth Tarkington in *The Magnificent Ambersons* ascribes the money-hoarding proclivities of that generation to their sharp recollection of want in the pioneer days. I imagine that the impulse back

of big corporate surpluses is the outcome of similar experiences. Such, at least, was the case in my small company.

With us it had always been customary to divide the earnings every month—the rule, I suppose, among partners. No sooner had I entered the business than, with no nest egg in the bank, I ran into cut rates in circulation, a strike, a depression, and the war. From that I reacted to a big surplus for us, none of which was loaned out on call. That became too great a responsibility during the bank panic, so I distributed it. Now that the panic is over, I might like to have some of it back in the treasury.

But whatever my successes or failures, or those of anybody else running a business, I am sure I can do it better than any outsider, whether his motives be good, theoretical, or hostile to our form of government.

Yours sincerely,
Robert R. McCormick

That tells a knowledgeable reader what McCormick thought himself to be: urbane, self-assured, polite to an old friend, yet not signing off too intimately as "Bert." It tells, too, what he thought to be the truth about his view of money. He was careful with it, he didn't lend it out on call and, as a fiduciary, played it safe with the ultimate owners when the going was close. He thought himself no chance-taker.

But the bank panic, far from being over in 1932, had not really begun. By the time Mr. Roosevelt took the oath of office on March 4, 1933, the money system of the great Republic was—and people then could hardly believe it then, any more than people later could quite imagine it—dead. It had stopped. There was no system. That is all one can say to describe the fact.

Mr. Roosevelt was elected on November 8, 1932, carrying all states except Maine, Vermont, New Hampshire, Connecticut, Pennsylvania and Delaware. On February 15, 1933, at Miami, Florida, as he was riding in an open car, Giuseppe Zangara, whose full history is not even yet satisfactorily clear, fired six shots. None hit Mr. Roosevelt. But for a country already racked with terrors, that was the last bearable threat. Since 1930, more than five thousand banks had collapsed. In Michigan, the very day before, the governor had proclaimed an eight-day "holiday" for all banks in the state.

This meant the bankers just shut the doors to everybody and huddled inside, rummaging blindly through their wrecked apparatus for an idea of what to do next. And out it came. Instead of circulating money, the local clearing house would issue "scrip," whatever that meant. It meant little tickets.

If a housewife should present one to a grocer he would, perhaps, take it as a promise that one day, somehow, it would be redeemed by somebody in lawful currency of the United States, with which to settle his own debts to others who had debts of their own, too. The housewife got the scrip from her husband, who got it in lieu of cash, who got it from the clearing house which let the employer have it as a debit against his unreachable bank balance, which might, or might not, be available as money again one day.

In the meantime, McCormick and Roosevelt kept up those "Dear Bert," "Dear Frank" exchanges, playing out the manner of eighteenth-century Whig and Tory gentlemen whose responsibilities were no greater than their magnanimity. Partisan scuffling had its time, its place, but also its limits. McCormick asked to see the President-elect just after the assassination attempt, and was invited up to Hyde Park for lunch the Sunday following. His note, dated February 22, 1932, said: "I'll be there," and added, "I feel that you are going over the top, and the least I can do is to wish you well." And, as usual, though it opened, "Dear Frank," it ended, "Sincerely yours, Robert R. McCormick." And it was in keeping that McCormick would see accession to power in terms of the old phrase of attack from the trenches in 1914–18. Just five days later McCormick apologized for intruding at such a moment of "many preoccupations," but with explanation that "I fear we are on the brink of making one of those irredeemable mistakes for which opportunity [of correction?] is very seldom offered." The explanatory word which would make sense out of that is missing, but in McCormick's correspondence, if it should run more than two paragraphs, such an omission was never impossible. In any case, he went on to the crucial point, which is plain:

"The connection between the Great Lake system and the Mississippi River system and Chicago, the transportation center of the nation, is just opening. Nobody can know how much water will be needed to make this waterway practically successful. If the amount set up in the Canadian treaty turns out to be insufficient, we will never be able to have it increased without paying some great international price for it."

McCormick went on to present an argument about the dangers of falling lake levels in dry spells, maps to show the watersheds on which the system would have to rely for volume, and his explanation that "I repeat that I only venture upon your time because I want to prevent an irreparable mistake."

Mr. Roosevelt surely can be understood for failing to give the matter full focus in his mind. In a few days he would be going "over the top," and his first encounter would be with the nation's monetary collapse. He had to declare a "holiday" for the whole banking business. But McCormick was alarmed by something even more critical to his mind, Chicago's portion of the water flow out of the Great Lakes and through the Sanitary and Ship Canal. The more water, the more Chicago, and the more Chicago the more *Tribune,* the more *Tribune,* the more McCormick. That is what makes the world go round. But at the moment there was some doubt the world could go round for anybody. Mr. Roosevelt sent the letter on to the Secretary of the Interior. On April 4, 1933, Mr. Ickes sent it back to the President, noting that "I am not in a position to answer the general objection raised by Colonel McCormick to the treaty," and that he had sent on to McCormick some Weather Bureau and War Department information on the regional water situation. That was silly. McCormick already had it and had so shown in his letter. Later generations of Middle Westerners and everybody else having an interest in Great Lakes water levels began to discover, after a great drought in 1960–65, that McCormick had not been so wrong in his apprehensions. But nobody could say he was an easy quitter. On May 6, 1933, he tried once more:

"It would give my wife and me great pleasure to have you and Mrs. Roosevelt stay with us when you come to Chicago to open the World's Fair.

"My house was a present from my mother, who held all the mansion ideas of her generation, and is therefore so much too large for us as to contain room for you and at least a considerable part of your staff.

"It seems to me you are making very good weather of it in the storm." The usual salutation and signatures were used, though now to a President well over the top and away. It turned out Mr. Roosevelt could not get to Chicago, after all, but he hoped "Dear Bert" would let him know when next in Washington.

That exchange in May of 1933 is the end. It would seem in retrospect neither party ever had expected to see their cordiality living past one full field test, anyhow. That came, soon enough. McCormick already had his grievance at having been fobbed off on Harold Ickes while trying to warn the President against Canadian guile and fitful weather. Too, once the bank crisis was met, Mr. Roosevelt began his Hundred Days of revolution short of arms. Few, today, would say he could have escaped attempting it, even if he had been the man to try; but at the time it was a revolution of incomprehensible parts to many a citizen. The central doctrine was to regulate all aspects of agriculture and industry on terms of autarchy and good order. In the years since, polemical economists and historians have found ways of describing the effort that soothe one or another political aim. It is fair to say that each ox bellowed accordingly as he was gored, none more mournfully than the American Newspaper Publishers' Association, within which the ordinary publisher hoped to find refuge against Canadian paper trusts, dangerous radicals in the old-fashioned mechanic arts unions and the even worse reporters who talked crazily of having a system of collective bargaining for themselves, too. As for McCormick, he had long since defined the privileges and responsibilities that went with his own office. In 1924, the Tribune Tower went up, pursuant to Raymond Hood's design, and McCormick found an audience of ministers, to which he intoned:

> The newspaper is an institution developed by modern civilization to present the news of the day, to foster commerce and industry, to inform and lead public opinion, and to furnish that check upon government which no constitution has ever been able to provide.

When the Blue Eagle of the National Recovery Administration rose on his horizon, all McCormick needed to do was out with his war horn, summon the faithful and attack. The Freedom of the Press was in trouble again, and his duty was plain. Now, exactly two years and three days after that cautiously warm letter of June 28, 1932, McCormick's revised appraisal of his fellow Old Grotonian was given in an editorial: "A Warning from Germany." It began by surveying the previous weekend, in which Hitler's Night of the

Long Knives had, with hog-butchers' dispatch, settled the issue of just who was running the Nazi dictatorship. The *Tribune* gave a concise description of life in the Third Reich not even the most prejudiced could fault as pro-Nazi. Then it turned to life in the United States as of July 2, 1934.

Any nation wishing to avoid Germany's fate, so the *Tribune* reasoned, must first deny itself to a dictator. And there is an infallible early warning if any presumptive dictator is on the prowl. The press is the device through which the people learn what the government is doing, therefore, the state of the press is the touchstone of liberty. And in the United States of 1934, so the *Tribune* held it, the free press was under siege. From there, McCormick never looked back. Even as death was overtaking him twenty years later, Roosevelt was still the center of his passion. No amount of repetition ever seemed to him a sufficient explanation of the enormities he had been asked to bear or his obligation to resist not in defense of his pocketbook, but in the name of honor. One thing is known. His pocketbook did not suffer. If his honor did, McCormick himself never once guessed it.

Of all the New Deal social change, just one actually got his endorsement, the Securities and Exchange Act of 1934. But it is also true that McCormick was sympathetic toward some of the most sophisticated and difficult philosophic concepts of the great revolution. Like some of the most radical-minded of economic determinists in the early New Deal, McCormick was all for Congressional actions which cut defaulting nations off from further borrowing in the United States and set bars against any future trading in armaments, which was itself condemned as the main provocation that had led the United States into needless war with Germany. There, the *Tribune* and the Communist Party in the United States saw Wall Street alike, not for the first time nor for the last. If it were within human possibility to do so, it would be warranted for some scholar of quality to build a satisfactory explanation. He will find the *Tribune* and the *New York Daily Worker* had many a thought in common about the causes of the First World War. And he will find them together again on world events between August of 1939 and July of 1941. But after that there was a difference of views not reconciled until McCormick, in 1945, began air flights all about the world to report on what he described as an over-blown, indefensible American Empire and its works of vanity in Europe, Asia and Africa. Much of the Soviet political literature between 1945 and 1955 reads as if it had been lifted from him, as his from it.

In the New Deal years, there came a steady stream of vituperation from Chicago. In the 1936 Presidential campaign, McCormick had telephone operators answer all calls with the announcement that so and so many days remained to save the Republic. He had a photograph cooked up to argue that soon the Social Security plot would have every working man tagged and numbered like a prisoner of war. When police and strikers fell to shooting before the gates of South Chicago steel plants, it was the day of the anarchists again, the Haymarket Riot of dread memory. McCormick put a rocket under the managers of the Illinois National Guard. One result was the assignment of Colonel George Catlett Marshall to go out and improve the troops. Marshall became a regular visitor at Cantigny.

But in the New York end of the Tribune Company during the New Deal, Patterson was reacting in a manner that defied sense. By 1933, the *News* was not only dominant in its field by the ultimate test of circulation, advertising and net profits, but a great money pump on a national scale. Patterson's skill at the invention and management of newspaper features was such that no matter how any publisher might hold back from other creditors he never neglected his credit status with McCormick's fearsome accounting agents. In 1933, as others were sunk in misery, the *News* was arranging a beautiful, new 42nd Street publishing plant. It suited Patterson to the marrow that in the lobby he could lay out a globe of the world and a set of weather gauges. Like McCormick, he was a great nuisance to forecasters and harassed them with theories on what makes the wind. Across the front of the new skyscraper he had a frieze laid on to illustrate Lincoln's saying that God must have loved the common people, he made so many of them. Not long after he saw five millions of his paper-dollar profits vanish in one market day, Patterson resumed a habit of his youth, stalking the common man. He spent more than one night in a Bowery flophouse and shuffled with the breadlines. He noted that still in 1933, the United States had not as much to offer in social welfare as Germany in 1913. And he went to the *News* with a change in marching orders. People were no longer interested in divorce trials. They wanted to know how to get jobs. Patterson allied himself with Franklin D. Roosevelt. In an editorial that was the true journalistic and political shocker of its time, he held that nothing less than a sort of dictatorship could save the United States. He would serve the dictator. And so he did, more nobly and with less reservation than any other journalist of significance in the country. All his scorn was laid against the very publishers who huddled somewhere behind McCormick and urged that headlong champion from the West on to an attack as furious as Patterson's battle for the New Deal in New York.

Patterson invited any governmental agency to investigate the Tribune Company and report whatever occurred to it. He denounced the Second Class mailing privilege as undeserved subsidy of the press and thought the whole Free Press doctrine, anyhow, should be restudied by Congress. In 1936, he was for Roosevelt with all the fervor McCormick put into the Republican campaign and opened up the *News* on its page opposite editorial to what he called a "Presidential Battle Page," with equal space for propagandists on each side. It was a national sensation and is of great interest yet to any student of political folkways. He continued the Battle Page until 1944, then killed it in the lamest moment of his life. He was simply unable to bear more of Roosevelt and unable to say so with his past disarming candor. He claimed himself afraid to go on with the Battle Page because of supposed risks of libel. In truth, Patterson had simply worn out in an agony of mind and body, but had no possible way of confessing it. He was far gone, by then, from the posture in 1937 that made him perhaps the only publisher of rank in the United States to support Mr. Roosevelt's attack upon the Supreme Court after it destroyed the legal architecture of the New Deal's ventures into autarchy. He had even forgotten that in 1937 he had been so close to the President that he was offered a Cabinet position, Secretary of the Navy.

Little wonder, then, that an uninformed partisan might say there must be something downright crooked about McCormick and Patterson, one hammering Roosevelt from the right and the other upholding him from the left, and between them, coining money for Tribune Company at a rate that dizzied even themselves. But there was nothing in their behavior either could see as odd. In every sense except the biological, they were true brothers. They had saved a family business as profitable as it was old, curious and fascinating, with only two misadventures, each quickly abandoned. The first thing to go wrong was a mass distribution magazine, named with Patterson's usual gift for the succinct, *Liberty*. Just who failed *Liberty* has never been made clear. Patterson more than put it into the top brackets of circulation, but somehow it never was able to crack the advertising market against the then entrenched combination of *Collier's* and the *Saturday Evening Post*. The more circulation the more loss. So the cousins unloaded *Liberty* to Bernarr MacFadden for his own failing paper in Detroit, and in the process made what came to be an acknowledged major blunder. They quit Detroit too suddenly, and further, let go some special paper mills in New York. A few years later, these were cherished as gold. On the whole, the *Liberty* venture had only served to insure McCormick's unchallenged dominance of the business end, for which Patterson had no taste, anyhow. And in New York, Patterson had an instrument of his own making that McCormick was far too intelligent to menace, even if he had wished to try. Each took the other at face as doing what he must.

As a matter of fact, there was nothing either of them could do about their status, anyhow, even if they had come to a fistfight on politics. By 1932, it was plain the daughters of Joseph Medill were not much longer for this world. Mrs. Patterson had quit Washington for Chicago at the end of the First World War. There, she died in September, 1933. George Seldes, on returning to Paris in 1920 from reporting the Kapp *putsch* in Berlin, went around to the Ritz for a call on Mrs. McCormick. When he told her where he had been she said in a sober, calm voice, "Well, God damn the Germans." And from there she called also for damnation of the Japanese, the Jews, the Roman Catholics. Nor by any oversight was the Almighty to ignore the French, for whom she had a special intention: "I fell out of bed in this damned country." Seldes went away thinking nothing more totally described the foreign policy of the *Tribune* than these curses of a dominant old lady who had been a mighty force of journalism in her day. He was, as in some other matters, totally incomprehending. What he heard was a cry of the heart from an embittered widow whose feckless husband's death a few months before lay heavy on her memory as she came again to Paris, where, long before, she had suffered through the ruin of all her ambitions for power and place. It was in Paris that her meddling in the Storer affair drove the patience of Theodore Roosevelt past the breaking point so that he dropped the McCormicks, too. Never, really, did Mrs. McCormick know herself as a mighty force in anything at all. Her husband and her fondled first son both died in strange circumstances. Her only real protector was her second son. Yet, he was never secure in her love and learned to defy her as the price of his own survival. There was nothing left, really, except France, which lured her against all her agonies. She died at Versailles, July 5, 1932.

At that, the sisters again came within an ace of shattering the family fortune. Except for Weymouth Kirkland's powerful law machine, it is difficult to see how the heirs of Joseph Medill could have held their stock together in the hard times of 1932–33. But it was done, and neatly, too. McCormick had his ten shares from Robert W. Patterson. And Patterson's daughter had her ten shares from Joseph Medill. After the death of her second husband, she had gone into court and taken as her legal name the one by which she came to be known best: Eleanor Medill Patterson. On May 5, 1932, she deposited eight thousand dollars in cash and these ten shares under a voting agreement called the McCormick-Patterson Trust. She thereby surrendered all the legal or equitable interest represented by those shares. Her brother and cousin were the named trustees and it was provided that she would succeed Patterson, on his death or disability. Meanwhile, she was the beneficiary of the trust's voting activities and could look to it for revenues proportionate to units of beneficial interest put in her name on the trust's books. The books of Tribune Company would be something else again. On May 6, 1932, McCormick handed over his ten shares and received from the McCormick-Patterson Trust a slip of paper noting that it had credited him with ten units of beneficial interest in trust holdings of Tribune Company stock. By the end of 1933, all stock in Medill's testamentary trust for the interest of his daughters had gone over, 262½ units of beneficial interest for each grandchild of Joseph Medill or successors in interest. This meant 87½ units directly to Medill McCormick's eldest daughter, Katrina, a like number to his widow and another 87½ units to her also as guardian for the younger daughter, Ruth Elizabeth McCormick, then just past her twelfth birthday.

All was legally secure within Tribune Company for the long haul. The McCormick-Patterson Trust was good, by law, for at least twenty years from the death of McCormick or Patterson, whichever survived the other. In the meantime, any attempts to alter the terms of agreement would have to carry the combined support of beneficiaries whose total interests would equal not less than 87.75 percent of all the units of interest represented in the trust. The clock was not to begin ticking until McCormick died on April 1, 1955, and by then just about everything and anybody of interest to him had already gone ahead.

CHAPTER FIFTEEN ★★★ On October 5, 1937, Mr. Roosevelt appeared in Chicago to dedicate a bridge joining the main stream of city traffic to a great, new driveway along Lake Michigan. The Outer Drive was a favorite *Tribune* project and not even the thought of New Deal thumbprints all over it could spoil such a great day for McCormick. For Mr. Roosevelt, it could hardly have been a more amiable occasion. On the horizon there was a *Tribune* billboard with one word, "Undominated," but the election of 1936 had put McCormick in his place. He had rejected the idea that, in a panic, people who wish to preserve their existing society quite logically experiment with money, business and social relations in hope they may hit on something that will save them from total ruin. And the country had, in turn, rejected McCormick. His one idea was to put all the governments, city, county, state and national, through something like a proceeding in bankruptcy in order to search them for concealed assets rightfully belonging to the taxpayers. With these returned, the taxpayers would then be able to build a new national health and, if wise, would thereafter hold government down to police work and record keeping. He now stood repudiated. And so Mr. Roosevelt had special pleasure, some of his staff thought, in accepting luncheon with George William Mundelein, the Cardinal Archbishop of the most populous single Roman Catholic congregation in the nation. The cardinal was one of Mr. Roosevelt's warmest admirers and a call at His Eminence's residence would have many satisfactions, personal and otherwise. But the cream of the jest was that McCormick's town house stood only a few doors down Astor Street. That was the sort of alarum with which Mr. Roosevelt delighted to divert himself in counterpoint to solemn occasions. And the address on the Outer Drive bridge had turned out to be, instead of a light gala, an occasion of profoundly solemn, not to say abrasive, experience for Mr. Roosevelt's own official family.

To this day, historians are still trying to crack the puzzle of just how Mr. Roosevelt came to use his Chicago visit as he did.

But as to what he had done, there was instant recognition. He had put the world on notice that his Administration would now throw its weight against powers which might seek to profit from aggressive war. To appreciate how revolutionary a departure this was from the New Deal in its domestic posture, it is necessary to know something of the inner tensions with which Mr. Roosevelt had been confronted from the start.

On the one hand, there were the old-line traditional Democrats who might be called, or at least called themselves, conventional Wilsonians. These were used to the care and nursing of a world market for tobacco, cotton and raw materials in general; and in banking, insuring, underwriting and distribution, both foreign and domestic. They were a mixture of the urbane and the provincial so dextrous that in the same individual an untutored observer might think he had met the one when in fact the other had evaded him. This group was exemplified in two elderly Tennesseans, Cordell Hull and Norman H. Davis. Mr. Hull was asked by Mr. Roosevelt immediately after the election in 1932 to resign from the Senate, where he had been a foremost advocate of lower tariffs and the internationalist outlook, to become Secretary of State. Mr. Davis had been one of Mr. Wilson's advisors at Versailles. He moved in and out of Mr. Roosevelt's service in communicating with the League of Nations. In between, he represented committees of bondholders who had bought amply, if not too wisely, in the world market of the 1920's. To all such as these, the London Economic Conference of 1933 was thought a first and last chance to revive a Wilsonian order among the powers.

But the Wilsonians did not have Mr. Roosevelt's mind all to themselves. There were in the early New Deal many who thought the United States should adopt something of what was called in

Italy the corporative state. They had no interest in the kind of operatic stomping around that was such a delight to the Italian premier, Signor Mussolini, but his arguments for putting economic and political doctrine into some orderly form were not altogether ignored, either by academicians or by business interests badly frightened in the desperate years of the Great Depression. The National Recovery Administration, the Agricultural Adjustment Administration, the Wagner Labor Act, the Guffey Coal Act and the Tennessee Valley Authority, all pointed American thought in the direction of autarchy, national self-sufficiency, detachment from foreign dependencies and, in sum, a rejection of the old Wilsonian themes. Two very different Democrats from Messrs. Hull and Davis exemplified such views.

Professor Raymond Moley, of Ohio, was one of Columbia University's leading academicians in the study of government and public law. Mr. Moley was also one of the very first of the group around Mr. Roosevelt which came to be known as his Brain Trust. When the New Deal came to Washington, Mr. Moley was followed about by journalists and high dignitaries to discover what his magic might be. Within six months he was out of government, embittered, frustrated and astonished to discover that Mr. Hull's rather austere, churchly public manner had nothing whatsoever to do with the Secretary's operating methods. In short, he had been thrown by a deacon. Mr. Moley put his experiences together in a book, *After Seven Years,* which has no equal for giving insight into the early collisions between those who wished Mr. Roosevelt to move for autarchy as against those who wished him to revive the Wilsonian view.

The high point of New Deal commitment toward autarchy was the 1936 political year. In that, Mr. Roosevelt's speech at Chautauqua, New York, on August 14 warned against Americans who would pursue "fools' gold" in attempting to corrupt the neutrality acts which had been flowing out of Congress in keeping with the undeniable national will. And he said:

> We can keep out of war if those who watch and decide have a sufficiently detailed understanding of international affairs to make certain that the small decisions of each day do not lead toward war, and if, at the same time, they possess the courage to say 'no' to those who selfishly or unwisely would let us go to war.

Nowhere was the theory of isolation, to use that hopelessly insufficient tag-line for a whole complex of views, more utterly embedded than on the campus of the University of Chicago. The embarrassment of being on the same side with McCormick was dismissed by saying "even a clock that has stopped is right twice a day." But it was a difficulty, to be sure. The chancellor, Robert Maynard Hutchins, spoke almost in *Tribune* language. And one of the university's most favored graduates, holding a title of rank in the New Deal, got out a work arguing that the road to happiness for American democracy lay not in extensive foreign trade and meddling in Europe's endless wars, but in developing the continent at hand. The author was Jerome Frank, called to Washington in May of 1933 as general counsel to the Agricultural Adjustment Administration and one of the most intense of the intellectuals of Middle-Western inflection who had aligned themselves with Rexford Guy Tugwell, the poet-economist who had once declared it time "to make America over."

In 1938, Jerome Frank was a member of the Securities and Exchange Commission. And it was then he got out his appeal, well after Mr. Roosevelt's proposal to quarantine aggressors had rocketed from a Chicago bridge to every chancellery in the world. In 1938, too, a word once thought the noblest in all the lexicon of diplomacy, "appeasement," began such a descent in esteem that even into the next generation it frightened any statesman to think any person, anywhere, might hold him guilty of considering such a solvent. And among the next generation of public personages few admitted to having heard that so distinguished a man as Judge Jerome Frank, late of the United States Court of Appeals, had once in 1938 issued a defiance of the times, entitled: *Save America First.*

There is no need to pursue here the historians' quarrel about Mr. Roosevelt's Quarantine the Aggressor speech, except to elevate one curiously nagging mystery few of them seem to have noted at all, much less explored. Norman Davis suggested the President say a word against isolationism. Mr. Hull's memoir told how the State Department worked up a brief on which to rest it. But neither saw the final text and each was frank to express shock at the daring line:

> When an epidemic of physical disease starts to spread, the community approves and joins in a quarantine of the patients in order to protect the health of the community against the spread of the dis-

ease. . . . War is a contagion, whether it be declared, or undeclared. . . . We cannot have complete protection in a world of disorder in which confidence and security have broken down.

Reaction was so sharp and so totally focused that Mr. Roosevelt had to issue a supplement, immediately. Sanctions against Japan, which was hard at gnawing away in China, were not his plan. He would concede, though, that he had an idea on how to force a settlement in Asia. But what was it? Here it is necessary to raise the still open question of just how much Joseph Medill Patterson had to do with Mr. Roosevelt's change of direction on that much debated day in Chicago. On September 5, 1937, Patterson wrote for permission to see the President and said explicitly he wished to discuss foreign policy. On September 12, Patterson went for a cruise down the Potomac with the President. And one of their companions was Norman H. Davis. Patterson wanted the United States and Great Britain to set a naval chain across the Pacific, tied to Singapore, Australia, Hawaii and the Alaskan Islands. This would bring Japan to heel. And on October 7, 1937, he began to broadside his argument with an editorial challenge: "Shall We Take Them Now, or Try It Later?" followed with a regular Monday morning series, "Two Ships for One." This, he kept up until Pearl Harbor.

It is the best evidence of what Roosevelt thought all this worth that, even after Patterson declined to become Secretary of the Navy, Roosevelt sent him the pen, anyhow, with which the naval reconstruction bill of 1940 was signed into law. In May of 1940, Patterson wrote privately to a friend in the army that he opposed the United States getting into another war, but that it seemed certain to happen. He hoped he would be acceptable to serve with troops in the field. When Mr. Roosevelt ran for his third term, Patterson was near to alone among principal newspaper proprietors to support him. Then, on December 17, 1940, Mr. Roosevelt announced his lend-lease formula, presented to Congress as House Resolution 1776. There, Patterson and Roosevelt parted.

The campaign that Patterson organized against Roosevelt in the hostile atmosphere of New York City was a fascination and a horror to Administration officials, some of whom had their own doubts whether they were more loyal to the President's leadership or to the doctrine in Jerome Frank's *Save America First.* Roosevelt's feeling toward Patterson became as fierce as Patterson's toward Roosevelt. Friends of each manipulated them together shortly after Pearl Harbor, trying for reconciliation. Patterson found himself standing in the President's office. He had come, he said, to ask for any service he could do best. Roosevelt, according to one who was present, let him stand, unanswered, for five minutes, then said:

"Joe, I want to give you one assignment. . . . I want you to go home and read your editorials for the past six months. Read every one of them and then think what you have done."

Many of the President's friends were open in their anguish. Frank C. Walker, the Postmaster General, made no hesitation in saying that, for all Mr. Roosevelt's behavior was human, it was a disastrous lapse of judgment and brutally unfair to one who had been his friend in many an hour of need. But nothing helped. From the White House, that day, Patterson walked a lonely, bitter way to his grave in 1946, saying his one aim left in life was to outlive Roosevelt.

If McCormick ever so much as reminded Patterson of the past, there is not anywhere an available record of it. The *Tribune*'s own appraisal of the 1937 speech was such as to give McCormick no cause to wish later it had been different:

"The crowd which gathered at the dedication of the new bridge yesterday heard Mr. Roosevelt deliver what may well prove to be the most important speech he will ever make."

Mr. Roosevelt, the *Tribune* held, hoped to ally the United States with England, France and any other open to persuasion for an attempt to use economic and financial boycotts as the keepers of a peace. It reviewed Mr. Wilson's diplomacy and found Mr. Roosevelt had grown up within it, was a party to it.

"At the dedication of the new bridge, Mr. Roosevelt repeated his declaration that he hates war. He repeated his determination to avoid it. The crowd applauded. He was expressing their inmost desire. The crowd also applauded Mr. Wilson when he campaigned on the slogan, 'He kept us out of the war.' They accepted his word and did not examine the meaning of his diplomatic acts. A month after his inauguration, America was in the war."

In 1917, as one of Pershing's staff investigators, McCormick took fully to the view that somehow the world is run mostly from behind an arras. The intrigues within the French Cabinet were to McCormick the essence of real power at work. And all he had seen or learned in his life came together in 1937 to make it plain. As McCormick understood events, Wilson was not trapped and beset by forces beyond his reckoning. He was a liar who had betrayed public trust; not driven, but driver. And in Franklin D. Roosevelt, he saw another Wilson, a President to put the United States into war against its will. It was a curiously high compliment to ability, if a low estimate of character.

McCormick's view of politics led him to a peculiar sort of intellectual company. Marxist doctrinaires in the twentieth century have shot fiction, journalism and history with their proofs that war comes at the beckoning of arms manufacturers, bankers and "merchants of death." These will the course of events and governments obey. There is no more total example of this formula than the literature of the National Socialist Party in Germany, which declared the world to be in mortal danger from a conspiracy of Jews. To save the world, therefore, the Nazi logic led from the robbery of bankers and manufacturers to the herding of tailors and grandmothers into gas chambers.

In the years after 1937, McCormick found himself accused of being one with Hitler and Stalin, both, in such projections. By 1941, the United States was split in doubt and indecision between those who adhered to neutralism, whatever that meant, and those who spoke for intervention, wherever that might lead. McCormick was an early party to the forming of America First, a political action meant to stay Mr. Roosevelt's cunning. It embarrassed him not at all that the literature of America First and of the Communist Party in the United States read much alike—until June, when the Communists were hard put to explain what had happened to the Molotov-Ribbentrop plan for peace in their time between Russia and Germany. Nor did it embarrass McCormick that both the name and a good deal of the language used by America First were straight lifts from speeches by William Hale Thompson in 1927. If anybody had asked him, he would have inquired what those had in mind who organized Bundles for Britain? There is nothing to be gained in reviewing here the day-by-day exchanges of abuse. It is a rare volume dealing with that period which has not its selection on McCormick and the *Tribune* all set out in the index, but very little in the text ever presents McCormick's effort as having any true foundation in the national mind. Just the same, the one-year Selective

Service Act of 1940, providing for registration of men between twenty-one and thirty-five, was renewed on August 18, 1941, for only eighteen months. This authority passed the House of Representatives by a vote of 203 to 202. Nor was the division on party lines, either.

The great foreign-policy debate that wracked the nation for the better part of five years inevitably suffered from a sort of Gresham's Law in political language, so that as he became frantic to the point of panic, McCormick shocked even his most urbane associates. Yet the *Tribune* in 1941 was not one whit more brutal than the *Tribune* of 1861. Nothing it had to say about Mr. Roosevelt was much different from the description of Cyrus McCormick as poor white trash from the Valley of Virginia with a predilection for man-stealing. Added to Chicago's tradition of extravagant political dialog was McCormick's own special problem. He had found himself invincible, so far. Not even Capone or the Great Depression itself had been able to defeat him. Who, then, was Roosevelt? And who were the President's friends, that they thought to intimidate McCormick?

Some of the things he did, before and after Pearl Harbor, led more than one person to think him crazed. He knew perfectly well that in a city of such polyglot identity as Chicago, ethnic and religious tags unsettle feelings very quickly. Yet he had not the least hesitation in ordering the "foreign-born" into news stories to disadvantage any he thought he could. He knew as well as anybody the special sensitivities of citizens having any Jewish attachments. Yet he went out of his way to group together in news columns, in cartoons and in editorials, names and faces of public men so identifiable, and to spell out as theirs attributes of great and undue power over the life of the country. To ask that they should hold him less than maliciously purposeful was unreasonable. Yet, he did as much, and in the same manner, against others. He put such men as Mr. Justice Felix Frankfurter of the Supreme Court, Secretary of the Treasury Morgenthau and Senator Herbert Lehman of New York, together as a triumvirate of significance. But he certainly did no less in grouping the President, Vice-President Henry Wallace and Harold Ickes, as three conspiring against civilized society. In point of fact, if there was any group of citizens entitled to feel especially marked by McCormick as class enemies, it would be those intellectuals of general public esteem known as Rhodes Scholars.

McCormick's favorite example of the native English demon was Cecil John Rhodes, late of Bishop's Stortford, Hertfordshire. Rhodes was born July 5, 1853, at the vicarage held by his father. His health was so delicate he did not go off to school but was taught in a local curate's grammar class for villagers. Even so, by the time he was sixteen the family physician decreed he would shortly die if not turned out for a long sea voyage. Thus the chance of empire sometimes turns, as do so many other affairs in this world, on obscure, unwonted individual choices of action. The eldest Rhodes son was already about as far from Bishop's Stortford as could be managed on earth, attempting to grow cotton in the African Natal.

It is generally suggested by Rhodes' biographers that he went to South Africa because he had been stricken with lung trouble. His subsequent career suggests something was far more disturbed in Rhodes' head. He was a desperate, unformed seventeen-year-old when first he looked upon the violent world of South Africa, so alien to Bishop's Stortford. On October 13, 1873, he was admitted to Oriel College, Oxford, tempered by events his classmates could hardly imagine, let alone credit as true. From then until finally passed for his degree on December 17, 1881, Rhodes gyrated between Oriel and Africa. He came as an outsider who had never been to a public school, who had no money, no powerful family, no splendid patron. He was older than any of his associates, even than some of his teachers. And he reeked of madness and visions. But, instead of saving souls for the next world, he would save humanity in this present. First, the gold and diamonds of Kimberly would make him powerful. Then, he would organize all human affairs according to his philosophy.

Critics and rebels against England, of every hue, race and political variety, have been well armed by Rhodes for their purposes. As for McCormick, whenever it struck him that English greed and pseudo-American vice were again threatening to unman the Republic, he would cause the *Tribune* to rediscover a frightfulness going under the short title of "Rhodes' Will." At the time Rhodes' celebrated vision fell upon him, he was just 24. To all of Oxford he proclaimed that God Almighty had explained to him the English were first race of the world and the more of the world England controlled, the better for all humanity. Whereupon, though as yet he still had hardly enough money to stay in college, he set to entertaining the vision by a method he continued until death itself managed to shut him up in 1902. He began to make wills. This 24-year-old delusional adventurer disposed his then nonexistent estate in trust with the Secretary of State for the Colonies and with a colonial Attorney General to promote a secret society which would devote itself literally to extension of British rule throughout the world. And as Chicago never tired of being reminded, it was a very special assignment of the secret society to work for recovery of the United States as part of the British Empire.

Apologists have protested that Rhodes was only a man of his time and called it unfair to measure his call for the secret society against Marx's Communist Manifesto or to compare his imperial vision with Hitler's ordinance for the thousand-year National Socialist state in Europe. It is true enough that the language comes only from the second of the serial fantasy called "Rhodes' Wills." But if the unctuous final version protests intent to establish world peace, the hard underlying spirit never falters. Rhodes was for "Britain First." And Last.

When Rhodes' estate was finally run through probate in 1907, something near $30 million provided scholarships at Oxford for young men, certified for "literary and scholastic superiority, skill at manly sports, qualities of manhood, and moral force of character." Five such potential leaders were to be selected from Germany. Sixty would be drawn from fifteen specified Crown Colonies. Two would be found in each of the United States. It was put about early that Rhodes had the impression there were only thirteen of these last, but that is now said to have been disproved by some Rhodian research expert.

In the working out, whatever else they may have accomplished, Rhodes' beneficiaries have not as yet succeeded in uniting the world under the British *Raj* or even in abolishing war. Colonials, by and large, have shown themselves uncommonly lacking in gratitude and have used their learning most in pursuit of political independence. As for the Germans, Parliament in 1916 passed a law setting aside the will's authority to let any more such cuckoos in the nest. The case of the Rhodes Scholars from the United States is not so simply told, even though the scholarships have always been highly esteemed and vigorously sought as means for outstanding young men to get ahead in what some regard as the world's finest intellectual companionate. At Oxford, an impression was formed in the early days that the American postulants were a credulous lot, without gifts worth anybody's notice. They were also, at first, up against some suspicions at home, exemplified in the *Tribune*'s theory that they were enrolled minions of empire. Time and performance have abated both wounding views, generally, but their patron's theory undoubtedly had effect on some Rhodes Scholars. More than one has supported such movements as The English-Speaking Union, and the even more direct commitment put by the Union Now movement. McCormick's reaction was to let it out that in general Rhodes Scholars were little better than Benedict Arnold. And to drive his point home, he several times had the *Tribune* run elaborate accounts of Arnold's attempt to justify treachery with the claim of intent to reunify the British Empire. Furthermore, he had the whole case all done up again as a melodrama and acted out on the television and radio for his Saturday night audiences with the full script in the next morning's *Tribune*.

Quite naturally, in all his years of making trouble for himself, McCormick never acquired a more faithfully industrious set of enemies than the Rhodes Scholars who have accumulated through the generations in halls of government and education the country over. Many thousands of always earnest, sometimes labored, words of self-defense have somehow not quite settled all questions. Rhodes' vision of the good society, as he put it in words, has been found repellent by men far less fractious than McCormick. To nullify the effect of the *Tribune*'s revelations, therefore, has always been uphill work in its own, special territory.

Nowhere on earth is the doctrine of purposeful causation more directly received as a holy popular faith than in Chicago. If the grain market should collapse, members of the Board of Trade appreciate instantly that evil combinations of New York banks made it their business to ruin credit in the Midwest. If a South Side beer garden should fly up in bits, the neighborhood would not even dare to whisper that someone had offended the Syndicate. If a suburban pavement be eaten with potholes, only the precinct heretoch has the power to secure its improvement, by exercise of that magic known in Chicago through the splendid term "clout." Let any newspaper handicapping artist suggest the outcome of a horse race and half the city bets that he must know something. The other half instantly perceives machinations of that well-known shadow-government which has designs to mislead innocents in all cases and gets money down on the opposite side. Of course, these habits expose universals of human temperament, everywhere necessary to relieve day-to-day tedium. But in Chicago they have special value as defense against the irritating notorieties of being called "the Second City," so that anything and anybody can be endowed with special mysteries, and speculations on intrigue become a high art.

A *Tribune* rerun and discursion on the awfulness of Rhodes' Will, therefore, was always as beloved to McCormick's audience as the dolors of *Cavalleria rusticana* to Neapolitans, each time new and fresh in emotional jolts. Just how much money did Rhodes really squeeze out of the Africans? Did he actually work up Jameson's Raid and start the Boer War all by himself? If the Scholars don't get paid out of a secret fund to promote British interests, why are they doing it for free?

By midsummer, 1941, the Roosevelt Administration had as one of its principal domestic aims intimidating McCormick, somehow. He had really gotten past the President's defenses in a fashion to match Theodore Roosevelt at work on Wilson in 1916. And for the way it all ended—having brought on pretty much of a disaster, one way or another, for everybody who touched the project—no man was more to blame than McCormick, himself.

In 1939, a long developing journalistic crash startled Chicago. Emory Thomason had started up his own paper in 1929, the *Chicago Illustrated Times,* for which McCormick professed vast tolerance. It had attempted to find an audience by local imitation of Patterson's New York style, but without much luck. The *News* was in diffuse ultimate ownership. Its publisher was Frank Knox, who had been the Republican candidate for Vice President in 1936 and in 1940 would take the position in Mr. Roosevelt's Cabinet Patterson had refused. But in 1939, what changed everything was Hearst's sudden surrender of the morning field. Gone were those bellowed counterpoint harmonies older than living memory, the cries of hawkers with rival morning papers to sell. Something went out of Chicago's sense of fun in 1939 when Hearst finally hauled down his morning flag and left the *Tribune* in possession of the field. The city felt older, uneasy. Any other publisher except McCormick could have seen that it was time to mute his brass. The second greatest metropolis in the United States was due that much tact. There is a well-established method for handling such problems. In any monopoly situation, the journalist with any wisdom at all adopts a tone of "yes, but," and "there is much to be said on both sides." In 1939, McCormick passed up an opportunity to conquer Chicago once and for all and to make it believe him worthy of its total trust. All he had to do was acknowledge that between black and white there is an infinitely varied shade of everyday grey in the affairs of men. Nothing more. He need only confess the President of the United States a man much like himself, concerned for human betterment, and, like himself, relying on effort to win against certain error. In his position of a monopoly on news and thought in Chicago's morning journalistic field, McCormick had in his hand power such as he had never known, to demonstrate that he really understood politics and had some sense of limit, some sense of self-discipline and some capacity to use with skill the positive, as against the negative, emphasis of his mind. Certainly he had such a capacity. His Canadian venture was, by 1939, well on toward maturing a truly spectacular industrial complex on the St. Lawrence North Shore at Baie Comeau. There he had played the pacific role of monopoly capitalist with concern only for things that count; getting the buildings up, the work force assembled and the operation going, among some of the most fractious elements of religious, ethnic, social and political disaffection to be found in North America. It would be hard to match Quebec stresses anywhere, then or now. Yet McCormick mastered every step with not one serious bobble. How was it, then, that the same man, in his native city, had so little political sense as to ride Chicago, after 1939, with an even harder hand than ever?

One view is that McCormick never learned politics, really, as he learned productive business enterprise. Certainly he never used it with anything of comparable sensitivity, or success, either. A variation on this view is that McCormick did not, at heart, consider politics very important, anyhow. There can be no denying that he *knew* politics, in that he had its persons, events and dates ever in his conscious thoughts and used all these in his language. But did he *understand* politics? Mayor Edward J. Kelly, his friend from their days on the Sanitary and Ship Canal, understood politics as the art of the possible. If that is what politics is, the art of the possible, then McCormick certainly never understood it, and he very probably didn't, in the very center of his soul, give a rap. It was nothing to compare with punching a button that set logs marching in one end of a building, only to march out the other end all neatly made over into roll, after roll, after roll, of beautiful white paper. And priced right.

In any case, if McCormick could really bear the thought of having Chicago hang on him worshipfully, his best chance came as Hearst surrendered, and the other publishers trembled to think what lay ahead for them. So what he did was to lay on worse than ever, until that midsummer of 1941 made it inevitable that Roosevelt would really go for him.

The truth about what happened next is at once so ludicrous, so shocking and so near to McCormick's own ineptitudes that it would scarcely be credited, except that it comes from witnesses who were, to say the least, hostile to his interest. Harold Ickes' *Secret Diary,* Volume III, covering the years 1939–41, is basic to the account here following. A second, almost equally essential source of information, is the biography of Marshall Field III by Stephen Becker, issued in 1964 under the *imprimatur* of the Field interests. It is from these, more than any other, that insight is given into the formation of the Roosevelt Administration's move to save Chicago from a man more than one holder of high office by then considered a true enemy of the public welfare. Marshall Field III was the grandson of the merchant prince who had saved Medill's day with a loan in 1873. In his middle age, Field III came into control of more than $100 million. He took a turn for good works and in New York, after others had lost heart, put himself in, alone, to finance the experiment of *PM,* an afternoon tabloid newspaper proposing to live only on circulation, free of every influence except the judgments of its editor, Ralph McAllister Ingersoll. But, somehow, though *PM* was beautifully turned out in typography, language and moral attitudes, it could not quite find an audience. Not even its attempts to annoy Patterson into a fight could get it anywhere. Patterson understood how to handle that sort of thing. He just kept on playing his own sort of game and left Ingersoll in frustration and doubt as to whether he even read *PM* at all. Patterson read it, all right, and with care, every day.

One day in early 1941, Field was in Chicago at a meeting of the

University of Chicago Board of Trustees. There he fell into discussion with William Benton, another trustee, about the spectacle of Chicago at McCormick's mercy. He would like to see a liberal morning paper in his native city and he would put money behind it. Benton had the highest reputation in advertising, promotion and related matters. Would he help?

Benton leaped into action. The *Secret Diary* is rich in notations of Mr. Roosevelt, Mr. Ickes, Mr. Benton, Mr. Knox and Emory Thomason in counsel. Mr. Benton quite sensibly did not underestimate McCormick's resources. He thought Field should open modestly and shove in his main troops, so to speak, only upon discovering the enemy weak spot through practical maneuver. Not for nothing did he have his reputation as one liberal with pocketbook talents that would impress even McCormick. He drew up a detailed plan according to his axiom and went to Florida for a rest. When he got back to the strategy board meetings, so he told Field's biographer, he felt as if he had somehow let down Field, Chicago, liberalism, Roosevelt, the cause of freedom itself. He discovered that which so often turns out to be the horror and nightmare of lawyers. His principal had been operating without him.

Thomason, it appears from the *Secret Diary,* was cowed at the outlook and spoke heavily of being ruined. His resources had been thin at the start and were now considerably the worse for wear. It was an open secret in Chicago publishing that McCormick long ago could have squashed Thomason and probably would have, except that he and Thomason really were friendly, for old time's sake, in spite of political difference. Nor was it in doubt that Thomason's main audience read his paper more because of his enthusiasm for Mr. Roosevelt in all things, rather than, as with the *Tribune,* because they found it irresistible, page by page.

Another competitor, and one even more spectacularly in Mr. Roosevelt's favor, could ruin him. It was only natural that he would hold it the best strategy for Field to come in as his banker. Let Thomason, the man who knew McCormick best, run the war. But he was up against a fox of long experience in Mr. Secretary Knox, who in his hard days as general manager for W. R. Hearst had learned the necessary art of grasping for cash in a hurry even while seeming to decline it. Mr. Knox let it be known that the *News* was making a barrel of money and he was very happy. Mr. Field could make Chicago a finer, better place without ruining anybody except, of course, McCormick. As for himself, Knox intimated sadness only at the thought that he might not see the grand climax. He was getting old and the public service now held him. He wondered if he would ever return to his heart's true love. And so, it was on.

Field signed commitments to Knox for equipment and plant that the Field biographer conceded ruinous. Platoons and squadrons of researchers, technicians of printing, promotion wizards and masters of every detail for getting out newspapers in cities which were not Chicago, all now appeared. A great pother and prize-giving discovered a name for the liberating force to come. It would be called *The Chicago Sun.* Its moral outlook would be, of course, impeccable, by the automatic process of being non-McCormick, and its dimensions would be overpowering. Field, everyone assured everyone else, "has got the money to do it." Nobody seemed to remember that just after the Civil War, indignant moralists hired Charles A. Dana to come out from New York and teach Joseph Medill to suck eggs. They, too, "had the money." As Melville Stone's memoirs tell, they had less a couple of years later, but they did have a handsome set of lawsuits with Mr. Dana, who retreated to New York. There, among his other triumphs, he became the center of a great scandal of journalism. He was discovered by Victor Lawson to be the chief among several high dignitaries of the Associated Press holding stock in its competition.

The wisdom of the experts, anyhow, was to abandon Benton's limited warfare doctrine and hit McCormick head-on, all-out, crush him down and kick him out, in one grand foray. Field would collect the credits. Knox would settle for cash. And so, on December 4, 1941, for the first time in more than two years, Chicago was again alive with the braying of the hawkers, holding aloft the sign in which to conquer. And what did the headline shout? The *Tribune* had crouched to spring against an assault on the order of: "Good Morning! The Sun Is Out!!" What the headline announced was: "Revolt Grows In Servia." Janissaries at the base of Tribune Tower put down their cleavers and puzzled over that one as McCormick sent Patterson a telegram reading: "Marshall's paper awful." He spoke for more persons than one. And, as he knew, the expense was hideous.

The *Tribune* had prepared against Field with all the high technical competence of a publishing system having resources to make any competitor think twice. A special cash fund of five million dollars was put on drawing account. A managerial force thoroughly trained, long in power and fierce in purpose, set about closing off the corridors through which Field would have to travel if he hoped to get anything back for his money.

McCormick had blundered once by mishandling his role as monopolist and brought on Field. Now, he blundered again, and it was a disaster for many more people than himself before he was done. A very good case can be made that it was a disaster of grave, long-range consequence to the very thing McCormick considered his prime obligation—or privilege, as one may like to put it—the idea of a press legally secure against governmental dictates.

Just one consequence of the final Battle of Chicago left the Associated Press under a sort of shadow from which it has never since emerged. Nor has anybody, in government, in journalism, in philosophy or anywhere at all, come forward with vigorous proposals to try for a *status quo, ante bellum.* The very essence of American journalism went through a metamorphosis in McCormick's working through of his emotions toward President Roosevelt, Harold Ickes, Marshall Field and their myrmidons. Journalistic historians have not yet begun to discuss the subject with any special candor, but their chance to do so remains quite open. Year by year, governmental agencies such as the United States Information Service have tested for means to get onto formal terms with the commercial press as producers of "news," not "government propaganda." Governmental assumptions to generate and qualify the flow of public information, typified in that example, have grown to a major bureaucratic obsession.

In his declining years, McCormick made a great deal of noise about such matters and much of what he said in diagnosis was recognized within the closed circle of newspaper proprietorship as all too true. But he never confessed error on his own part. It is impossible to think he ever had the faintest notion that the major blunder, if not crime, was his own. Just the same, it was.

It was not difficult for the *Tribune* intelligence services, rooted in every part of Chicago's financial, advertising, printing and political establishment, to make a close appraisal of what Field was losing in consequence of being taken in by Knox. He was a very rich man, to be sure, but his whole life's record was thoroughly well known to McCormick, who had been a friend since their childhood days. Field was not of an aggressive temper, nor was he a lunatic, either. The times, as much as any combination of people, had rushed him far out over his head. He had no idea yet of what it meant to challenge so thoroughly emplaced an adversary, but events would show him, and in a hurry.

McCormick's proper cue, again, was to mute his brasses. Field could make no advance against the *Tribune* head-on, and any advance he might make at all would come first out of the three afternoon papers already in a state of advanced cannibalism toward each other. Even the *News,* for all that it would thrive as landlord and lessor of machinery, would suffer dreadfully in advertising and circulation. Thomason's paper probably would be first to crack. Would Thomason hold still for virtue's sake, if offered cash? Let all the competitors suffer in silence. Watch for a buy. Patterson was sure it would work. So was Mrs. Eleanor Patterson. Both urged McCormick to lie low. And Weymouth Kirkland, out of his many lines of independent information, went to McCormick early, with word that Field had been stunned at the sight of his bills. He urged McCormick to let nothing personal creep into what should be treated as an ordinary business competition. Instead of finding out what McCormick wanted and giving it to him, Kirkland, for once, offered unasked advice. And Mrs. Patterson, after a final attempt to talk reason, came back to Washington in exasperation, to report: "Well, it's Bertie against the world. . . ."

McCormick's idea of muting his brasses and allowing Field to retreat was to come out on July 26, 1942, with:

> Ralph Ingersoll, editor of *PM,* has been shamed into entering the army as a volunteer after his draftboard had refused to grant him a deferment requested by his boss. It remains to be seen whether Ingersoll's friends in Washington will obtain a commission and a nice safe berth for him. Whatever his value as an editor, and it isn't much, he has had a real value to his owner. The publicity given to Ingersoll as a draft dodger has detracted attention from Marshall Field as a slacker. Field is of age to volunteer. He cried for war before it came. Now that it has come, he lets men like MacNider and O'Hare do the fighting while he skulks in his clubs, night and otherwise. No one

would suggest that he is indispensable to *PM* or to anything else. The term to fit him and all the herd of hysterical effeminates is coward.

Two days later, the *Sun* carried a single sentence under the heading, "Editorial of the Day." It read: "You are getting rattled, Colonel McCormick."

To call McCormick "rattled" just then was to be more kind than accurate, for he was near to following his grandfather William into a total loss of emotional control. There could never be any warrant for putting a business contest with Field in the terms of that editorial. In the First World War, Field had enlisted as a private in the First Illinois Cavalry, as nobody knew any better than McCormick. He went to the front in August of 1918 and came home a captain, after taking part in the battles of St.-Mihiel and the Meuse-Argonne. No man ever said Field was other than an excellent soldier, devoted to his duty.

If McCormick ever wrote Field an apology comparable to that sent Ford, none in the present Field establishment know of it, nor is there any reason to think it was done. Privately, he offered the remarkable excuse that Field had never confessed it was McCormick who got him a commission in 1918.

When McCormick's day to die came on in 1955, Field was himself in decline and had little more than a year of life to go. Thomason had died in 1944 and three years later his paper was taken over by the Field interest, which converted the whole into a single morning tabloid, the *Sun-Times,* achieving by long roundabout Benton's original plan. Knox had died in 1944, too, and his *News* was now in the hands of John S. Knight, who had papers in Detroit and Miami, and wanted to get along with everybody. Hearst had died in 1951, but his evening paper was still trying to hang on. It was plain that McCormick had missed all boats. But the Field paper was as graceful as it was generous in its mortuary expressions.

Ten years later, with McCormick and Field both faded in public memory, journalism in Chicago amounted to the Tribune Company operating in mornings, as always, with the *Tribune,* and afternoons with Chicago's *American,* taken over from the liquidators of Hearst's unbearable extensions. The Field publications consisted in the morning *Sun-Times* and the afternoon *News.* Again, Chicago was painfully quiet and the competition was on a gentlemanly order, though McCormick would not have thought it free of menace. Yet, in light of his own performance in 1941–42, the working out should not have surprised anybody.

CHAPTER SIXTEEN ★★★ Hearst's crash in Chicago was no isolated misadventure. In 1932, he had played a crucial role in securing the Democratic nomination for Mr. Roosevelt, but soon discovered that would get him little. Mr. Roosevelt understood Mr. Hearst's ideas of friendship with Presidents as well as he understood what McCormick was up to with those "Dear Frank" letters in 1932. So, nothing worked and Hearst turned away.

In his days of glory, Hearst had let the capital slip away that now he needed to outdo McCormick as best friend of the savings bank depositor and defender of the Free Press against the ravages of government gone mad. Boycotts in circulation and advertising, plainly enough generated by political actionists, brought his bankers down on him. Hearst teetered so near to bankruptcy that at the close of business, one weekend in 1937, his chamberlains told him they dared not issue checks against the payrolls that would be due for settlement on the Tuesday upcoming.

In his business offices from Los Angeles to New York there was panic. Hearst, himself, was in an emotional and mental collapse. Two ladies saved him. One was Marion Davies, the motion picture actress he was never free to make his wife, but on whom he had heaped gifts until she had a substantial fortune in her own right. More than once she had offered Hearst all of it but he had refused, and now he refused again. In Washington, there was Mrs. Eleanor Patterson, hired five years before on the intervention of

Hearst's most gifted editor, Arthur Brisbane, to see if she might liven his moribund morning effort, the Washington *Herald.* Most of Hearst's executive staff had thought that just another of his wild shots. They got a great shock on discovering Mrs. Patterson not only took her job as a mortal challenge but also that at the art of survival in Hearst's Ozymandian court she was able and ruthless. No other editor, after all, could wink at Marion Davies in a crisis and retire to the powder room for a little nip and a swap of giggles about the machinations going on in the shadow of the Great King.

Unknown to Hearst, Miss Davies called Mrs. Patterson in Washington on the crisis weekend. Together, the ladies arranged with Hearst's general manager, Thomas J. White, to cover the deficit in his bank account on Monday morning. Altogether, they risked more than two million dollars that nobody could say they would ever see again, and on no better excuse than that they just loved Hearst as he was, including all his cranks and wiles.

Even so, all they bought him was a little time to start hauling down his flag with such dignity as he could muster. In Washington, as in Chicago, Hearst had morning and evening productions, the *Herald* and the *Times.* One of Mrs. Patterson's earliest efforts, at which she had been restrained by one of Hearst's terrified lawyers, was to buy up an old but ruined morning paper, the Washington *Post.* It was not the least of Hearst's operating problems that the *Post* had fallen to one of Mrs. Patterson's friends of long standing, Eugene Meyer, a banker and financier of great ability, who immediately began to pour in capital and force the pace of an already severe competitive struggle. And so, as the liquidation began in 1937, Mrs. Patterson took the *Herald* off Hearst's hands under a lease-option contract set against his debt to her. By 1939, she had both papers, and converted the whole into something not previously seen in metropolitan journalism. She decided to run the paper all day under the combined name, *Times-Herald,* keeping unchanged its editorial, cartoons, household hints and other such diversions, but making over the news columns any hour of day or night something freshly interesting might come along.

Somehow, it worked. Mrs. Patterson found herself commanding first place in circulation and going away. It was a position she never lost as long as she lived. Her most difficult problem was to bring up the volume and quality of advertising. For that, she reasoned nothing would so strengthen the *Times-Herald* as a demonstration that it had been accepted by other newspapers for a reliable performer.

Her principal competitors, the *Post,* and the Washington *Evening Star,* made much of the fact that for many years they had been members of the Associated Press, the world's dominant cooperative news service. Mrs. Patterson set out to become a member of the Associated Press. And so she did. But before she was done with the matter, her Cousin Robert in Chicago, not to mention a great many other people, could have wished Hearst had never had the impulse to let such a woman loose on journalistic premises. For as it turned out, Mrs. Patterson's pursuit of admission to the Associated Press set in motion forces that in the end put McCormick at odds with not only the Government of the United States but also the main weight of journalism, itself, all over the country. Just one side effect of his intransigence was to force a test between government and press, the long-range effects of which are by no means yet fully measured between the antagonists, themselves, let alone understood by the country at large. It is a tangled story, but nobody who has ever attempted to examine it has ever said it was less than curious.

The Associated Press began in 1848 as an exclusionary effort of six New York newspapers to control news in the great metropolis and dole it out, suitably colored, to approved publishers in cities worth being influenced. The coming of the telegraph and the Civil War only made the New Yorkers try harder to dominate all the news traffic and compose it to suit their local purposes.

It was Joseph Medill who broke them. He formed a western Associated Press and guided it to a victorious settlement with the eastern monopolists. Then came a great journalistic scandal, about which little is said, even yet, in gatherings of publishers. A rival system calling itself the United Press, no connection with the present news service called United Press-International, engaged in a rate and news war with the Associated Press. Victor Lawson, who had picked up where Joseph Medill left off as leader of the Middle-Western newspapers in their unremitting struggle for place, produced proof that some principal eastern publishers and officers of the Associated Press itself were heavy investors in the rival United Press. Of these, Charles A. Dana was the one whose conduct most shocked his colleagues, for Dana had always presented himself as a moral and ethical arbiter, downright brutal to any man caught out by his own investigations.

When the dust settled, there was a cooperative of publishers who had agreed to share costs and individually discovered news through a pooling system that experience had taught them to put under the strictest possible discipline. Melville E. Stone was called back from his untoward retirement to be general manager. He was one man they felt they could trust, not only for his purposes but for his judgment in action. They were right.

Journalism rests its case on five plain questions: "who?", "what?", "when?", "where?", "why?". It is astonishing what power these little words have to turn up answers that grip the interest of the world. But first the world must be disposed to believe the answers reflect an earnest effort to get at the whole case at hand, and that they were given as represented.

Under Stone's hand, the Associated Press learned to handle the five questions in such a way that its reputation—and the character that supports the reputation—are its one supreme asset. It is believed. AP mistakes are so few, and AP credibility in the world so nearly universal, that the United States Information Service has for years plagued the Board of Directors for permission to quote the AP in Voice of America broadcasts. It confesses people will believe the AP who won't believe the government of the United States, even in cases of each reporting the same matter the same way.

So far, the AP has not been shaken out of refusal. Its experience with governmental overreaching ranges from backwoods sheriffs in Mississippi to operators in the murk of great capitals around the world. To pursue the five questions at a minimum risk of passing under a yoke from which it could never again escape, therefore, the AP declines to let itself be used as the validating authority for anything any government says, anywhere, any time.

AP operations have always rested on fundamental judgments of policy, which are the obligation of member-publishers elected to the board of directors. Among these, there is a keen appreciation that news is a property, has a value, and as the Voice of America case shows, the AP does not automatically pass it out to everybody who thinks he ought to have it, and nothing more said.

Decision-making on news as property has its difficulties. What, for instance, is to be done about a publisher who steals an AP dispatch and uses it without due permission? W. R. Hearst held several AP memberships through his individual newspapers, yet his separately managed news agencies were caught using Associated Press reports in their dispatches. Several very rough lawsuits put a stop to that.

And what about the AP member who doctors an AP dispatch to make it read the way he likes—for whatever reason—and still puts out the fraud under the AP logotype? None other than Robert R. McCormick, a director of the AP of many years' standing, let his passion against Franklin D. Roosevelt drive him to order that AP dispatches in the *Tribune* dealing with sore subjects be amended to language that suited him. Aside from any other consideration, the consequence was self-mutilating. The changes were so clumsy and the wording so contrary to AP practice he was caught, immediately.

Nor was it a trivial matter, either. There could be no possible explanation that made sense, and for a director of the AP to so far transgress was genuinely shocking. There was a serious move not merely to reprimand McCormick, in person, but to make a public record and throw the *Tribune,* one of the AP's oldest and most stalwart members, out in the cold. Robert McLean, who was by then president of the AP, kept the voices down. If McCormick was grateful he showed it in a strange way. As the complications here being unraveled wore on toward their climax, McLean finally made a direct and personal appeal to McCormick. Would he, for the sake of the total membership, and preservation of its then imperiled authority to handle its own affairs, yield a position taken in self-interest? The answer was a flat no. If he couldn't have his own way, McCormick would bring down the whole house. He brought down the whole house and the rest of the story is just how he did it and what difference that made in the world.

In solving problems which deal with its property right in its own news discoveries, the AP has never had much trouble except the time and expense necessary to uncover miscreants and get them before a chosen tribunal, a court of law or its own board of directors. But there remains a further aspect of basic policy and from the very earliest times, it has been a hard one to handle. Who has a right to become an AP member, anyhow, and on what terms?

The tricky proposition of who to let in, and when, had never been solved in any reliable way from the Civil War days when Joseph Medill began his long, and successful, campaign to bring down the New Yorkers. They had been a major help to him. They were crude in their attempts to tie up the telegraph lines, browbeat their publisher-clients and doctor their dispatches to benefit New York at other cities' expense. And in dealing with public authority, when it became curious about their ways, they were both obtuse and haughty. As much as anything, their manners kept them in hot water with Congress and in the courts, until, finally, they lost out all around.

And in all its evolutionary adjustments to a changing world down to the time Mrs. Patterson asked for admission, the Associated Press had never been entirely easy in its mind about the problem of how far to go in rejecting applicants.

The 1939 rule-book was an undoubted work of legal art, tediously laced with ifs, buts and subtended qualifiers of what the board and the membership might do. But in practice the approach was pragmatic. In cities where AP service was not already being fully used, a publisher need only start up his paper, run it enough to demonstrate that he was no fly-by-night gambler. Then, he would be admitted. Such occasions, of course, were never many, and by 1939, very unlikely. AP memberships never lay long wanting for users.

It was a fairly relaxed matter, also, to buy out some publisher who already held a membership, so far as the AP itself was concerned. No doubt there would have been some outcry if, for example, Al Capone had presented himself with documents to show he had taken over the Chicago *Tribune* and now wished that newspaper's long-held AP membership transferred over to his own venture. Nothing in the book said the members couldn't do just that. Nothing in the book said they must. It was a matter of taste and discretion.

But beyond there, the rules took a sharp turn. Anytime a publisher applied for AP membership, any already admitted publisher who looked on the applicant as a competitor could almost take it as certain that his veto would stop the new applicant. It was odd, but that's how it worked.

When Mrs. Patterson discovered her fellow publishers in Washington were not very excited about getting her into their club, therefore, she sought out Thurman W. Arnold, Assistant Attorney General in charge of antitrust activities. Why, she wished to know, was Arnold not investigating the Associated Press? Arnold was often a guest in her house and as often a guest with her in others. It was a time of peak antitrust actions against monster combines of finance capital in mining, manufacturing and merchandising. Arnold even held a suit forming against investment banking, itself. Yet, he never knew what evening would find him accused, in semi-public, of running away from a bunch of newspaper publishers. His own words are best: "Cissy Patterson got me to feeling I was yellow." With that, the glacier began to move.

Arnold took the matter up with the Attorney General, then Robert H. Jackson. Word of Mrs. Patterson's gambit by now was well known in the higher circle of journalism. Robert McLean came down and offered Mr. Jackson opportunity to suggest any changes in the AP bylaws that did not affect the right of the membership to say who could belong and how miscreants must be controlled. Arnold discovered the Roosevelt Administration was not interested in having him initiate any antitrust suit against the Associated Press or any of its member papers.

But he was not done. Mrs. Patterson, alone among Washington publishers, had taken Mr. Roosevelt's third term accession as, if not the best of all possible choices, better than the Republican offering. Therefore, Mr. Arnold arranged a conference, shortly after the election, to discuss the AP matter in terms of practical politics. First, he invited her to sign a formal complaint in her own right. She demurred. Was it not the Government's business to prosecute such matters? Then Mr. Arnold tried his final maneuver. Mrs. Patterson had supported Mr. Roosevelt in 1940. Just a letter from her, if not a formal suit in court, would be enough. Mrs. Patterson left. In a little while, she put the *Times-Herald* at one with the *Tribune* and her brother in New York, all out to keep the United States from the drift to war, as the three saw it. Inevitably, this led to an all-out row with the Roosevelt Administration that never let up until the last of the combatants died.

And that was the state of disorganization all around, as Marshall Field came into Chicago with the *Sun*. There was little doubt in any mind whether Field would sign a complaint against the *Tribune*, the

Associated Press or anybody connected with either. Several books have been devoted to the details of all that followed, not to say many pages of testimony in courts and Congress. And at the most critical moment imaginable, when his fellows in the AP directorate were doing their best to turn the corner without a fight, McCormick blew up everybody, including himself, with a performance that guaranteed without doubt the unremitting enmity of the governmental power. He got it, and all his journalistic fellows had to stand consequences with him.

The Chicago *Sun*'s natal day was December 4, 1941. That same morning, the *Tribune* broke a news story that for farreaching potential, can be matched against the one in 1919 which, so Mr. Roosevelt thought, "broke Woodrow Wilson's heart." The *Times-Herald* carried it, too, but in New York, Patterson's editors used some circumspection, for which he was soon grateful. They passed.

In Washington, no matter what war is raging elsewhere, there is one in which peace never comes. That is the war between Federal agencies to convince Congress one bureau is entitled to more tax money than the next. An especially close combat was on, in 1941, between the air and ground forces. Papers of the most secret character were taken to the Capitol which showed a war plan more heavily committed to a land army than airmen thought proper. To this were annexed the most forthright estimates that the United States must throw its weight with Britain and France or all too soon face Hitler alone. It was a thesis of gravest meaning, in military terms, and the most dangerous provocation in the politics of the day. It bore the endorsements of General George C. Marshall, Chief of Staff of the Army, and of the Chief of Naval Operations, Admiral Harold Stark. There were men in uniform who would have stood with their bodies between that document and knowledge of it by the German high command. And within a matter of days after it was made public, the German general staff recommended to Hitler that he cut his losses in Russia at once, set himself behind a Fortress Europe and prepare to break the United States attack sure to come by 1943, the year the document itself designated as the best early chance to act. His refusal is regarded by more than one military analyst as the moment of his ruin.

Harold Ickes' *Secret Diary* records something, but by no means the total of reaction in the Cabinet as the war plan was made public. Immediately, the question was raised whether McCormick might not now be arrested for, if not quite treason in the strict meaning of the Constitution, certainly for the gravest sort of next available charge. Mr. Roosevelt ordered investigations, of course, both by civil and military agencies. What he got back, and in short order, tied his hands. He could not go against McCormick without grave embarrassment to General Henry H. Arnold, chief of his air force. The precise details of how the war plan got to Capitol Hill and from there to the *Tribune* are not even yet fully documented. Senator Burton K. Wheeler of Montana, once one of Mr. Roosevelt's strongest supporters in domestic New Deal efforts, but by 1941 one of his most total critics, said in his autobiography he got the document from an air force captain and gave it to a *Tribune* reporter. McCormick's fantastic "letter to Sawyer," that triumphant account of military innovations which soon followed the War Plan story into the news of the day, was handed over by Roosevelt to General Arnold to analyze for whatever sense there could be found in it. That appeared to be the President's idea of getting even with everybody at once. Copies of McCormick's letter and Arnold's analysis were widely republished and, in a time of general gloom and apprehension, gave the country a moment of diversion.

Within the AP directorate, the *Tribune*'s December 4 explosion was recognized instantly, aside from any importance in general it might have on other fronts of war, as a very special disaster on its own. The War Plan story now settled all doubt. There was no way to deflect an all-out attack by the Department of Justice on AP rules for admitting members, except one. If McCormick would climb down, move for Field's admission and otherwise humble himself, there was a chance the rest of the storm would pass.

Robert McLean has furnished some previously never disclosed details. McCormick's reaction to that thought was to tell some publishers he would start newspapers in competition with them, if they did not join him against Field. Others he cajoled with concessions in the use of the *Tribune*'s feature services, so widely prized. He began to tie up votes for his side in any floor fight. And as it became apparent just such a fight was sure to come at the Associated Press annual meeting for 1942, McLean found that McCormick, in more ways than one, held an extraordinarily powerful hand.

The Washington elders were in no simple position themselves.

Frank B. Noyes, president of the *Evening Star* company and a friend of McCormick since their youth in Chicago, was also a just retired president of the Associated Press. Mr. Meyer, while of no such rank in the AP, was certainly one of its most respected members. And how, now, were they to stand on the matter of the Chicago *Sun?* McCormick's position toward Field was precisely their own toward Eleanor Patterson, who had filed her claim for membership with the AP board of directors exactly as Field had done. But unlike Field, Mrs. Patterson had managed to have it both ways. Having started the governmental mind to suspecting the AP's whole membership policy, she now made a great public to-do out of her refusal to sign the formal antitrust complaint, as Field was quick to do. Then, the Government's intervention in aid of Field made it literally impossible to keep her out.

McLean has furnished a long memorandum impressive in its account of McCormick's performance within the AP directorate. At the least, he was hard to bear. At one point, he even threatened to go after the Board itself. McLean was generous enough to add that he really doubted McCormick was entirely aware of the position in which he had now put himself. In final effect, though, it was plain the old days were gone for good. Something within the AP board's inmost feeling about itself was shattered.

On that very point, Eugene Meyer took the floor at an open meeting of the whole membership and in the most delicate language observed that publishers ought not to let political matters blind their judgment in considering the existential situation. Some may have puzzled over his obliquities. But one who understood exactly was McCormick. Meyer had the identical problem with Eleanor Patterson that McCormick had with Marshall Field. It could happen to anybody. McCormick never came near to getting a public endorsement of equal worth in the whole AP wrangle. And in his final significant act as a journalist, he showed Meyer his appreciation in an astounding way. At least it astounded journalists and politicians the country over who imagined that McCormick was in every situation, always the same.

Of course, as anybody except McCormick would have known from the start, the only way to save the Associated Press from being overhauled by government was to keep it out of court, given the climate of the times and the nature of the partisans. It was to stay out of court that McLean had tried.

No doubt it would be unfair to say McCormick, single-handed, drove all before him into the courtroom, and wanted it that way from the start because he was spoiling for a showdown with Roosevelt. And no matter to what degree such an urge was governing him, McCormick really did cherish the illusion that he was right on the law, the facts and the equities. He was foolish enough to think he would win, in the end, against all odds.

And quite as one might have expected, it all came out the opposite way. The courts held against McCormick and against the AP, without recourse. The rules of membership collapsed, and the day of the AP as a self-governing cooperative was done. Now there was no longer safe ground on which members knew to stand in keeping competitors out. Nor, of course, would there be need to spend money on alternative and inferior news services. Hearst's own was first to collapse. The United Press, which had come up in the twentieth century as a straight commercial property organized around the Scripps-Howard chain, was hard put, but managed. Disciplinary powers within the Associated Press were left in a state of suspended animation, where they have been ever since.

Once McCormick had been put down there were second thoughts. Perhaps, for all that had been gained, something might have been lost. One publisher who wished to see what it all meant, in the long view, was Henry R. Luce, who had at one time or another used *Time, Life* and *Fortune* to analyze McCormick's performances with less than total approval. In December, 1942, Luce had a conversation with Robert M. Hutchins at the University of Chicago. What now was the state of the free press, under the Constitution, and what of its future? This question cost Mr. Luce $200,000 in cash. That was the amount he contributed to a Commission on Freedom of the Press, organized by Mr. Hutchins. Another $15,000 was forthcoming from *Encyclopaedia Britannica,* of which Hutchins was a director and the University of Chicago, a sort of beneficial owner.

Mr. Hutchins formed a body of philosophers, legalists, seminarians, anthropologists, financiers and historians to ponder the question. For the better part of five years the commission sat. Professor William Ernest Hocking, who had retired from a career of philosophy at Harvard, was chosen to put together the commission's finding. This may be read in a slim volume offered by the University of Chicago Press. Its title: *Freedom of the Press, A Framework Of Principle*. It would be inappropriate in this book to attempt any precise judgment on the commission's work, but it does seem reasonable to say that such a thing was an odd consequence of McCormick's refusal in 1941 to heed Weymouth Kirkland's advice on how to compete with Marshall Field.

The stresses of the long fight left scars within the AP directorate. Robert McLean formed the opinion that once McCormick found he could no longer use the AP by-laws in his personal battles he was uninterested in helping solve the AP's problems of adapting to the change. Whatever it signified, McCormick declined to let himself be renominated for the board.

Any twinges he might have felt about how he should conduct himself in a time as grave as that of the United States after Pearl Harbor, the AP suit anesthetized. He developed notions of persecution to the degree that he could believe general public limitations on food, drink, gasoline and marginal luxuries were aimed at him in person. One evening at table, as his cousin, Mrs. Patterson, made some small apologies for offering him a rather meager bit of meat, he glared at his plate and burst out that he knew, all right, but "they won't get me. I killed a beef." It would be easy to think McCormick was cold, selfish and heartless. He was, in fact, under the impression that Roosevelt's agents were after him, and saw it as a matter of his personal honor to outdo them.

And so it went throughout the war. McCormick considered himself in a state of siege. He was right, too. The Government of the United States was after him on every front. His tax returns, the *Tribune* paper supply, every one of the many practices of any corporation, were watched for openings. The detailed list is long and hardly worth reviewing. They didn't get him. And it is only fair to say that in his way McCormick kept the Government under siege, too. He didn't get it, either, though he did ruin the days, and nights as well, for a great many dignitaries from the President down.

He was never so delusional as to forget the importance of turning out the best possible newspaper, in the technical sense, of his life. All the skill and imagination of the staff were concentrated on giving proof that the *Tribune* would let no Chicagoan be neglected.

And it certainly did a surpassing work. No city had a reputation to match Chicago at unsparing service on the home front. *Tribune* reporters at sea, on land and in the air, and *Tribune* photographers, to the extent they were permitted, did some of the finest and bravest accounts of the war. And McCormick showed himself, for all his total loss of control in other things, still capable of generous attitudes toward those who followed him in his headlong career. Publishers, generally, made much in print about the bravery of their representatives. McCormick sent a *Tribune* reporter a $5,000 bonus for one single feat in the Pacific. He announced in the city room that when the war was over, the *Tribune* not only meant to take back every man and woman that had gone into uniform, but would also keep every added member of the staff on hand at the war's end. Furthermore, it was not talk. He did it.

As the war permitted, the *Tribune* set up operations not only in Europe but in Asia, too. It published in the Philippines, as promptly as its agents could assemble a plant, once General MacArthur was returned. In Europe, it scrambled for a toehold as the armies battled into Germany and, as usual, had problems with military governing authorities who felt *Tribune* politics reason enough to deny it any place in the life of the troops. But to no avail. The *Tribune* had its overseas editions again as long as the troops were there to read them.

It was inevitable that McCormick would be in trouble sooner or later on a matter of military censorship. When it came, the Department of Justice moved a grand jury in Chicago to inquire whether the *Tribune* had violated the laws on espionage and the censorship codes. Secretary of the Navy Knox initiated the action and Francis Biddle, as Attorney General, had the burden of bringing off such case as there might be. While he was in the midst of his effort, suddenly the Navy Department refused any further information. Mr. Biddle called off the grand jury and, in his own words, was left feeling like a fool. All the whole thing accomplished was once more to convince McCormick that he was persecuted and that he was invulnerable. The whole truth of the case has never yet been put on public record.

The great naval battle off Midway Island, June 3–5, 1942, changed the course of the Pacific War. From Pearl Harbor to Midway, Japan had the advantage. After Midway, the United States knew that it could win. United States cryptographers had made the difference. The Japanese codes and ciphers were broken, so their fleet movements were known, and Midway was an American trap. Great advantage lay with keeping the clue to victory well out of sight. Shortly after the battle, a *Tribune* correspondent just returned from the Pacific wrote an interpretation of the Midway encounter such that naval authorities assumed the Japanese would surely realize he had given away the secret. William D. Mitchell, who had been Attorney General for Herbert Hoover, presented the Government's case. There are many unsubstantiated accounts of why it all collapsed in the midst of action. One version was that the navy suddenly had second thoughts about blaring the word all over Washington and Chicago that at bottom the violation, if any, involved codes. How this was overlooked in the beginning it would be difficult to fathom. Another version held there was not one whit of evidence to show any *Tribune* executive or reporter had done a single thing to warrant complaint of any willful violation. And a third doctrine, supported by grand jury testimony, was that well before the Battle of Midway news that the United States had the Japanese fleet in its sights for a battle was freely discussed in Washington. If any real secrecy about code-cracking were at stake, governmental talk put it in jeopardy before the *Tribune* even had a story to write. In final fact, there was nothing to justify the charge, unless one is to say that McCormick had just goaded the Administration beyond endurance. Men in office, too, can be driven by critics to use their powers in fits of personal disorientation.

In 1957, a Commission on Government Security sat to review experiences in war and peace, with a view to reconciling the country's wish to know, against the Government's wish to keep its own counsel. The chairman of the commission explained its responsibilities by illustration. He said that after the battle of Midway the Japanese were "tipped off" (his words) by the *Tribune* and changed their code. If this had not happened, he reasoned, "Japanese sea power could have been finally and completely destroyed many long and bloody months sooner."

At precisely the time he was giving out this version, a press censorship manual for the armed services was issued in which the Government's handling of the Midway case in 1942 was analyzed as a classic how-not-to-do-it that had invited Japanese attention far more than the original publication. The manual's words were:

"As students of the Pacific War know, the Japanese did not realize that the code had been broken and on other occasions the fact that this knowledge had been kept from them enabled our forces to pull off a coup."

In 1964, both the Navy Department and the Department of Justice issued official memoranda asserting no knowledge at all about the conflict in official view. The Navy Department held that careful search disclosed "there is no official record in the Navy Department concerning the incident in question."

McCormick, naturally, got in what he no doubt considered the last word. Mr. Biddle went on from being Attorney General to serve on the International Military Tribunal at Nürnberg in 1945. There was not universal approval. Victors in a war could hardly hope to give an altogether clear appearance of impartial justice in trying the vanquished. The *Tribune* was loud in criticism that the Nürnberg trials were a kangaroo court. Still, when Mr. Biddle came on to Chicago in 1948 to lecture on the trial at a luncheon of prominent citizens, it was thought only polite to ask McCormick, a fellow Old Grotonian of the guest and in his own right a town spectacle. McCormick's secretary wrote that she had been directed by her employer to say he did not care to dine with a murderer. Not unremarkably, that was what Mr. Biddle most vividly recalled of McCormick thereafter. It was also an exceptionally good illustration of how far McCormick eventually fell in self-indulgence at invective, exaggerated language and grandiosity of manner. He had suffered much travail all his life and none of it had taught him to hold his tongue. But at least one change for the better had come by then into his gloomy presence.

In 1939, the first Mrs. McCormick died and a funeral was held at Cantigny that McCormick's cousin, Mrs. Patterson, thought near to parody. Death came after a long illness, and illness had been preceded by an even longer period of despondency. The difference in ages left McCormick and his first wife little enough to do together as she found herself less able to ride and to carry on the household flair to which her husband was accustomed. Still, when she died, McCormick had a detachment of troops turned out. He had a horse led behind her casket, stirrups crossed and eyes hooded in black, as if she were a fallen general. At her grave the three rounds were fired and Taps blown on the bugle as the colors of the

United States were folded. No doubt it was all, in McCormick's mind, entirely in keeping with her due as the daughter and sister of generals, and himself, after all, at the graveside.

In the early years of the war, he made a few efforts to find feminine companionship, without really trying very hard. But then, as he was driven to notice his households were falling shabby for the lack of a woman's touch, he invited some aid from Mrs. Maryland M. Hooper, whose husband's wholesale coal handling company had the *Tribune* as a client. The Hoopers had for some years rented a house from McCormick at Wheaton, and Mrs. Hooper had been a special friend of the first Mrs. McCormick, approximately twice as many years younger than McCormick as the first Mrs. McCormick was older. It is not too difficult for a skilled mathematician to work all that out, if he feels it worth doing. In early December, 1944, Mrs. Hooper and her husband divorced. On December 22, 1944, she became McCormick's second wife and immediately dust began to fly in his various households, which by now were: one in Chicago on Astor Street, the Cantigny estate at Wheaton, a considerable amount of property at Boynton Beach, Florida, and quarters in Canada at the mill towns. In New York, McCormick still held onto his rights of eminent domain at the old Ritz-Carlton, but in Washington made a particular uproar that there was not a fit hotel in the city. This allowed him to stay with his cousin at Fifteen Dupont Circle as a matter not only of family courtesy, but also as an absolute physical necessity.

Deaths and dissolutions had by now forced him to think hard about the future of the *Tribune*. Robert McLean was startled to hear McCormick say at a public gathering he hoped it would not be a case of pearls before swine for him to leave everything to the employes. In Philadelphia that kind of talk was not done, but McLean decided McCormick and the *Tribune* understood one another well enough. Nobody had shown offense.

Finding just the right relative to carry on after him was a matter about which McCormick's choice was narrowed by events beyond his control. He had no child of his own. Medill McCormick's son died in a fall off a mountain in New Mexico. Then Mrs. Courtlandt Barnes, eldest of two daughters in Medill McCormick's marriage, decided that her *Tribune* inheritance was what she called "blood money."

There was a very emotional exchange. McCormick finally agreed to buy her out, subject to approval by an attorney of her choosing. It was many years later that Mrs. Barnes learned McCormick, in turn, made a handsome profit on her interest in selling it off to Tribune Company employes.

The second daughter in the Medill McCormick marriage was very young and he hardly knew her at all in the time of his dealing with her sister.

In 1946, Patterson's death was the knock of warning that got to McCormick without recourse. He began to put his house in order. His first act was to find an occasion that suited him and announce that the Medill McCormicks' second daughter, by then married, was on assignment from him to prepare for a life of carrying on, as McCormick put it, "in the spirit of Joseph Medill." And so, in a little while she had at it. But in even less time, she was interrupted, and blamed McCormick. All of which summed up to a blow for him, for her and for others, of lethal effect.

In 1948, he was in Paris when the knock came again. A phone call told him Eleanor Patterson had followed her brother out of life. McCormick turned to his wife and said abruptly: "Cissy's dead." Then he strode off to the next room and Mrs. McCormick heard him through the door, rumbling, in a sort of tune, "Now I am the last leaf on the tree, the la-a-a-a-ast leaf on the tre-e-e-e-e-e!" And so he was, indeed. But, for all that had happened so far, the next six years of McCormick's life were as full of challenge as any he had ever seen.

At the war's end, he was ready with his own answer to the idea of the United Nations. In McCormick's mind, there was nothing for the United States to gain out of adventures offshore, but if there were no way to enforce reason against this mania, there was a way to insure against loss of sovereignty. Let the nations file application for admission to the United States under the terms of the Constitution. The Union had started with thirteen states. In 1945 there were forty-eight, and though nobody mentioned the fact just yet, there were already firm intentions to increase this number to fifty. And, at bottom, the very reason was to get Alaska and Hawaii beyond any claims that, as territories, they were subject to the jurisdiction of some extranational establishment of the United Nations. When he got no takers of his personal new order for the world, McCormick put it all down as proof the powers were not really interested in a good thing.

As soon as wartime restraints would let him, he began to plan toward an inspection of the world. And before he was done, he had covered nearly every part worth seeing. He even tried to persuade his pilot to fly past Cape Horn, the terror of seamen for centuries. But the pilot had more sense than that.

The travel began in 1945 with a run by boat up Lake Michigan and out to Baie Comeau, to lay the groundwork for a third expansion that carried the Tribune Company on into hydroelectric power, aluminum smelting and a still-expanding variety of heavy industrial projects far beyond any ordinary publishing company's reach. His memoir on Canada, generated by that trip, argues that a yarn-spinner of real gift was lost when McCormick convinced himself that he must be a law-giver and political philosopher. In between accounts of shooting rapids with Indian guides in the old days and new days of raising vegetables and milk cows in regions thought impossible for such things before, he took care to warn Girl Scouts always to carry a compass, know the stars and the signs on trees.

It was the atomic bomb that at last shattered McCormick's lifelong confidence in Fortress America. At first, he ran for the traditional military exit: for every weapon there comes a counterweapon. But his head cleared of this bromide faster than some others did as he had at the books and forced himself to restudy all he had ever known about physics, chemistry and electronics. But what really got him was curiosity. How McCormick conducted himself is best discovered by reading the second volume of David Lilienthal's diary, *The Atomic Years, 1945–1950*. Each managed to stifle old antipathies. As Lilienthal rather dryly conceded in his diary, they even became friends, of some curious kind, and McCormick got to see the works. In 1947, well ahead of the generality, McCormick came up with a plan for the *Tribune*'s defense. He laid in pineapple juice for thirst quenchers and application to burns, ordered axes, helmets and food supplies, a complete order of standby publishing rules. It was every bit sensible, too, and in a few years even the Government was trying to catch up. But McCormick conceded the bomb to be a dark shadow on the world. He could not see any way it could ever be lifted. For once, he admitted a problem beyond his solving.

In 1947, too, he rented air passage to Peking and took his wife, who knew it all from girlhood. He felt the end of China was not far off. While stopping over in Manila he heard that surplus B-17 bombers were going up for sale. Within forty-eight hours, his agents had snapped up a perfectly good bomber, with spare engines and all accessories for fifteen thousand dollars, total. While he was inspecting China, Korea and Japan, it was being adapted for his further purposes.

In 1948, he took off in his B-17 with Mrs. McCormick, secretaries, photographers, reporters and a recording staff, for ten thousand miles of flying around Europe. He visited Iceland, Scotland, Northern Ireland, Eire, Belgium, Luxembourg, France, Spain and Portugal.

Six months later, he flew 13,500 miles around Latin America, taking in Colombia, Ecuador, Peru, Chile, Argentina, Uruguay, Brazil and Venezuela. The great provocation of this trip was a call on Juan Perón, in Buenos Aires, for there again the urge to make trouble seized him. He remarked that Perón's formulations were in much patterned on the New Deal in the United States. If he expected mobs to march on the *Tribune,* he was disappointed. He hardly got any kind of press at all on that one. In 1950, he did better. He covered 24,000 miles in six weeks. Again he went to Spain and got himself into print twice. The first time was on discovering that some sign painter had put the flag of the deceased Spanish Republic on the side of his B-17. Then, he called on Generalissimo Francisco Franco and on leaving designated the Spanish chief of state the father of modern warfare. That got excellent results. All liberal publications were furious, as McCormick flew on to Greece, Egypt, Pakistan, India, Ceylon, Thailand, Saudi Arabia, Turkey, France, Italy, Denmark and, again, Iceland.

In Greece, he was utterly charmed by the King and Queen, and even more so at the work being done by Americans engaged in reconstruction under the Marshall Plan. The plan itself he condemned, for he had fallen out with the plan's author, after all their long friendship. Sometime in the early part of 1943 he wrote the war-harassed general, taking care to address him only as "Dear Marshall" to signify a personal and nonofficial communication. He had an idea how better officers could be selected from competent civilians, as against regulars low in brains and drive. Someone in the *Tribune* secretariat put the wrong initials on the letter and it went astray for six months. When at last it reached the chief of staff, General Marshall halted his pursuits of war, wrote McCormick apology for the delay, took responsibility for it on his own staff, and then very carefully delineated the logic for continuing selection of officers according to existing plan. It did no good. McCormick was sure he had been snubbed and said Roosevelt had reduced General Marshall's backbone to rubber. If so, it was knowledge Mr. Roosevelt never discovered for himself. He complained several times that General Marshall somehow was not the sort of man he could manage to call "George."

But, for all his dislike of the Marshall Plan as an idea, McCormick found it, as a process, irresistible. His broadcasts of Americans laying highways, building dams, doing over the war-shattered world, reveal him as a frustrated outsider, longing to have off his coat and get into the great adventure. Here were Sanitary and Ship Canals by the dozen. But all too late.

He interviewed the Premier of Egypt and the Prime Minister of India. To keep his standing as provocateur, he glared at the provincial reporters clustering before him on his landing at Karachi, in Pakistan, and asked: "What place is this?" The next day, newspapers all over Europe and the United States had squibs that suggested McCormick had expected to come down somewhere near Bloomington, Indiana. It was just the sort of boob-snatcher he liked best to remind rival publishers he should never be out of their thoughts. He fell into a handsome quarrel with the Danes and denounced their government for a specified list of socialist shortcomings. And for all that the Egyptians told him how the *Tribune* had kept their courage up in days of struggle against English colonial brutalisms, he spotted some flaws in their constitution. These, he denounced on the air. The Egyptians did not hear, or if so, failed to understand. They continued in error.

He inspected the beginnings of American commercial oil developments in Saudi Arabia, and there also made arrangements that the gift of a stallion be shipped home to his youngest niece, then high in his favor. He was never more near to letting himself confess his true emotions than in trying to explain the difference between European and American approaches to life in the Middle East. There were no American bugles, no pennants, no trappings of empire, and, to give his very words, "no Mrs. Hauksbee." There, surely, he wasted a shot. It was hardly likely that one in a thousand of his audience would know her as Kipling's lady of intrigues in *Plain Tales from the Hills*. But being out of phase with the popular taste was no novelty in McCormick's approach to pleasure. After the war, some notion led the British Foreign Office to assign an Old Ludgrovean as consul general to Chicago. He was Berkeley Gage, a descendant of General Thomas Gage who did so much to help George III lose the American Colonies. Gage soon established himself as a regular at McCormick's dinner table. During the Christmas holidays in 1951, he admitted that he could sing a little. McCormick, always ready to prove that Groton sadist had not been altogether fair about his own talents, rose, and with his arm around the consul's shoulders, rattled windows panes with—"Pull, Pull Together," the Eton boating song.

Shortly afterward, a touring member of Parliament, Woodrow Wyatt, put into Chicago and told Gage he would like to call on McCormick. The consul general advised against it. His work was nervous enough, and no man could tell what would happen if a British Socialist put a foot wrong at the top of Tribune Tower. But Wyatt went anyhow. He found McCormick so congenial he summoned up nerve and told him about Gage's warning, to which McCormick replied amiably there was nothing to it, the British Empire was no longer important enough to require his concern.

For 1952, he had much more serious projects on his mind. In little less than a month, he took in twenty thousand miles to scout Liberia, the Belgian Congo, Uganda, the Sudan, Libya, Malta, Morocco. And in France, he set about to see if he could also take in, or on, General Eisenhower, then commanding the SHAPE operation in Paris. McCormick's candidate for the Republican nomination was Senator Robert A. Taft, but it was well known that the Pocketbook Gang around New York had the general on its mind. McCormick wished to see whether yet another man of the Middle West was marked to follow the path of Thomas E. Dewey and Wendell Willkie into the clutches of the Gang.

General Eisenhower has recalled the encounter as polite and nonpersuasive either way, though it lasted more than an hour. He escorted McCormick to the door, and as he turned back, saw his own staff collapsed in laughter. They told him that Mrs. McCormick, following in the wake of her lord and master, had saucily flipped back her coat to show on her suit lapel a large button, reading, "I Like Ike." Years afterward, Mrs. McCormick said she couldn't remember a thing about it, but she did remember very well that her husband came straight home, determined to stop the Pocketbook Gang or blow up the Republican Party. In 1952, after the smoke cleared away, it would have been easy to say he had done neither. But political changes do not always come in an instant or in exactly the way partisans would prefer. After the Republican Party had finished its experience of 1964, McCormick's performance in the Eisenhower year looked less like a failure and more like a time-delayed bomb. Those least surprised at its explosion were his old associates on the *Tribune*.

In the *Tribune*'s Washington office the proudest archive is a telegram from McCormick to Arthur Sears Henning who was then bureau chief. The telegram is timed and dated 12:20 P.M., March 4, 1929, and it was McCormick's verdict on President Hoover's inaugural suggestions that the Government might lead and not follow public opinion on domestic reform and foreign affairs. The message reads: "This Man Won't Do!" Whenever some junior member of the *Tribune* organization has since wondered about the official case for McCormick's right to claim the second sight, that pronouncement has been quoted to prove that time proves McCormick right. His verdict on Hoover was not unique, of course, either at the moment or as the course of events unfolded. But other critics thought Hoover proposed to do too little. McCormick objected that Hoover wanted to do too much.

Whether McCormick had sound ideas on how to advance the selfish interest of the United States is an arguable proposition, but it would not be sensible to dismiss his grasp of the Republican Party's topical history, its inner organization and the relation of its public platforms to private expectations. From 1912 to 1952, he was almost always a delegate to its national conventions. He rarely neglected to have with him an elaboration which he would read to the hushed membership of the Platform Committee. They would attend him as if he were George Washington, delivering the Farewell Address. Then he would withdraw and the members would get on with their juggling, in hope of a lucky combination that would produce a victory at the polls. And so it went for forty years. On May 24, 1952, McCormick took to the air and began a grand summation of his life's feeling:

> Every commitment we make on the mainland of Europe or Asia is a serious danger to our national future, undertaken solely for the benefit of American individuals and companies and foreign countries fattening on our bloodmoney. . . .
>
> That is why every believer in Americanism, every lover of freedom, must eschew *NATO,* the North Atlantic Federation, the United Nations, and all the evils they have in store for us, and with them, their leaders.

There was the challenge, flat and plain. On July 12, 1952, as the party ended its convention in Chicago, McCormick took the occasion to say that in 1912 the same party's convention in the same city had been "thoroughly under the control of corruptionists led by Senator Nelson W. Aldrich of Rhode Island and Boies Penrose of Pennsylvania." These had put the party under the service of their pocketbooks and the harvest had been the Bull Moose revolt with Theodore Roosevelt, the election of Woodrow Wilson and all the world's disaster.

The three Republican conventions preceding 1952 struck McCormick as in the same vein. The machine had put up its pocketbook candidates and left the party's rank and file with nowhere to go. The public would not vote for such men. As for the Eisenhower-Nixon ticket, this was McCormick's verdict:

"I have not the slightest idea that the present candidates, nominated on its platform threatening the existence of our Republic, can be elected."

On August 9, McCormick confessed himself without a candidate. Senators Taft of Ohio and Byrd of Virginia would not leave their posts. Ex-President Hoover and General MacArthur were unwilling to end their great careers with a certain defeat. The conventions of 1956 would be so timed that third-party electors could not be chosen after them, so:

"If a third party is to be formed, it will have to be formed before the conventions, and a candidate will have to be found who can accept defeat in 1956 just as Frémont did in 1856, with the idea of having a victorious party in 1960, just 100 years after the Republican Party carried the country."

On August 23, 1952, McCormick uttered the call:

"I think the time has come to organize another party. I will not say a third party because there have been over thirty parties in the history of our country. I will not say a new party because we must draw upon people of similar beliefs in both of the old parties."

He then read off a list of candidates for the Senate and some other offices below the Presidency, a sampling of patriots to be supported and evil-doers who must be defeated. He invited listeners to write in for a complete set of the good and the bad. The next week he reported that the mail received was the largest in the history of his broadcasting, which by then was a standard, popular Saturday-night performance not only on the *Tribune*'s own radio and TV station, WGN, but also on a network across the Middle West.

The title of the patriot movement cannot be thought an accident of senile maundering. No man of his day knew the topical details of American political history better than McCormick. If any there be who do not know what he meant when he called for the formation of "The American Party," the place to look for an answer is in any standard dictionary of American political history and see a cross-reference, "The Know-Nothings." The gesture was calculated and the diagram plain. Nor did McCormick let it go at talking on the air. He proceeded at once to work out an action committee, "For America." The last two years of his life were concentrated as much on its organization as on his perfection of the way the *Tribune* was supposed to operate with him gone. Nor is it the wildest nonsense, either, to say that he was as effective in the one effort as in the other. In 1964, Tribune Company of Illinois had the healthiest year of corporate enterprise in its long history. In 1964, just four years behind McCormick's schedule, the Republican Party suddenly found itself in the grip of men the generality professed not to know. And whether the Presidential campaign that followed was an ignominious ending to effort by the new men or a beginning of political action even more strictly pursuant to McCormick's model, no man could really know. But one thing was undeniable. The

Republican Presidential campaign for 1964 was, at last, McCormick's own. And the *Tribune* performed as if McCormick, himself, were back at that great marble slab of a desk, running it with his own hand.

CHAPTER SEVENTEEN ★★★ McCormick's last flight, in more ways than one, came in 1953. He was now rid of the B-17, and so put himself in the hands of the commercial airlines for ten thousand miles that took him through England, France, Italy and Germany. It was a sentimental journey, with side trips to places he had been in his childhood. He made a special point of having a day at Ludgrove. To look at him, one could hardly imagine that such a vigorous, questing old man would, in a matter of weeks, take blows from which he could not recover. The least was a bout with pneumonia. The worst struck at his pride, his family feeling and his professional reputation.

To McCormick, the Tribune Company, taken as a whole, was never a mere corporate machine for making him rich. It was a world in which he could let himself go, building and operating among people of skill who really didn't care about his politics but enjoyed his ingenuity and drive at all the elements of converting trees to home-delivered papers. And as for the *Tribune* itself, the newspaper in Chicago, it was his child, his friend, his truest and closest companion. He had saved it and it, in turn, many a time over, had saved him. McCormick was never more eloquent, nor did he ever more reveal his own sentimental heart, than in saying once: "A newspaper is a living thing."

He did this in the course of discussing the mistakes of Joseph Pulitzer, who could not really bear to give up and so in his will had laid out a course so strict it led to the ruin of his best newspaper, the New York *World*. McCormick said, more than once, that nobody should try to manage after his own day is done. And yet . . .

Control of the Tribune Company had come down from Joseph Medill. Where was it to go next? McCormick would have been less than human if he had not cared. And, of course, the McCormick-Patterson Trust had been formed precisely to keep control where it had been, in the hands of Medill's blood heirs. But the trust could not work its magic, lacking the will of beneficiaries to hold fast. Or lacking their wit, either. The first break against it came in 1936, as McCormick's niece, Mrs. Barnes, demanded to be let out. Ten years later, Joseph M. Patterson was dead and his executors had tax problems the trust could do nothing to solve. The effect was that while stock control remained within the trust, the people it represented were changing identity. The interests of McCormicks and Pattersons were eroding. So far, new interests were in the hands of employes of the Tribune Company and in form removed from actual power to intervene in company policy. But for how long?

McCormick had few alternatives in seeking the next possible unifying family figure. He chose his brother's youngest child, Ruth Elizabeth McCormick.

Not long after her twentieth birthday, Miss McCormick married Maxwell Peter Miller, Jr., and the two young people set out at LaSalle, Illinois, to learn journalism through the well-tried route of their own shop in a small town. In 1945, McCormick brought his niece into the Tribune Company as a director and provided a future for her on the board of the McCormick-Patterson Trust. Her career at practical management, of course, he could not stipulate. It was part of the original agreement that Mrs. Eleanor Patterson would succeed her brother as McCormick's cotrustee in event he died before her. And so it turned out, but the arrangement was not a happy one. Patterson's death had shaken McCormick, as it had shaken his feminine cousin. They had life-long bonds of affection, to be sure, but neither especially admired the other's judgment in facing up to the world. And most of all, they were challenged on every side by events beyond their power to understand, not to say control.

McCormick showed a tendency toward positive interventions in the management of the *News*. In a strict sense of corporate administration, he was utterly correct in all he did. The *News* had been run by Patterson in a highly personal style. It had matured in his daily presence, and with him no longer there, the executive staff were at an emotional ebb. The *News* was too valuable a property to let slat in the wind. But McCormick was, as only he could be, insensitive to a lonely woman's need for reassurances.

The two old people fell into open quarrel. In early July, 1948, McCormick received from Mrs. Patterson a bulky letter, hand-carried from Washington to Cantigny. She spelled out her objections and threatened to form a combination against McCormick, drawing in Patterson's daughter Alicia, who had married the financier Harry Guggenheim, and with him built a most successful newspaper for the Long Island suburban life centered around Garden City. Mrs. Patterson indicated that she and the Guggenheims would now set about to chop McCormick down, but for exactly what offense she did not say.

McCormick's answer was to take off for Europe. If he was in the least intimidated, he did not show any sign of it and afterward, in fact, professed himself puzzled. It never occurred to him, apparently, that as much as anything, Mrs. Patterson was just harassing him to shift the burden of her own fears and troubles.

Her sudden death on July 24, 1948, hardly two weeks after that challenge to fight, gave McCormick relief from one set of problems, but brought new ones. Later he put out the story that it was his idea immediately to buy Mrs. Patterson's Washington paper, the *Times-Herald,* make it over into what he called a latter day "Fort Necessity," and from such as base, reintroduce the United States to the "burocrats." If he really had such a plan from the start he went about it in a peculiar way.

Mrs. Patterson, like her brother, left an estate which put its administrators to some tests of ingenuity. She had owned the *Times-Herald* as direct private property, not through a corporate structure, and there were no precise devices to evaluate it for tax purposes. Her interest in the Tribune Company, though ultimately corporate, was also difficult to appraise. There was no general market for McCormick-Patterson trust units and such demand as there was had already been fairly well met in the liquidation following her brother's death.

Mrs. Patterson's will called for acts which made it plain there would have to be some serious cash accumulated. It could only come from sale of her Tribune Company interest. She left the *Times-Herald* to some employes. She left her daughter a life income and other property. She distributed a considerable further amount among friends, all of these taxable to her estate rather than to the beneficiaries. Property beyond this was to go in trust for some individuals and for charitable and welfare purposes. At first, the will was withheld from probate until a *caveat* by the daughter was withdrawn. Finally, in February, 1949, Mrs. Patterson's estate was in the hands of her named administrators. McCormick met with them and was entirely courteous, even friendly, but showed no disposition to help in marketing McCormick-Patterson Trust units. On the contrary, broad hints were dropped that the administrators would bear in mind, of course, the McCormick-Patterson trustees would have to consent in writing to any transfers of interest. Nor did McCormick have any helpful thoughts concerning the *Times-Herald.* Instead, he let summer wear on to the customary July meeting of the Tribune Company directorate at Baie Comeau, far out on the North Shore of the St. Lawrence. He was absorbed with plans for hydroelectric power and aluminum-smelting project which, in spite of all his subsequent distractions, he did bring off.

But in 1949, as so long ago with Keeley, his Canadian pleasures were shattered by news of action to the south that demanded immediate reaction. The directorate were loaded into company planes and rushed to Chicago where they could sit, legally, to act on the bad news. In New York, J. P. Morgan & Company had been making inquiries among possible buyers of McCormick-Patterson Trust units. In Chicago, a financial advisor to His Eminence Samuel Stritch, successor to Mundelein as Cardinal-Archbishop, talked of having seen figures. And in Washington, Eugene Meyer, in an attempt to buy the *Times-Herald* for merger with his *Post,* had made a formal tender to take up any trust units not placed elsewhere. The Tribune Company had only hours in which to make up its mind what to do.

This account is not dedicated to exploring the details of all the executors and beneficiaries in Mrs. Patterson's estate had before them, but only to recording McCormick's performance. The net was that the Tribune Company bid in the *Times-Herald* and made a sufficient market so that no McCormick-Patterson units reached

Mr. Meyer, Wall Street, or churchly muniment vaults. McCormick announced Mr. and Mrs. Miller would come on to hold Fort Necessity. The Tribune Company's business had never been better. McCormick himself was now beyond anybody's warning that what will work one place may not in another. Money was poured into plant and equipment so the *Times-Herald,* as a product, shone as never before. All the *Tribune*'s unmatched operational techniques put it it in the customer's hands in the best type, on the best paper, with the very best flourish. But, somehow, it did not read quite the same. Some gathered that all McCormick really wanted to do was show Washington he thought it contemptible. Then, he quarreled with his niece. He never chose to discuss the matter, but Mrs. Miller was understood to say that she had resigned on discovering she was denied "a free hand." How anybody with even the most modest experience would have expected "a free hand" in McCormick's service it is difficult to fathom.

Shortly after she left the paper, Mrs. Miller divorced and in a little while remarried to Garvin E. Tankersley, who had been city editor of the *Times-Herald*. McCormick came to Washington and called the executive force into conference. In solemn, weary tones, he said that "the people in Chicago all think I am the only one who can handle the situation here," and so he would run the *Times-Herald* directly. Certainly it was true the paper now could be saved by nobody except McCormick. And so, after the usual round of fights with the Washington hotels, which he considered provincial beyond imagining, McCormick set up in one large Washington house after another, always kept fully staffed for his brief appearances. He gave the paper what attention he could muster. But nothing relieved its troubles or his.

Early in 1954, McCormick went to his house at Boynton Beach, Florida. He was by now sagging quite visibly and the winter around Chicago was no more difficult for him than the round of business. Kent Cooper, the retired general manager of the Associated Press and one of McCormick's warmest admirers, called on Eugene Meyer and Philip L. Graham, Meyer's son-in-law. Would they be interested in buying the *Times-Herald* if he could persuade McCormick to sell? It was a pointless question. Meyer had been trying to buy the *Times-Herald* from the day of Mrs. Patterson's death. He and Graham flew at once to Florida. In ten minutes, McCormick showed Meyer his appreciation for that moment of standing together in the Associated Press fight of 1942.

People not well acquainted with either Meyer or McCormick were astonished. They need not have been. In politics, to be sure, Meyer had shown himself capable of adapting to the times, though nobody could properly say he had ever been one of Mr. Roosevelt's unqualified admirers in all things. But Meyer and McCormick were contemporaries, could regard each other as Yalemen who had more than earned their "Y in Life" after graduation. And in journalism, Meyer had shown himself worthy of McCormick's respect. He had been a tough competitor, he had learned while doing, and shown himself under stress to be a gentleman. So, why not? Cooper tried to make a big mystery out of the whole thing. He claimed it all his own idea and said McCormick had specifically directed him to tell Meyer "he never would have got that paper if you hadn't thought of my selling it."

Now McCormick began to give off signs of increasing emotional and physical distress, but found it difficult, sometimes, to keep in mind exactly what had upset him. One of his principal executives was summoned to Florida on urgent business. McCormick showed off a set of bedside buttons. It seemed that when he punched for his valet he kept getting a chambermaid, or an airplane pilot. Instead of his usual vigorous gloom and its side-effects of danger, his demeanor was just one of sadness.

In Chicago, the postwar generation had come to view him, to the extent that it did so, at all, as somewhat like the Water Tower down on Michigan Avenue, the city's great symbol of survival from the fire of 1871. The old man and the old granite monument were each impediments to traffic, but each had a sort of antique grandeur as reminders that Chicago had lived.

Motorists who were careless could discover the tower had no idea of moving out of their way. And any who thought senescence had put McCormick out of action should have listened to his broadcasts for 1954 as he worked over William Hale Thompson, Franklin D. Roosevelt and laid down points on his own life story he thought historians would need to know. And it should be mentioned again that right to the end he kept his concern for the political regeneration he had announced in 1952.

McCormick's granite was not of the substance, however, as all his associates now had to accept. In 1953, on his return from that final inspection of the great world, he had come down with pneumonia. Then he showed symptoms of cirrhosis of the liver and genito-urinary distress. He complained of feeling cold. In December, 1954, he had a last conference with Weymouth Kirkland, to be sure about his will. On September 4, 1870, Robert S. McCormick was in Paris. There, he watched the mob storm the Bourbon Palace and head for the days of the Commune. He inscribed a pair of cufflinks with the date and wore them through all his own career. When he died, McCormick got them. Now he passed them on to a cousin, Brooks McCormick, executive vice president of the International Harvester Company. He added a hope that Brooks McCormick's son would be given them, too, once the boy had reached an age to "appreciate and preserve them." He gave full quittance of all debts except for purchases of real estate or beneficial interests in the Tribune Company, and ordered all written evidence destroyed. He chose one portrait of his mother for the Chicago Art Institute and one of his father for the embassy in Paris. The rest of his family art, "including all portraits of myself," all his books, manuscripts, guns, library on freedom of speech and freedom of the press, statues, medals, photographs, silverware, army commissions, furniture—everything in the house, really, and in his office at the *Tribune*—would be arranged as a museum of his life interests there on Cantigny Farm. A special building was to be a center of research on the doings of the First Division in all wars. It is all there just the way he wanted it. To see it costs not a penny and thousands do, some perhaps wondering just who it was that provided them such a show.

To his wife, McCormick gave some privileges of distributing less important personal effects and the right to stay at Cantigny, if she chose, as its chatelaine. She chose not. He also left her one million dollars in principal to be paid out in ten annual instalments. To a number of *Tribune* executives, members of the law firm and old friends, he left a thousand dollars each, as Joseph Medill had done, just to show he cared for them. He took care of his secretaries and household forces in the manner of a grand duke, and of course provided for a semistate funeral, mausoleum and the physical management of the museums.

Everything else he deeded over to the Robert R. McCormick

Charitable Trust, except a small income to an aged relative in Texas and provision for $100,000 a year to his wife for life, once she had received her principal sum. The objects of the trust were to care for sickness, distress or need among active or retired Tribune Company employes resident in Illinois; to aid "worthy and deserving children" of these employes in education; to do as much for Illinois widows and children of army officers; to promote free speech in Illinois and principles of Constitutional behavior; endow beds for the Passavant Hospital in Chicago; run some scholarships at the Citadel, a military school in South Carolina, and give to Chicago's united charities and to Northwestern University. There was a long recitation of legalisms intended to preserve the McCormick-Patterson Trust's control of the Tribune Company's stock. But nothing for Groton, nothing for Yale; not even something for Ludgrove. The will was dated December 18, 1954. On January 4, 1955, he added a minor codicil giving money to his two step-daughters and another relative he just remembered, but changing nothing in the main work.

He was taken out to Cantigny to wait, and became fearful of the nights. *Tribune* reporters who had roamed the world with him in good times and bad, now really moved at the sight of McCormick fighting death in feebleness and agony, took turns with his pastor at the night watch. And it gave him some dim pleasure to find his favorite bulldog, Buster Boo, in the room whenever he cleared up. So, when he felt himself better, all the friends made up a little book of mementoes and signed it. Buster Boo put on his paw mark.

McCormick was difficult to fathom, as to his niece. Did he wish her there or not? In his will he had asked that her son Mark be given a chance on the *Tribune*. But he said nothing about her daughter, nor about her, as beneficiary of anything he owned. Mrs. McCormick, one of her daughters, and a woman neighbor waited out the last night.

And so it was that at 2:47 A.M. on April 1, 1955, surrounded by women who could say nothing to him as he had nothing for them, in his grandfather's house that had been Red Oak in the days when the prairie rolled from its door and a boy could ride his pony, disturbed by nothing worse than the chime of cowbells and the piping of the meadowlarks, McCormick died in his sleep.

The years had done something to relieve the stress for authors of obituary literature. His contemporaries were mostly gone and the war in Korea had confused many people's memories about events before. In the main, McCormick made a smooth enough passage over into a marmoreal Chicago town character.

Not that he went any too quietly, at that. To some, he was an object of concern to the end. A distinguished Chicago attorney who came on to Washington some years later, said:

"Why, when I saw the *Tribune* first page every day, I felt the old man was aiming it straight at me. And when I saw it with his picture on it, saying he was dead, I felt relieved."

It would have pleased McCormick to know.

Yet it would not do to suggest that was the whole story, either. There was in Chicago a thorough appreciation that the death of McCormick meant the death of a type which had made it one of the world's most interesting and versatile communities. The city was quick to give him a monument that would have delighted his heart. McCormick was always a believer in the promotion of exhibits and fairs. He caught the spirit from the Columbian World Exposition in his grandfather's day and he made it pay, too. His last municipal effort was just such a thing. He ordered the *Tribune* to put fifty thousand dollars into underwriting a commercial exhibition on a piece of land down on the lake front, and he was a great fan in attendance at the showing of diesel locomotives, automobiles, dog food, prefabricated kitchens and all the wonders of American trade he considered the essence of civilization.

The exhibition did so well it not only paid off its underwriting, but became a permanent show, as well. At the suggestion of a reporter on Marshall Field's newspaper it was called McCormick Place.

And so in his native city, McCormick finally was acknowledged as a citizen who had done much and done it very well, indeed. He worked hard all his life at enterprises of great use to civilized society. He also made a great profit out of his work for himself and for others. And as for the newspaper that was the center of his effort, any institution so embedded in a city's life has also, perhaps even in spite of itself, acquired merit. And if it has shown bias in appreciation for McCormick's useful side, surely that cannot do harm to any other man. There was attention enough given his failings, by others.

In death as in life, McCormick was commonly called, by both admirers and critics, an "aristocrat." He fully agreed and more than once said so, in plain words. Nobody was ever taken in by his occasional feeble attempts to curry support with descriptions of himself as "middle class."

But what is an American aristocrat?

Aristotle thought of aristocracy as a form of government in which education and discipline are qualifications for suffrage or office-holding. Aristocrats were the few men who would hold power in common among themselves and exercise it, not selfishly, but in the interest of the many under their care. Such a noble concept has never been very much of this world. Long, long ago, aristocracy took the form of an oligarchy, a privileged order of power distinguished by birth or fortune.

As American distinction goes, McCormick's family connections can be described as privileged, but not anciently so. He liked to give an impression that the McCormicks in Virginia were grandees. The house McCormick's great-grandfather built still stands. It is called Walnut Grove, and is now maintained by the Virginia Polytechnic Institute as a sort of combined museum and experimental farm. An imaginative visitor can easily be persuaded to feel it touched with an air of melancholy, empty now of vivid, antagonistic life long drifted away. But no amount of fantasy can conceal its physical form. It is a plain red-brick farmhouse of the sort common to the Virginia back country. It wears no trace of connection with Tidewater splendors. And on the other side of his heritage, not McCormick, his mother or anybody else could erase Joseph Medill's determined simplicities, or those of his wife, either. They rose because they were able, but also because there was room for such a rising, too.

If an American cannot claim privilege descended through generations, endowed with "old" money and many ancestral performances in high public office, then how is he to be an aristocrat?

In 1813, John Adams was writing Thomas Jefferson about the afflictions of Polish kings, who were notable as victims of the aristocrats who chose them to reign but would not let them rule. Adams thought "your *aristoi* [Jefferson's natural aristocrats of virtue and talents] are the most difficult animals to manage of anything in the whole theory and practice of government. They will not suffer themselves to be governed."

No American could look down on McCormick with hauteur, if the mark of the aristocrat is resistance to being governed. His very letter to Franklin D. Roosevelt in 1932 saying that however badly he might run his business he could do it better than it could be helped by government is explicit evidence. The fact that he was proved wrong ten times every day in no way impressed him. He just didn't believe it.

Unlike most men, McCormick was able. Like most men, he was vain. And it was his most severe affliction that no experience of his life ever broke his spirit enough to free him of his vanities and fill the vacant spaces in his days that, in the end, became so bleak.

McCormick's greatest vanity was to think himself a historian and teacher of social values. He felt he used the *Tribune* justly, but no man of his intelligence could have believed it, given any degree of detachment. McCormick also used the *Tribune* to make a great deal of money and did his best to kick the liver out of anybody who tried to interfere. It never occurred to him that he shouldn't.

His ideas on social value were of no real persuasive force with anybody except himself. So, too, must it be said McCormick's idea of history was more than a little simple. But it would have done no good to mention there are those in the world who say historians should be accurate about the future, tentative about the present, and guess about the past. And he would only have turned away on hearing it argued that the facts of history are points in human psychology. And so, it is through knowledge of McCormick's view of history that it is possible to take his measure, at last.

He was powerfully informed, thoroughly intelligent, and when he chose, a forceful reasoner. He was industrious and he accomplished much. For all the high coloration put on his behavior because of his role as public man, Chicago gained from McCormick's presence and is now that much a better city because he lived in it, and lived exactly the way he did. The rest of the world, though it had to put up with much from McCormick, at least managed to outlast him.

Which is not to say that McCormick could not have made a very different showing if he had been really as close and as broad a student of historical possibilities as he thought he was. McCormick saw history as something he could use in his business. Whatever he stumbled on that didn't fit, therefore, he threw out of his mind.

And so for all that he did pick up in roaming the world, that habit of rejecting whatever did not fit caused him to miss a great deal more that happened every day, right before his eyes.

A NOTE ON SOURCES ★★★ The foundation of fact preceding includes not only written but verbal information from McCormick, his family connections, and a broad variety of personages with whom he had transactions in business.

Of his family, for reasons they understand, I single out here only his widow for special mention. Mrs. McCormick made available letters, documents and photographs, and in personal interviews supplied data otherwise not to be had. I am very much in her debt, if not less so to others here unmentioned.

I thank the officers and directors of the Tribune Company of Illinois, and the trustees of the Robert R. McCormick Charitable Trust, collectively, for permissions to quote from Chicago *Tribune* editorials, from various of McCormick's other writings and broadcasts, and for permission to reproduce cartoons and other matter held under copyright. Help was given further by Daniel D. Calibraro, J. Loy Maloney, John Park, Robert H. Roach, the late Arthur A. Schmon, Charles Smutny and Walter Trohan; and I would be remiss if I should not here express very special appreciation to J. Howard Wood, president of the Tribune Company and chairman of the board of trustees of the Robert R. McCormick Charitable Trust.

The Tribune Company's law advisors were equally generous and I wish to note special thanks to the late Weymouth Kirkland, to

Howard Ellis, Keith Masters, Willis D. Nance and Perry Patterson, for their individual contributions.

For information of special bearing on McCormick's personal relations with Presidents of the United States, I thank first former President Dwight D. Eisenhower and with respect to the late President Hoover, I mention the Hon. Lewis L. Strauss; Pierre Salinger and Thomas J. Walsh, in connection with the late President Kennedy; also, in the cases indicated, Representative James Roosevelt and Elizabeth B. Drewry, director of the Franklin D. Roosevelt Library; and Philip C. Brooks, director of the Harry S. Truman Library.

For special information concerning McCormick and the Associated Press, my particular thanks to Benjamin M. McKelway, Robert McLean and Paul Miller, as presidents; Mark Ethridge as a director; the late Kent Cooper, Frank Starzel and Wes Gallagher as general managers; and for insights into McCormick's sale of the *Times-Herald* to the Washington Post Company, to Alfred Friendly, Edward Folliard, Marquis Childs and J. Russell Wiggins; also, in connection with McCormick and his Freedom of the Press specialty, James A. Bear and Theodore F. Kuper, of the Thomas Jefferson Memorial Foundation; Robert M. Hutchins, of the Center For Democratic Institutions; and Henry F. Luce, in connection with the organization of the Freedom of the Press inquiry at the University of Chicago. Finally, for verifications pursuant to the antitrust actions involving McCormick, my most special thanks to the Hon. Thurman W. Arnold, for information not otherwise available.

In connection with research on the grand jury investigation following the Battle of Midway, I wish to thank especially the Hon. Francis Biddle, Attorney General Nicholas Katzenbach and Assistant Attorney General J. Walter Yeagley; Rudolph Winnacker, historian to the Secretary of Defense; Rear Admiral R. E. Eller, director of naval history and Lieutenant Commander D. K. Dagle, chief of the magazine and book branch of naval history; also the Hon. Loyd Wright, in his capacity as chairman of the Commission on Government Security.

For special researches in Chicago, I am grateful for help from Professor Herman Pritchett, head of the department of political science at the University of Chicago, and his associates, Hadley P. Arkes, Michael Goodkin and Mark Warden. I received special help, too, from the Virginia Polytechnic Institute, from the American History Division of the New York Public Library and from so many persons at the Library of Congress I am forced to collect all of them for a single expression of gratitude for their skill and interest. I am grateful to the Illinois Historical Society for permission to quote from Walter Trohan's "My Life with the Colonel," and to the Chicago Historical Society for information concerning Medill and McCormick family papers. For correspondence between McCormick and General of the Army George C. Marshall, I am deeply indebted to Forrest C. Pogue, director of the Marshall Research Center, and for information on Yale activities to George Richards, secretary of the Class of 1903.

Among the many individuals who gave special help or comment, I am obliged to G. E. Allen; Herman Edelsberg; Professor John Kenneth Galbraith; the Hon. Averell Harriman; Julie Hollobaugh; James W. Irwin; Arthur Krock; Edward D. Lapping; the late A. J. Liebling; the late General of the Army Douglas MacArthur; Merrill C. Meigs; John Dos Passos; Harold Taylor and Roy A. Wyckoff, Jr.

I thank Edward Bennett Williams for reading this manuscript and for encouraging evaluations. I am most grateful to Adam Yarmolinsky for many discussions, and for the Foreword, especially valuable to one seeking to communicate with a generation which had hardly entered the arena as McCormick left.

Finally, to Ashbel Green and John Gudmundsen, for editorial counsel and guidance, my deepest appreciation.

It is not possible to do McCormick full justice here in the matter of a bibliography. General, special, political and social American histories from 1847 forward almost invariably somewhere touch on McCormick's family or the *Tribune*. Research must start with the paper's microfilms and bound files which, except for a few years, are complete and can be found in numerous libraries. The Tribune Company has published a series of official histories, of which the best are: *The WGN* (1922), commemorating the *Tribune*'s seventy-fifth birthday; and three volumes of *The Chicago Tribune, Its First Hundred Years* (1943–45–46), bringing the account up through 1900. The special memorial issue of the paper for June 10, 1947, has much material for any person interested in Chicago's total life, aside from its attention to the history of the *Tribune* itself. The

Canadian venture is described in Carl Wiegman's *Trees to News* (1953).

On Chicago and Illinois politics, the Merriam and Masters accounts are well supplemented by such as *Big Bill of Chicago,* by Lloyd Wendt and Herman Kogan; and *Lowden of Illinois,* by William T. Hutchinson. Then, too, important material is found in George H. Mayer's *The Republican Party, Ballots & Bandwagons,* by Ralph G. Martin; Samuel Hopkins Adams' *The Incredible Era;* and Henry F. Pringle's *Life of Theodore Roosevelt.*

McCormick family histories and special studies fill near to six inches of space in the Library of Congress index card files, but any reading into these must begin with William T. Hutchinson's two volumes on Cyrus H. McCormick. There are special glimpses of McCormick's parents in T. Bentley Mott's *Twenty Years a Military Attaché;* and some facts in John Tebbel's *An American Dynasty;* but no source more useful than McCormick's own broadcasts of memoirs and family history, taken properly by anyone who has grounded himself independently.

Histories of Chicago's journalistic and general social life are also beyond enumeration here, but no inquiry should overlook Burton Rascoe's *Before I Forget;* A. J. Liebling's *Chicago: The Second City; Deadlines & Monkeyshines,* by John J. McPhaul; *Chicago,* by Edward Wagenknecht; *The Chicago* [River], by Harry Hansen; and *The Illinois,* by James Gray; and for two uncommonly informed glimpses into vanished aspects of the older city, Arthur Meeker's reminiscence, *To Chicago with Love;* and Edgar Lee Masters' little known *Levy Mayer and the New Industrial Era.*

APPENDICES

August 6, 1932

Dear Frank:

A line to thank you for your hospitality to me. I enjoyed every minute of it.

Your general's driver took me to Peekskill very cleverly. I told him I thought he ought to become a racing car chauffeur. We made the train by seconds.

Presumably you will want some relaxation from the strenuosity and monotony of the campaign. I am therefore sending you under another cover a copy of John Boettiger's book on the murder of Jake Lingle. You will find it interesting, and also get an insight into the author.

As my eyes struck the enclosed clipping I recalled your remarks about the people who wish to tax corporation surpluses in order to force their distribution.

Booth Tarkington in "The Magnificent Ambersons" ascribes the money hoarding proclivities of that generation to their sharp recollection of want in the pioneer days. I imagine that the impulse back of big corporate surpluses is the outcome of similar experiences. Such, at least, was the case in my small company.

With us it had always been customary to divide the earnings every month—the rule, I suppose, among partners. No sooner had I entered the business than, with no nest egg in the bank, I ran into cut rates in circulation, a strike, a depression, and the war. From that I reacted to a big surplus for us, none of which was loaned on call. That became too great a responsibility during the bank panic, so I distributed it. Now that the panic is over, I might like to have some of it back in the treasury.

But whatever my successes or failures, or those of anybody else running a business, I am sure I can do it better than any outsider, whether his motives be good, theoretical, or hostile to our form of government.

Yours sincerely,
(Signed)
Robert R. McCormick

Governor Franklin D. Roosevelt
Executive Chamber
Albany, New York

Papers of Franklin D. Roosevelt, Democratic National Committee–Box 164
GENERAL SERVICES ADMINISTRATION, *National Archives and Records Service,* FRANKLIN D. ROOSEVELT LIBRARY, Hyde Park, N. Y.

February 27th, 1933.

Honorable Franklin D. Roosevelt,
President Elect,
Hyde Park, New York.

Dear Frank:

The only reason I bother you in your many pre-occupations is that I fear that we are on the brink of making one of those irredeemable mistakes for which opportunity is very seldom offered.

The connection between the Great Lake system and the Mississippi River system; the connection between the Mississippi River system and Chicago, the transportation center of the nation, is just opening. Nobody can know how much water will be needed to make this waterway practically successful. If the amount set up in the Canadian treaty turns out to be insufficient, we will never be able to have it increased without paying some great international price for it.

I enclose a map showing the climatic conditions of the United States, which shows that most of the watershed of the Missouri River lies in the arid regions. The Mississippi River above its confluence with the Missouri and Illinois is very small and its head waters are in regions of minor rain fall. Both these rivers flow through areas of great evaporation. I do not think that water storage is practical for them.

If you will look at the map you will see that the weather conditions of the Ohio, and especially of the Tennessee River, are entirely different. You can ascertain that these smaller rivers supply more than half the water that passes Memphis and that their flow is much more regular throughout the year. We have floods in the Mississippi and the Missouri every Spring and low water every Fall.

I repeat that I only venture upon your time because I want to prevent an irreparable mistake.

Yours sincerely,
(Signed)
Robert R. McCormick

Papers of Franklin D. Roosevelt, O.F. 156
GENERAL SERVICES ADMINISTRATION, *National Archives and Records Service*, FRANKLIN D. ROOSEVELT LIBRARY, Hyde Park, N. Y.

April 4, 1933.

My dear Mr. President:

I am returning to you herewith the letter addressed to you under date of February 27 by Colonel McCormick, of the CHICAGO TRIBUNE, with respect to the pending St. Lawrence Waterway Treaty.

I am sending to Colonel McCormick today information from the Weather Bureau with respect to the rainfall in the upper Mississippi Valley, and a further report from the War Department on the matter of storage dams for that region. When you turned this letter over to me, I gathered that this was what you wanted me to do.

I am not in a position to answer the general objection raised by Colonel McCormick to the treaty, so I am sending his letter back to you.

Sincerely yours,
(Signed)
Harold L. Ickes

The President,
The White House.

Inclosure.

Papers of Franklin D. Roosevelt, O.F. 156
GENERAL SERVICES ADMINISTRATION, *National Archives and Records Service*, FRANKLIN D. ROOSEVELT LIBRARY, Hyde Park, N. Y.

May 6, 1933

Dear Frank:

It would give my wife and me great pleasure to have you and Mrs. Roosevelt stay with us when you come to Chicago to open the Worlds Fair.

My house was a present from my mother, who held all the mansion ideas of her generation, and is therefore so much too large for us as to contain room for you and at least a considerable part of your staff.

It seems to me you are making very good weather of it in the storm.

Yours sincerely,
(Signed)
Robert R. McCormick

Honorable Franklin Delano Roosevelt
President of the United States
Washington, D.C.

Papers of Franklin D. Roosevelt, P.P.F. 426
GENERAL SERVICES ADMINISTRATION, *National Archives and Records Service,* FRANKLIN D. ROOSEVELT LIBRARY, Hyde Park, N. Y.

May 16, 1933.

Dear Bert:—

It is fine of you to ask me to use your house while I am in Chicago but, as you now know, I shall not be there. I have been a long time in writing to thank you but I was waiting to see how things turned out in order that I might know definitely whether or not I could get away. However, I would only have been in Chicago a few hours and would not have had any time for a visit.

It was more than generous of you to offer to let me share your own home. Do let me know when you are coming to Washington.

Very sincerely yours,
(Franklin D. Roosevelt)

Colonel Robert R. McCormick,
The Chicago Tribune,
Chicago, Illinois.

Papers of Franklin D. Roosevelt, P.P.F. 426
GENERAL SERVICES ADMINISTRATION, *National Archives and Records Service*, FRANKLIN D. ROOSEVELT LIBRARY, Hyde Park, N. Y.

THE AMERICAN PARTY *

I think the time has come to organize another party. I will not say a third party because there have been over thirty parties in the history of our country. I will not say a new party because we must draw upon people of similar beliefs in both of the old parties.

The Southern Democrats will never vote the Republican ticket, and many old-line Republicans will never vote the Democratic ticket, so I suggest that we form the American party, to which all people thinking as we do can subscribe, and to which people in both party organizations disagreeing with us cannot subscribe.

We will follow Jefferson and Lincoln while we repudiate Truman and Dewey.

I swallowed Willkie in '40, Dewey twice in '44 and '48, candidates foisted upon the majority by sharp practice, but now that the Democrats have taken over our party by voting in Republican primaries by the ruse of falsehood and corruption and can be expected to do it again four years from now, I will be imposed upon no longer.

I can see no benefit in changing "Me, Too" Dewey for "I, Too" Ike, who was nominated and is entirely surrounded by men who know exactly what they want—which is not the good of this country.

His chief newspaper supporters are Democratic New Deal papers. They have been urging him not to support the Republican nominees devoted to America. They want the continuation of the Marshall Plan, with money going to Europe and mink coats coming back.

He is the candidate of effeminates like the All-Slops and Childses, the Fleesons, the Schiffs, and the Luces, who are urging him to denounce American-minded senators and support the "free" world. They use that word with falsehood on their tongues. They mean for him to support socialism in Europe as a prelude to bringing it here.

Governor Stevenson is the nominee of the CIO, for which the present Democratic party is merely a false face, and which intends to destroy utterly private initiative and private property.

Between these two candidates no choice is left for the voters. As Franklin Roosevelt said, "They planned it that way."

---

* An address by Colonel Robert R. McCormick, editor and publisher, *The Chicago Tribune,* August 23, 1952, broadcast over WGN, WGNB and The Mutual Broadcasting System.

Do not vote for either of these candidates. Concentrate on voting for patriotic candidates for Congress in both parties.

It is time, therefore, that we organized ourselves into another party from which Truman Republicans and the Truman Democrats will be excluded.

It has been hard for me to reach this opinion because my grandfather founded the Republican party.

My grandfather first proposed the name Republican in 1848 and publicly in 1852.

A study of the demise of the Whig party and the birth of the Republican party made clear to me that this opinion is sound.

As early as 1854 a meeting at Ripon, Wisconsin, resolved that should the Kansas-Nebraska Bill pass, the older organizations should be abandoned and a new party organized to be called Republican. After the bill was passed by the Senate, another meeting chose a committee of five to organize the new party in Wisconsin. Michigan held its convention of anti-slavery Democrats at Jackson, also in 1854. The repeal of the Missouri Compromise was denounced and a state ticket was nominated which helped to bring together the anti-slavery people regardless of former party adherence. At a later convention called at Jackson, the name Republican was adopted and a platform accepted. The Free Democratic ticket had been withdrawn and that party organization abandoned. A Republican ticket was nominated with a Republican majority in the legislature and three out of four congressmen.

Also in 1854 a convention in Vermont met at which anti-slavery resolutions were passed. State committees of the parties nominated a fusion ticket from which a legislature was elected which sent to the United States senate an anti-slavery Whig and a Free Soiler.

In Massachusetts a convention met at Worcester in 1854. The Know-Nothings were successful in the election, but their legislature sent Henry Wilson, the Republican nominee for governor, to the United States Senate.

At a convention in the village of Strong, Maine, in 1854, they assumed the name of Republican. A candidate for senator was nominated, but failed of election in the fall.

Allegany County, New York, elected county officers who called themselves Republicans in the fall of 1854 after being nominated at a convention held in Angelica. The Anti-Nebraska conventions did not result in the formation of a new party because the Whig platform and ticket agreed sufficiently with the sentiment of the conventions.

The Ohio convention of 1854 did not adopt the name Republican, but nominated Anti-Nebraska candidates for Congress and all were elected. Pennsylvania remained Democratic.

In Washington, D.C., thirty members of the House met at the call of Israel Washburn of Maine and talked about forming the Republican party.

Interest in the new party continued to grow during 1855. On June 17, 1856, the Republican convention met in Philadelphia. Delegates represented every free state, the territories of Kansas, Minnesota, and Nebraska, the District of Columbia, and the states of Delaware, Maryland, Virginia, and Kentucky. In that election eleven states went Republican: Connecticut, Iowa, Maine, Massachusetts, Michigan, New Hampshire, New York, Ohio, Rhode Island, Vermont, and Wisconsin. Many state and congressional officers were elected. Congressional officers were also elected in some of the states which went for Buchanan, especially those in the North. In the election Buchanan (Democrat) received 174 electoral votes, Frémont (Republican) 114, and Fillmore (Whig) 8.

In 1854 Lyman Trumbull was the "Anti-Nebraska-Democratic" candidate for the United States Senate in Illinois. He received the votes of the Whig members of the legislature from Lincoln and was elected. In 1860 both Lincoln and Trumbull were elected as Republicans.

Following this procedure, I propose that we support those American-minded men who run as Republicans until they find it politically desirable to run as Americans and members of the American party.

In states where the Republican party has been betrayed, such as New York and Massachusetts, I think we should support the patriotic candidates for Congress on the Republican and Democratic tickets and put up American candidates where both candidates are international New Dealers.

If I were a resident of Virginia, I would vote for Senator Harry Byrd. Every patriot in Wisconsin will vote for Senator Joseph McCarthy.

Every patriot should vote for:

William F. Knowland of California
John J. Williams of Delaware
William E. Jenner of Indiana
J. Glenn Beall of Maryland
Charles E. Potter of Michigan
James P. Kem of Missouri
Zales N. Ecton of Montana
Hugh Butler of Nebraska
John W. Bricker of Ohio
Edward Martin of Pennsylvania
Arthur V. Watkins of Utah

Harry P. Cain of Washington
Vivian Kellems of Connecticut

Every patriot should vote against:

Henry Cabot Lodge Jr. of Massachusetts
Edward J. Thye of Minnesota
Irving M. Ives of New York
Ralph E. Flanders of Vermont

The list of congressmen to vote for is too long to broadcast. It will be included in the pamphlet reprint of this address which may be obtained by writing to the *Tribune*.

I think the American party should nominate candidates for the Presidency and the Vice Presidency in 1956.

Everywhere we find anger, disgust, and even despair. I share the anger and disgust, but not the despair.

From the time of the American defeat on Long Island in 1776 down to the American defeat on Long Island in 1952, from the time when the capital was burned in 1814 by an exterior enemy to the present when it has been betrayed by domestic enemies, it has often appeared doubtful that the Union could be saved.

Our economic stability, greatly threatened toward the end of the last century, has been brought nearly to ruin by the New Deal. During all this time people have despaired, but the courageous ones have held steadfast and fearless, so we must persevere.

With malice toward none; with charity for all; with firmness in the right, as God gives us to see the right, let us strive on to finish the work we are in. . . .

CONGRESSMEN TO VOTE FOR:

ALABAMA—*For:* George M. Grant and George W. Andrews.

ARIZONA—*For:* Harold A. Patten.

ARKANSAS—*For:* E. C. Gathings, W. F. Norrell, and Oren Harris.

CALIFORNIA—*For:* Hubert B. Scudder, John J. Allen, Jr., A. Oakley Hunter, Ernest K. Bramblett, Thomas H. Werdel, Gordon L. McDonough, Donald L. Jackson, Carl Hinshaw, Norris Poulson, Patrick J. Hillings, and John Phillips.

COLORADO—*For:* William S. Hill and J. Edgar Chenoweth.

CONNECTICUT—*For:* Antoni N. Sadlak.

FLORIDA—*For:* A. S. Herlong, Jr. and Dwight L. Rogers.

GEORGIA—*For:* Eugene Cox, E. L. Forrester, James C. Davis, and William McD. Wheeler.

IDAHO—*For:* John T. Wood and Hamer H. Budge.

ILLINOIS—*For:* Edgar G. Brown, Richard B. Vail, Fred E. Busbey, William E. McVey, Robert R. Siegrist, Richard W. Hoffman, Timothy P. Sheehan, Edgar A. Jonas, Marguerite Stitt Church, Chauncey W. Reed, Noah M. Mason, Leo E. Allen, Leslie C. Arends, Harold H. Velde, Robert B. Chiperfield, Sid Simpson, Edward H. Jenison, William L. Springer, Charles W. Vursell, Phyllis Stewart Schlafly, and C. W. Bishop.

INDIANA—*For:* Charles A. Halleck, Shepard J. Crumpacker Jr., E. Ross Adair, John V. Beamer, Cecil M. Harden, William G. Bray, Earl Wilson, Ralph Harvey, and Charles B. Brownson.

IOWA—*For:* Thomas E. Martin, Henry O. Talle, H. R. Gross, Karl M. Le Compte, Paul Cunningham, James I. Dolliver, Ben F. Jensen, and Charles B. Hoeven.

KANSAS—*For:* Albert M. Cole, Errett P. Scrivner, Myron V. George, Edward H. Rees, Clifford R. Hope, and Wint Smith.

KENTUCKY—*For:* James S. Golden.

LOUISIANA—*For:* F. Edward Hebert, Edwin E. Willis, Overton Brooks, and Otto E. Passman.

MAINE—*For:* Charles P. Nelson and Clifford G. McIntire.

MARYLAND—*For:* Edward T. Miller, James Patrick Devereux, Jerry Toula, Samuel Hopkins, Frank Small Jr., and DeWitt S. Hyde.

MASSACHUSETTS—*For:* William H. Bates, A. L. Goodwin, Donald W. Nicholson, Richard Wigglesworth, and Joseph W. Martin Jr.

MICHIGAN—*For:* George Meader, Paul W. Shafer, Clare E. Hoffman, Gerald R. Ford Jr., Jesse P. Wolcott, Ruth Thompson, John B. Bennett, and George A. Dondero.

MINNESOTA—*For:* August H. Andresen, Joseph P. O'Hara, H. Carl Andersen, and Harold C. Hagen.

MISSISSIPPI—*For:* Thomas G. Abernethy, Jamie L. Whitten, Frank E. Smith, William A. Winstead, William M. Colmer, and John Bell Williams.

MISSOURI—*For:* Thomas B. Curtis and Dewey Short.

MONTANA—*For:* Wesley A. D'Ewart.

NEBRASKA—*For:* Carl T. Curtis, R. D. Harrison, and A. L. Miller.

NEW JERSEY—*For:* T. Millet Hand.

NEW YORK—*For:* Henry J. Latham, Frederic R. Coudert Jr., John C. Butler, W. Sterling Cole, William E. Miller, Harold C. Ostertag, Ralph A. Gamble, Ralph W. Gwinn, Katherine St. George, J. Ernest Wharton, Bernard W. Kearney, Clarence E. Kilburn, William R. Williams, John Taber, and Daniel A. Reed.

NORTH CAROLINA—*For:* F. Ertel Carlyle, Graham A. Barden, and Woodrow W. Jones.

NORTH DAKOTA—*For:* Ushur L. Burdick.

OHIO—*For:* William E. Hess, Paul F. Schenck, William M. McCulloch, Cliff Clevenger, Clarence J. Brown, Jackson E. Betts, Thomas A. Jenkins, John M. Vorys, Alvin F. Weichel, Frank T. Bow, J. Harry McGregor, and George H. Bender.

OKLAHOMA—*For:* Page Belcher.

OREGON—*For:* Harris Ellsworth and Walter Norblad.

PENNSYLVANIA—*For:* Benjamin F. James, Karl C. King, Paul B. Dague, Ivor D. Fenton, Samuel K. McConnell Jr., Walter M. Mumma, Alvin R. Bush, Richard M. Simpson, James E. Van Zandt, Leon H. Gavin, Carroll D. Kearns, Louis E. Graham, and Harmar D. Denny Jr.

SOUTH CAROLINA—*For:* Mendel Rivers; W. J. Bryan Dorn, Joseph R. Bryson, and John L. McMillan.

SOUTH DAKOTA—*For:* Harold O. Lovre and E. Y. Berry.

TENNESSEE—*For:* B. Carroll Reece, Howard H. Baker, and Tom Murray.

TEXAS—*For:* J. Frank Wilson, Olin E. Teague, William R. Poage, Wingate H. Lucas, Frank N. Ikard, Kenneth M. Regan, Omar Burleson, Walter E. Rogers, O. Clark Fisher, and Martin Dies.

VIRGINIA—*For:* Edward J. Robeson, Watkins M. Abbitt, Thomas B. Stanley, Richard H. Poff, Burr Harrison, Howard W. Smith, William C. Wamplar, and Joel T. Broyhill.

WASHINGTON—*For:* Walt Horan.

WISCONSIN—*For:* Lawrence H. Smith, Glenn R. Davis, William K. Van Pelt, Charles J. Kersten, Alvin E. O'Konski, and John W. Byrnes.

WYOMING—*For:* William Henry Harrison.

GETTYSBURG
PENNSYLVANIA
November 12, 1963

Dear Frank:

It is a great many years since you, as a newsman, used to drop into my office in the old State, War and Navy Building for a chat.

It was during those years that I first saw Colonel McCormick. He was apparently quite a friend of General MacArthur's and since, for two years or more, I occupied an office right next door to the General's office, I more than once had the opportunity to chat with the Colonel briefly.

However, the only serious conversation I ever had with him took place during my days in SHAPE, just outside of Paris, France. Colonel McCormick with his wife came to call on me at my headquarters office. His purpose was to talk about politics and the forthcoming election campaign of 1952. We discussed such matters as the theory of isolationism, collective security, the lack of Republican success in the Presidential campaigns since 1928, and the surprise election of President Truman in 1948. Respecting a number of these subjects he remarked several times, "I don't know that I agree with you exactly, but I do respect your opinion and your frankness."

The conversation lasted for an hour or so and at its end I escorted the Colonel and his wife down the hall to the main entrance merely to say a courteous farewell. As we approached two or three of my staff officers I noticed that all of them were wearing big, wide grins—a circumstance that caused me, after the departure of the McCormicks, to question my staff as to the reason for the laughter. General Persons, who was among the group and who was rocking with merriment, finally was able to reply, "As the Colonel and his wife approached us Mrs. McCormick turned over the lapel of her suit coat, on the back of which was a button that read, 'I Like Ike!' " Since the Colonel was, of course, an ardent supporter of Senator Taft for the Republican nomination, it was easy to see why my staff found Mrs. McCormick's gesture a bit amusing.

Other than the above I do not recall any other incidents and possibly even this is not worth recording.

In any event it was nice to hear from you after all these years. With best wishes,

Sincerely,
(Signed) DWIGHT D. EISENHOWER

Mr. Frank C. Waldrop
4900 Loughboro Road, Northwest
Washington 16, D.C.

INDEX

ABOUT THE AUTHOR ★★★ Frank C. Waldrop is a journalist turned cattle breeder. He was born in Alabama, reared in Tennessee, and since 1933 has been in Washington, D.C., as observer and participant in the life of the Capital, in both its official and private aspects, throughout the most significant years of American experience in the twentieth century.

After a preliminary try at the soldier's life, Mr. Waldrop began as a reporter on the Nashville *Evening Tennessean* in March, 1928 and in 1929 went to New York with Hearst's *Evening Journal.* In 1930, he returned to Nashville as city editor, then managing editor, of the *Evening Tennessean.* In 1933, he came to the Washington *Herald,* with which publication in its successor forms he remained for 20 years, lacking one month. In that period he held every journalistic role from reporter to editor-in-chief and partial owner, without any exceptions. Of his experience he writes: "No journalist could ever have hoped to have so close a view and such a free hand in so many interesting projects as I did in those 20 years and no man at all is entitled to ask for more. I think I was lucky beyond all reason to get in when I did, where I did, and luckier still to get out in time to find an entirely different career just as intense and in its way, even more demanding."

Since 1953, Mr. Waldrop has twice served as a consultant to the Department of State on technical matters, and was a consultant to the House Select Committee on Science and Astronautics which drafted the first laws in human history to authorize research into the general universe. He is also an amateur at genetics, as applied to beef cattle. In 1937, Mr. Waldrop collaborated with Joseph Borkin in writing "Television: A Struggle for Power," the first such effort to survey an industry that was not yet in existence; and in 1942 he edited "MacArthur On War," a collection of official papers by Douglas MacArthur to that date.